OTHERS UNKNOWN

OTHERS
UNKNOWN

◆

THE OKLAHOMA CITY

BOMBING CASE

AND

CONSPIRACY

◆

STEPHEN JONES

AND PETER ISRAEL

PUBLICAFFAIRS

New York

Published by PublicAffairs™, A Member of the Perseus Books Group.

Printed in the United States of America.

Book design by Jenny Dossin.

Photo of defense team by Joel Silverman.

Library of Congress Cataloging-in-Publication Data

Jones, Stephen, 1940–
    Others unknown : the Oklahoma City bombing case and conspiracy /
Stephen Jones and Peter Israel. — 1st ed.
        p.   cm.
    Includes index.
    ISBN 1-891620-07-X (HC)
    1. McVeigh, Timothy—Trials, litigation, etc.   2. Nichols, Terry,
1955–   —Trials, litigation, etc.   3. Oklahoma City Federal
Building Bombing, Oklahoma City, Okla., 1995.   4. Bombing
investigation—Oklahoma—Oklahoma City.   5. Bombings—Oklahoma—
Oklahoma City.   I. Israel, Peter, 1933–   .   II. Title.
KF224.O39J66   1998
345.766'380264—dc21   98-40572
                                                                             CIP

First Edition

10 9 8 7 6 5 4 3 2 1

This book is dedicated to:

The District Court of the State of Oklahoma, Fourth Judicial District,

the Honorable Ray Dean Linder, Chief Judge,

The United States District Court for the Western District of Oklahoma,

the Honorable David L. Russell, Chief Judge,

and

The United States District Court for the District of Colorado,

the Honorable Richard Matsch, Chief Judge and Presiding,

May it please the Court.

For now we see through a glass darkly; but then face to face.
Now I know in part.

—PAUL'S FIRST LETTER TO THE CORINTHIANS, 13:12.

CONTENTS

PART IV

INTRODUCTION

The bombing of the Alfred P. Murrah Federal Building in Oklahoma City was the greatest act of terrorist violence ever committed in the United States. Timothy James McVeigh and Terry Lynn Nichols were accused, tried, and convicted in the bombing conspiracy. Whatever one says about that verdict—and, as McVeigh's counsel, I will have a great deal to say in these pages—it strains belief to suppose that this appalling crime was the work of two men—any two men. I believe it came about because of foreign involvement. I also believe our government might have prevented the whole thing—if it had been paying attention.

This book is an attempt to explain what happened and why.

. . .

Many people ask me—an Oklahoman, someone who knew people who were killed in the bombing—how in the world I could have represented a man like Timothy McVeigh. It wasn't an easy decision, as I'll explain in the chapters to come, but it wasn't as difficult as some might think. Even a man accused of the worst act of terrorism ever committed in this country—especially such a man—is entitled to the best possible defense. This concept is a cornerstone of our system of justice. My colleagues and I in *United States v. McVeigh* sought to provide such a defense.

As in any criminal proceeding, of course, it wasn't up to us to prove anything. Our task was simply to convince a jury that there was reasonable doubt as to our client's guilt. Our efforts to present such a case, however, were thwarted and finally defeated. The fact that this happened in an American court of law was the shared responsibility of the judge, the government, the press, and even, I must concede, members of the defense team, for which I take full responsibility. But it wasn't just those of us in the Denver courtroom—lawyers, jurors, judge, and Timothy McVeigh—who suffered because of this. All of us lost—all Americans. Because a government theory full of holes carried the day. Because the "others unknown" who helped plan and execute the bombing are still out there. Because the whole tragedy might have been averted but wasn't. And because until we know what really happened, we can't hope to prevent other similar tragedies perhaps carried out by some of the very people who helped destroy the Murrah Building.

Those responsible in the federal government would have us believe that the bombing was an open-and-shut case, quickly solved and aggressively prosecuted. If that is right, then it is staggeringly unique. Think of the bombing of the U.S. embassy in Beirut in April 1983. Sixty-three people were killed, and to this day there is not a single arrest or conviction. In December 1988 Pan Am flight 103 was destroyed by a bomb, killing 270 people. As of today there have been no arrests or convictions. In November 1995 an American-run military training center in Riyadh, Saudi Arabia, was bombed, killing seven. Again, no arrests or convictions. In June 1996 another bomb killed nineteen Americans in Dhahran, Saudi Arabia. No arrests or convictions. And of course there was the October 1983 bombing of the U.S. Marines barracks in Beirut. Two hundred forty-one Americans were killed, and fifteen years later there has not been a single arrest or conviction. Again and again, the same pattern, whether it is in Karachi, Pakistan, or over Lockerbie, Scotland: The crimes remain unsolved and unprosecuted. And in the World Trade Center bombing, an attack that took place not in the Middle East but in New York, on our own soil, the perpetrators were a group of Islamic radicals. Given all this, does it seem so far-fetched that what happened in Oklahoma might not be as simple as the government said?

The real story of the bombing, as the McVeigh defense pursued it, is complex, shadowy, and sinister. It stretches, weblike, from America's heartland to the nation's capital, the Far East, Europe, and the Middle East, and much of it remains a mystery. There may be many reasons why this is so, but perhaps the most important has been the U.S. government. And in the end, the Oklahoma City bombing conspiracy may not merely be the crime itself but also the systematic, deliberate attempt of our federal government to prevent all of us from finding out what exactly happened on that terrible April morning.

The McVeigh Defense Team, October 1996

(Front row, left to right, Karen Warner, Shelly Hager, Ann Seim, Stephen Jones, Renae Elmenhorst, Karen Olds, Kathryn Irons, Trish Pierpoint; back row, Randy Coyne, Mike Roberts, Jim Hankins, Andy Murphy, Amber McLaughlin, Scott Anderson, Ann Bradley, Rob Nigh, Mandy Welch, Sam Guiberson, Jerry Merritt, Robert Warren, Dick Burr, Bob Wyatt, Desi Milacek; not pictured, Cheryl Ramsey and Chris Tritico.)

PART
I

1

"BABY KILLER! BABY KILLER!"

April 19, 1995, 9:30 A.M. eastern daylight time. Department of
Justice, Washington D.C.

The call had been routed from the central switchboard. James
Miller, a receptionist in the Executive Secretariat, took it. That was
part of his job, answering the "nut line," so called because that was
where the central switchboard of the Justice Department sent the
crank calls and the prank calls. People, for instance, who felt like
threatening the attorney general, or the United States of America,
or the world.

While Miller was talking on the phone, two fellow employees
stopped by his work station. One was Kimberley Tolson, a "correspondence analyst," the other a courier for the criminal division
who had a delivery to make. The courier's name was Russell Stuart
Green.

Since Miller was still on the phone, Tolson signed Green's log
sheet for the delivery; Miller, reaching across his desk, time-
stamped it.

The time stamp read 9:38 A.M.

(Actually, the clock inside the stamp was running six minutes fast.
The real time was 9:32 A.M. eastern daylight time.)

Miller hung up the phone.

"This guy's saying some federal building in Oklahoma City just blew up," he told the others. "He's saying he's standing across the street, watching it."

"Yeah, right," Kimberley Tolson said over her shoulder, heading back for her desk, while Green, with a straight face, said, "Hey, don't you think you need to tell somebody about that? Like the president?"

Eight days later, James Miller was interviewed by the FBI about this call. Miller quoted the anonymous caller as having said, "I'm nobody special. The federal building in Oklahoma City has just been bombed. I'm standing across the street from it. I can see it from where I'm standing."

There was only one problem with this, but it was an enormous one.

The time according to the time stamp on Stuart Green's log sheet (allowing for the six-minute correction) was 9:32 A.M. eastern daylight time.

That made the time in Oklahoma City 8:32 A.M. central daylight time.

The explosion that destroyed the Alfred P. Murrah Federal Building, on Fifth Street in Oklahoma City, wouldn't happen for another thirty minutes.

9 A.M. central daylight time.
A twenty-foot rental truck, yellow with black lettering, the largest of the two-axle models in the Ryder line, had pulled up in front of the Alfred P. Murrah Federal Building in Oklahoma City, Oklahoma. It parked near the front entrance, under the overhang, just below the America's Kids Day Care Center on the second floor.

Moments later, the truck blew up in a blinding, deafening explosion.

The truck itself, the air outside it, the very construction material of the building—its glass facades, its concrete—all became part of a giant, exploding blasting cap of unimaginably destructive force. The shock wave, known technically as the detonation front, burst in every direction from the explosion at blinding speed—greater than 9,000 feet per second, or 7,000 miles per hour—and with a pressure, at the point of explosion, on the order of 1 million pounds per square inch. A huge chunk of the building was blown in and out. The shock wave hurled, dismembered, and crushed bodies. Dozens of people—men, women, children—were flung indiscriminately into the abyss below, amid furniture and building materials, where the explosion had opened up a crater some thirty feet deep. In the blink of an eye, six women, all employees of the Federal Employees Credit Union, sitting in a semicircle in front of the desk of their director, Florence Rogers, fell to their instant death, leaving Mrs. Rogers staring out at blue sky and the fractured roof of the Oklahoma Journal Building. The blast that ripped away the floor stopped two and a half inches from her desk. A Marine Corps recruiter, Captain Michael Norfleet, had been making a telephone call to Washington D.C. to see whether Sgt. Benjamin Davis had been accepted into Officers Candidate School. The line was busy, however, and Norfleet got up and walked away. Sergeant Davis himself came over, sat at the captain's desk, and was found by rescue workers several days later, dead, still sitting at the desk. Stories like these were multiplied hundreds of times about people who, by luck or fate or act of God, survived while others didn't. Husbands and wives perished, as did parents, grandparents, siblings, aunts, uncles. There were more than two dozen sons and daughters who lost both parents, more than two hundred who lost one. And in the final death toll were nineteen children.

Meanwhile the shock wave surged up, outward, literally lifting the building, causing beams and slabs to collapse. Almost simultaneously, the upward thrust was replaced by a devastating vacuum at the core of the explosion, which pulled and twisted the entire front half of the edifice and ripped it into the crater below. Smoke curled into the sky. All over downtown Oklahoma City, alarms went off. All this in the blink of an eye. At the Oklahoma Geological Survey Station in Norman, some sixteen miles away, the first shock registered at 9:02:13 A.M.

When the explosion occurred, the United States Courthouse one block away trembled as if caught in an earthquake. More than one hundred 36"-by-54" windows shattered and flew into the courthouse. Inside, heavy courtroom doors were jammed, rooms were flooded with broken glass, and judges' chambers were turned into piles of plaster, fallen ceiling tiles, and broken glass. Shards of glass peppered and scarred desks, courtroom furniture, and walls. But the courthouse was far from the only other building damaged. As far as twenty blocks away, windows cracked and blew out, and in the adjacent street and parking lots, cars, flattened and twisted, caught fire and burned like vehicles abandoned on a battlefield.

Alerted by the concussion of the blast and the pillars and plumes of smoke now rising in the morning sky, crowds of Oklahomans, civilians as well as rescue workers, converged on the blast site, and medical teams set up triage stations at its perimeter. The media arrived on their heels, some of them in helicopters. Fire, police, and emergency medical systems were swamped with phone calls, and thousands of alarm systems had been triggered throughout Oklahoma City. Inside the courthouse and the remaining structure of the Murrah Building, there was pandemonium. The halls quickly became jammed with screaming, panic-stricken people and a stifling mixture of dust and acrid smoke. The courthouse exits had been destroyed by the blast, making evacuation excruciatingly slow for everyone. No one had any idea what had befallen them or those far less fortunate in the Murrah Building. Terror and shock permeated the courthouse, the trapped survivors of the Murrah Building, and the occupants of surrounding buildings.

The response of the city's emergency services was instantaneous and massive, and Federal Emergency Management Agency (FEMA) units were en route to Oklahoma from all parts of the country within the hour. Rescue efforts at the site had to be halted just before 10:30 A.M. because of a second bomb scare, but they resumed almost immediately, continuing all day and into the night, despite high winds and thunderstorms, and for days thereafter. The destruction was simply unparalleled in our society and shocking not only because of the death toll that rose from day to day but also because of where it took place—in the very heartland of America.

168 people dead (or possibly, as we shall see, 169).

503 injured.

320 structures in the area surrounding the Murrah Building damaged.

Approximately $651 million in recovery costs.

A whole populace in mourning, and a rising riptide of anger that would never ebb.

The Republican governor of Oklahoma, Frank Keating, stated that the bombing was unlike anything he had ever seen in his years as an FBI agent, U.S. attorney, and law enforcement official in the Reagan and Bush administrations. Without a doubt, Oklahoma—and the nation—had just experienced the worst case of domestic terrorism in the history of the United States.

An hour and a half later that same April morning, a patrolman for the Oklahoma Highway Patrol, Charles Hanger, pulled over a 1977 pale yellow Mercury Marquis on Interstate 35, some eighty miles north of Oklahoma City. Hanger stopped the car because it displayed no license plate. The driver, a young man named Timothy McVeigh, told Trooper Hanger that he was returning to Junction City, Kansas, from Arkansas. Concealed under his left arm, however, was a loaded .45-caliber Glock pistol, and Trooper Hanger promptly arrested him for having no tag or insurance verification and for carrying a concealed weapon. Hanger drove McVeigh to the Noble County lockup in the courthouse building in nearby Perry, Oklahoma. The locked yellow Mercury was left on the side of the highway.

Before the day was out, federal law enforcement officials had already traced a vehicle identification number (VIN) upon what appeared to be the rear axle of the Ryder truck. It had been blown sky-high in the explosion and landed more than a block away, narrowly missing a driver and his wife and children. Through Ryder headquarters in Miami, officials traced the VIN to a rental agency in Junction City, Kansas, which had rented the truck, two days before, to a man who had identified himself as Robert Kling. Employees at the dealership agreed that Kling had been accompanied by another man, and they helped FBI artists prepare composite sketches of them. They were labeled UnSub #1 and UnSub #2 (Unidentified Subjects #1 and #2), later to be known as John Doe #1 and John Doe #2. The following day, Thursday, the FBI by showing these drawings door to door in Junction City came up with a match for UnSub #1. According to Lea McGown, manager of the Dreamland Motel in Junction City, UnSub #1 had been a guest at the motel April 14–18, 1995. But Robert Kling wasn't the name he'd used. He'd registered as Timothy McVeigh, and he'd given his home address as Decker, Michigan.

That night, an FBI SWAT team descended on the farm of James Nichols in Decker, Michigan. James Nichols was the older brother of one Terry Lynn Nichols, who lived in Kansas. But it wasn't until the next morning, Friday, through a routine phone call and check, that the investigators discovered that a Timothy McVeigh was already in custody in the Noble County Jail in Perry, Oklahoma. He was facing state misdemeanor charges for the missing license plate and the concealed weapon. In fact, Judge Danny G. Allen was on the verge of setting bail in his case.

The FBI could hardly believe their luck.

We've got him! The bomber's been caught!

In no time, they arrived in Perry in force, the media with them, and the crowds that had already formed outside on the courthouse square were shouting, "Baby killer! Killer! Baby killer!"

Before the linking of McVeigh to the bombing was made public, most Oklahomans, myself included, had no idea what had happened. Some, at first, had even thought a gas line had exploded. Then, quickly, the disaster became a bombing, intentional, a terrorist act. The morning of the explosion the FBI was known to be looking for a brown Chevy pickup truck and two men of Middle East extraction—Arab types—who had been seen running from the Murrah Building just before the blast, and before noon that same day David McCurdy, former U.S. congressman from Oklahoma and former chair of the U.S. House Intelligence Committee, proclaimed that the bombing was the work of Middle East terrorists. This made weird sense. The similarities to the World Trade Center bombing, including the use of a Ryder truck, could not be ignored, and Oklahoma City had a large Muslim fundamentalist population, including even some former members of the Iraqi Republican Guards who had been taken prisoner in the Gulf War and had refused to return home. Whoever the perpetrators were, though, both the U.S. attorney general and the president of the United States called for the death penalty for the perpetrators, and the FBI announced a reward of $2 million for information leading to their arrest and conviction.

Only 3 million people inhabit our whole state, and Oklahoma City itself has been called the largest small town in America. It seemed, in those awful first days, that each and every one of us knew somebody who knew somebody who'd been there. And knew somebody else who would have been there, but for luck and God's grace. The sense of involvement, of participation, was unavoidable. We stayed glued to our television sets, horrified by what we saw but unable to turn away from the repeated images of the victims, young and old, living and dying. We saw the bleeding, tear-stained faces, the gallant rescue workers, the nurses and doctors running toward the site, the now-classic photograph of the Oklahoma City fireman cradling the body of the dead child, so tenderly. That weekend we watched broadcasts of the memorial service in Oklahoma City attended by President Clinton and the First Lady. Those of us old enough to remember realized that we'd done the same thing more than thirty years earlier. November 23, 1963. Dealey Plaza, in Dallas. John F. Kennedy, assassinated. Then, the riderless horse in the nation's capital.

Nor was this the only déja vu. John Doe #1, we were told that Friday (McVeigh's name had not yet been released to the public), had been located. The media, obviously, had been tipped off for the occasion. It would have been easy to take the prisoner away from the Noble County Courthouse in Perry, maintaining maximum security—a truck could have backed right up to the doors of the building—but the FBI supervisors had another purpose. They wanted to show off their quarry. They wanted to control that very important first impression. So John Doe #1 was led out into the afternoon sun, for all the world to see, by two FBI agents.

He was a tall young man with a crew cut, a chiseled jaw, an impassive expression, a military bearing. His eyes seemed fixed on some faraway point. From somewhere off-camera the jeerers and hecklers could be heard. The young man was wearing the orange jumpsuit of a prison inmate, but apparently no bulletproof vest. He was shackled and handcuffed.

We would see this same image of him literally hundreds of times on our television screens and in print. This was what the government wanted us to see. He may have been identified as Timothy James McVeigh, but those of us old enough to remember "saw" in him the ghost of Lee Harvey Oswald.

2

"MR. JONES, CHIEF JUDGE RUSSELL DESIRES YOU CALL HIM"

I'd been on a two-day trip to Dallas, and it was late in the afternoon on Friday, May 5, by the time I headed north on U.S. 81. I was going home to Enid. U.S. 81 follows the old Chisholm Trail, which was once a main cattle-drive route from Texas up through Oklahoma to Abilene, Kansas. Most of it is now a four-lane highway some thirty miles west of Oklahoma City. Never heavily traveled, it crosses through flat farmland, with now and then a gentle swell in the terrain—wheat fields mostly, with cattle and occasional oil pumps, some of which have been pumping steadily since the 1920s—and small towns like Okarche and Kingfisher and Hennessey, where the speed limit drops briefly from 65 to 25 mph and the tallest buildings are the grain elevators.

En route, I called ahead to Enid on the car phone, telling my people in the office not to wait for me, and when I rode up the empty elevator to the eleventh floor of Broadway Tower, to the law offices of Jones, Wyatt & Roberts, I found that they'd taken me at my word. The premises were deserted.

As for me, I thought it would be a good time to catch up on some work. I knew Sherrel, my wife, wouldn't be home till much later that evening, and the children were all away. But when I entered my sanctum sanctorum, lined with wood paneling and bookshelves and framed photos and memorabilia, I found a message taped to the back of the tall leather chair behind my desk.

It was from Karen Olds, our receptionist, and it read:

"Mr. Jones, Chief Judge Russell desires you call him. He wants to talk to you."

Judge Russell's home number, as well as that of his office, was included.

I sat down at my desk. I had known David Russell for years, all the way back to the University of Oklahoma Law School. We'd both worked for Dewey Bartlett—I when Bartlett was governor, David when he was a U.S. senator—and then, after David was appointed U.S. attorney in 1975, we'd found ourselves on opposing sides in several cases. It so happened that I'd been in his personal office, talking with him, the very moment President Reagan called to tell him he'd named him to the federal bench, and so I'd been the first of his colleagues to congratulate him. We were friends, not close friends but good ones, and I'd always found him to be a fair judge. But federal judges, particularly the chief judge of the Western District of Oklahoma, don't go about calling lawyers just to chat, and they don't leave their home phone numbers either.

I tried Judge Russell's office, but he'd long since left. And then his home, but all I got was an answering machine. I left word, telling him where I was, and left my own home number too.

And I thought of the bombing.

Two weeks before, on April 21, when Timothy McVeigh was identified as John Doe #1 and charged, Susan Otto, head of the Federal Defender's Service in Oklahoma City, had taken over his defense. She had recruited John Coyle to join her. Coyle was a well-established and rather flamboyant Oklahoma City criminal lawyer. I'd heard that they'd tried to step down after the first weekend, Otto out of conflict of interest—her own office, in the old federal courthouse building, had been damaged in the bombing, and she knew many people who'd been caught in the catastrophe—Coyle, so he said, because he'd received numerous threatening phone calls and his wife had insisted he drop out. But Judge Russell, in turn, had made them stay on the job at least through the preliminary hearing the following week and until he found the two replacements McVeigh was entitled to by law.

I didn't envy him his task. Yet I'd heard that he'd been besieged by telephone calls, letters, and faxes from out-of-state lawyers, some of them highly qualified, others less so, all of them seeking appointment as McVeigh's attorney.

Inevitably, there'd been some measure of speculation around the office that we ourselves might be called in. I was one of the naysayers. For one thing, we were too small, just six lawyers at the time. For another, although we were a litigation firm, and although I'd represented more than two dozen defendants in capital cases during my career, criminal law was not our main practice. Among our major clients during the early 1990s were out-of-state insurance companies that retained us to defend them in Oklahoma litigation, and I also represented Enid's newspaper, Phillips University, and the recently elected governor, Frank Keating.

Sherrel had raised the subject too. What if I was asked? She'd always supported me in the past when I'd taken on unpopular causes, but this—the bombing—was just too close to home, she felt, too emotional. People were so angry, so vengeful toward McVeigh, and who could blame them? Hadn't our own friends, Don and Sally Ferrell, lost their thirty-seven-year-old daughter, Susan, who was a lawyer for HUD?

I'd reassured Sherrel. It wasn't going to happen. In addition to the rage that would be directed at any Oklahoma lawyer who defended McVeigh, the case was simply too large, I thought, for an Oklahoman to be appointed. In my estimate, Judge Russell would be better advised to recruit a federal defender from out of state, and if (to come back to that Friday afternoon) he wanted to talk to me now, I imagined it was to solicit my opinion of this or that candidate.

My house was dark and empty when I got home later. It had been thundering all evening—typical spring weather in Oklahoma—and when I pulled into our driveway, some five miles north of town, the sky was pitch-black above my head and strong winds tore through the trees, the cottonwoods, elms, and sycamores that adorn our property.

Then, around 9:30 P.M., the phone rang.

I was on my way downstairs, and I went into the library on the first floor to take it. For some reason, I remember, I didn't turn on the lights. Perhaps this was because, having lived in this grand and wonderful home for almost two decades, I could navigate every corner of it comfortably, even in darkness.

I heard a voice say, "Mr. Stephen Jones?"

It sounded as though it was coming from a great distance.

I acknowledged my name and the voice went on, in a bureaucratic tone, "Mr. Jones, this is the Department of Justice Watch Command Center in Washington, D.C. Please stay on the line for Chief Judge Russell from Oklahoma City."

Why on earth was a telephone call from Oklahoma City to Enid being routed through Washington?

Then I heard Judge Russell's voice, and the voice from Washington cut in again, saying, "Your honor, Mr. Jones is on the line. This is a secure telephone," and then Judge Russell spoke again.

"Stephen," he said, cheerfully enough, "I guess you know why I'm calling."

"Well, judge," I answered, reaching for the legal pad and pencil I always keep near my phones, "I've been assuming it must be about those basset hounds." David Russell and I had both purchased dogs from the same breeder.

"No," he chuckled in reply, "not this time." Then: "Let me come right to the point. I'm calling to see whether you would accept an appointment, under the Criminal Justice Act, to represent one of the individuals who has been, or will be, charged in the Oklahoma City bombing."

And there it was.

I caught the phrase—*one of the individuals who has been, or will be, charged*. As of that Friday, only McVeigh had been charged, but I knew the judge was careful with words. Clearly he was indicating that there would be others, and the reason a secure line had been used was probably because I was one of the few people outside the court and the Department of Justice who now knew it.

He waited for me to answer. I hesitated. I remember, at that particular moment, hearing the wind again, working the trees outside.

"Well, judge," I heard myself reply, "I'd have no professional problem with it."

I meant this in a formal sense, that is, that as a member of the Oklahoma bar, I believed in our obligation to defend the unpopular and the indigent, even when it came to someone accused of such a barbarous crime as Timothy McVeigh.

"The judges and I have talked about this matter," he went on, "and you're one of four we agreed that I should call. Since Arlene has already announced that they'll be going for the death penalty, under the statute we'll need two lawyers minimum for each defendant."

By "judges," he meant the six judges of the Western District, of which he was chief judge; "Arlene" was Arlene Joplin, who'd once worked for me and who was now head of the Department of Justice's Criminal Enforcement Division for western Oklahoma.

"May I ask who the others are?" I said.

"Yes, you may," he answered, "but two of them have turned me down, and one is still thinking about it."

We talked on. Since I'd never been appointed to defend someone at trial under the Criminal Justice Act, I asked him to tell me a bit how it worked, and he did, walking me through the mechanics of the system. Among other things, he said I would be compensated at the hourly rate of $125. I asked him about staff, investigators, expert witnesses. All such expenses were authorized, he said, but they had to be approved in advance by the court.

"Well, judge," I said finally, "may I ask why you've called me?"

"Certainly."

"To put it another way," I corrected, facetiously, "what did I do to aggravate you guys?"

He laughed with me.

"We had three reasons, since you ask," he said, his tone more familiar now. "The first is that you're an excellent lawyer. You've tried many cases before me, and I think you're first-rate, and as far as I know, you have no conflict of interest in the matter."

"That's correct," I said. "There's no conflict of interest."

"Secondly, you have a reputation for very high ethical standards and adherence to ethics—that's been my experience—and that's very important to us."

I thanked him for that.

"And third, you have an established career and you don't practice just criminal law. You won't use this case to advance your own interest at the expense of the client's."

I took this as a high compliment, and I told him so.

"I'm not saying it to be complimentary," he said. "It's what we talked about."

I was to hear later, from Ted Lidz, the administrative director of the Federal Defender's Service, that I had been Russell's choice from the beginning, but that there'd been some opposition to using a lawyer in private practice rather than a public defender or someone associated with one of the death-penalty centers that did appeals work. According to Lidz, Judge Russell, swamped with applications, had decided to let others play out their own candidates before insisting on his.

"Well," I said, "let's do this, if it's possible for you. I assume nothing's going to happen until Monday. Could you give me twenty-four hours? I'd like to talk to my family and a couple of other people. I think I'd like to talk to the governor too. I've never been in a case— well, certainly I've been in cases that were controversial and where I thought there was some personal risk. But I've never been involved in one where I thought my family might be in jeopardy, and my associates too. Or even the building I work in. I'd like to think about that aspect of it."

"I've no problem with that," Judge Russell said. "In fact, that's exactly what you should do. When can you get back to me?"

"What about 6:30, tomorrow night?"

"That'll be fine."

I 'm not sure whether I thought the following thoughts alone or whether I aired them after Sherrel came home. I know I sat right there for some time, not moving, in the darkness of the library. I remembered, when I was seven, standing outside my parents' apartment in Houston, Texas, and hearing the boom from Texas City, more than sixty miles away, when two ships loaded with ammonium nitrate exploded in the harbor, flattening much of the town and killing more than five hundred people, including all twenty-three members of the Texas City Fire Department. I remembered that when I was nineteen and a week away from going to college, the elementary school I'd attended, the Edgar Allen Poe School, was bombed by a man from Seminole, Oklahoma, who'd carried the bomb himself onto the school premises. Martin Kelley and I, who had summer jobs together, rode in the first ambulance to arrive on the scene and the image that greeted us—I'll never forget it—was a young boy, eight or nine or ten, staggering around a corner of the building with his right arm blown off. I remembered going to Christ Church Cathedral every Christmas Eve for years and hearing J. Milton Richardson, dean of the cathedral and later bishop of Texas, preach the same sermon on what Christmas Eve meant to a dying child.

I knew that, of the 168 victims of the Oklahoma City bombing, nineteen were children under the age of six.

But I thought too of other lawyers who, in our history, had been called upon to defend controversial cases. Of John Adams, our second president, who, with Josiah Quincy, had been pressed into service to defend Captain Preston and other redcoats charged with the Boston Massacre. Of U.S. Sen. Reverdy G. Johnson, who had represented Mary Surratt against charges of complicity in the assassination of Abraham Lincoln. Of former New York Governor William Seward, who'd represented a freedman accused of murdering a whole family.

Each of these men had honored the call and obligation to defend the despised, the damned, the outcast, and each had suffered calumny and abuse for what he did. The Oklahoma City bombing case, I knew full well, would attract national, even worldwide attention, and everything I did, if I took it on, would be scrutinized as through a microscope. In addition to the question of physical risk, there were professional, economic, and social consequences I would have to face. Defending Timothy McVeigh would win me no new friends, and I thought about the effect it might have on my existing clients, as well as among my friends and neighbors in Enid, where I had lived and worked for more than thirty years.

"Jonesy? Are you there?"

It was Sherrel's voice, calling out to me from our back entrance, then again from the kitchen.

I called back to her.

"What on earth are you doing," she said, by this time in the library doorway, "sitting here in the dark?"

And I answered, "Booter"—Booter being one of my nicknames for her—"that call you were afraid would come has come."

"Oh, my God," she said. "What are you going to do?"

She came in and sat down next to me in the darkness. We talked about it for a long time then—about ourselves, the children, the case. I know we said the things husbands and wives say to each other when something that could change their lives is at hand, my telling Sherrel that if she didn't want me to do it, I wouldn't, and her telling me that if I wanted to, I certainly should, and I also remember that we never turned the lights on.

The negative factors were easy to line up. We joked a little—a kind of gallows humor—about how we lived five miles out of town, in a big house in a deserted area, and were sitting ducks for any marauders. And how John Coyle had withdrawn because of the death threats. And about the danger to our children. Stephen Mark and John, the two oldest, were living in California and Texas respectively, but Edward and Rachael were home often. And what about my mother, who also lived in Enid? Then there was Jones, Wyatt & Roberts. Naive though I might have been then about some of the consequences, I already knew the case would be all-consuming, that it would monopolize my law practice for as long as it lasted. And what of Sherrel's political future? If my own aspirations were over—a convinced and lifetime Republican, I'd run for office four times in Oklahoma, lastly as the Republican nominee for U.S. Senate, and had been defeated four times—Sherrel's had just begun. She'd stood for the state legislature the year before, had lost in the Republican primary by six votes, the closest election in Oklahoma. Already, the governor and Tom Cole, his chief political adviser, had been talking about her running in 1996 against a popular local Democrat, State Senator Ed Long. But what effect would my taking on a highly visible, and hugely unpopular, defense have on her chances?

Unpopular causes, unpopular cases. I'd never shirked them. Some twenty-five years before, I'd served as general counsel to the Oklahoma Chapter of the American Civil Liberties Union (ACLU), which, to some people in our part of the country, was tantamount to being a card-carrying communist. (I later resigned from the organization, however, when the national ACLU came out for the impeachment of President Nixon. As a young man during the mid-sixties, I had worked for Mr. Nixon in New York as his personal researcher, when he himself was in full-time practice, and I thought—then and now—that he was a much-maligned president.) In that same turbulent period, I'd defended a long-haired and nearly blind college student, Keith Green, who'd been arrested for carrying a Vietcong flag into an ROTC formation at the University of Oklahoma. My insistence on representing him had cost me my job with the Enid firm I'd worked for and had propelled me into practice on my own. Later, I'd represented Abbie Hoffman, the famous radical Yippie, when Oklahoma State University refused to let him speak on campus.

And then there were two murder cases that had propelled me, whether I liked it or not, into statewide notoriety. On Labor Day 1974, when I was the Republican nominee for state attorney general, Marvin Thrasher, his wife and two children were brutally murdered in their small frame house north of Woodward, Oklahoma. A week later, a young drifter, Bobby Wayne Collins, was arrested and charged, and a Woodward lawyer, Romain Mossman, was appointed to represent him. Criminal law, though, was outside Mossman's usual practice, and he telephoned me and asked if I would take over the defense. I agreed. The facts of the case, though, were so brutal, the crime so horrible, that emotions ran strongly against us, and even though I obtained a change of venue to Enid, Bobby Collins was convicted and sentenced to death. Although, on appeal, a divided court upheld his conviction in a narrow decision, it also vacated the death penalty.

Ten years later, a prominent local businesswoman, Sue Caton, was arrested and charged with the first-degree murder of her sometime business partner and former lover, Jack Kretchmar. This was not a court-appointed case. Mrs. Caton paid us a handsome fee, and we secured her release on bail. Inevitably, the ingredients of sex and violence, unrequited love and murder, plus the accused's prominence in the community fanned and inflamed the local rumor mills, and, once again, we obtained a change of venue. At trial, Sue was acquitted of murder, convicted of manslaughter, and served less than eight months, during which period she came home every weekend.

Still more recently, there was the case of Roger Dale Stafford. Stafford was a notorious serial killer who'd been on death row in MacAlester Prison in eastern Oklahoma ever since his conviction in 1979. Nine years later, in my only federal court–appointed work before Judge Russell's call, the court had asked me to take over his appeals, and we had managed to keep him alive for another seven years. Time was now running out, though, and later that summer, at Roger Stafford's request, I would be a witness at his execution.

Unpopular causes, unpopular cases. Although Collins, Caton, and Stafford may have enhanced my reputation as a criminal defense lawyer, they, along with my old association with the ACLU, doomed me politically and, in the eyes of some of my more self-righteous neighbors and fellow citizens, tarnished me and my family in the process. I, in turn, had always taken my constitutional duty seriously. The Sixth Amendment is quite explicit—"In all criminal prosecutions, the accused shall enjoy the right . . . to have the assistance of Counsel for his defense."—as is the standard set forth by the American Bar Association with regard to the counsel: "All qualified trial lawyers should stand ready to undertake the defense of an accused regardless of public hostility toward the accused or personal distaste for the offense charged or the person of the defendant."

Over and over again since, I've been asked the question, "But how could you defend someone like McVeigh?"

"Because I was obliged to," I've answered. And to those willing to listen, I've added that it is also the duty of the advocate to defend his client with all the skill he possesses.

How, alternatively, could I turn it down, once it was offered, and ever look myself in the mirror again? What would be the sense and rationale of my career as a lawyer? And how, if I refused it, could I ever again walk into the U.S. courthouse in Oklahoma City and appear in front of those very judges who'd called on my services?

Obligation, yes, but there was something else too. I think of it as the Wardlow Lane factor.

As long ago as I can remember, I was fascinated by lawyers and politicians. They were my role models. A distant relative of mine on my grandmother's side was the great and famous criminal defense lawyer in Houston, Percy Foreman. Foreman was a big, barrel-chested man with prematurely graying hair, piercing eyes, and an instinct for the dramatic. Even before the Supreme Court rulings in *Escabedo*, *Miranda*, and *Mapp*, he saved all but one of his first-degree murder clients from death row. People hired Percy Foreman, it was said, because "he carried the keys to the jail in his pocket."

Another early hero of mine was Thad Hutcheson, scion of a well-known and respected Houston family who ran a determined but losing campaign, as a Republican, in a special "sudden death" election in 1957 to fill the remaining term of Price Daniel in the U.S. Senate. On occasion, I would visit Thad Hutcheson's law offices in downtown Houston, and I still remember the faded pictures on the walls of members of the Harris County bench and bar, the horsehair black sofas, the attractive young strawberry-blonde secretaries, and the book-filled lawyer's offices. I would gaze reverently at those rows upon rows of law books, in their gray or tannish covers, with gold lettering and polished to a sheen with oiled cloth.

Jim McBride, my high-school history teacher, gave me a copy of *Lanterns on the Levee*, the autobiography of William Alexander Percy, the uncle of the novelist Walker Percy and a small-town lawyer in Greenville, Mississippi. I read and reread it. I began to devour books about lawyering and politics, and the "romance" of both—I can think of no other word to describe what I felt—infused me. Then, when I went to "the Forty Acres," as the University of Texas in Austin was known, I felt I had everything a young man could seek. The great and near-great came to speak on our campus. The library, even then, was one of the largest in the country, and I got permission from my government professor, O. Douglas Weeks, to patrol its closed stacks. Just across Guadalupe Street, members of the still embryonic civil rights movement were protesting the decision of local theaters not to seat Negro students on the main floor, and less than a twenty-minute walk away was the pink granite pile of the Texas State Capitol. On its second floor was the Texas senate, otherwise known as "the Club," and the acknowledged leader of the Club was Wardlow Lane.

The thirty men and one woman in the state senate lived a hardly less regal existence than the members of the British House of Lords, and their chamber was no less splendid, with its floor-to-ceiling windows, its haunting portrait of Stephen F. Austin, its large mural canvas of the Battle of the Alamo, and its thirty-one desks spaced evenly inside the gold railing. This elegant room became the center of my every political interest, and it was there that I first became acquainted with a legendary man—the short, stocky, grumpy, curmudgeonly senator from Shelby County—who has influenced me ever since.

To political Texas during the fifties and early sixties, Wardlow Lane was the epitome—the very bastion—of conservative laissez-faireism and noblesse oblige privilege. In a collection of prima donnas, he was prima donna number one. He controlled the Texas senate. Wheeling and dealing, needling and cajoling, at times even physically intimidating, this rural, gnome-like *generalissimo* ran his political arena in a crude, brilliant, and, to some, infuriating style.

But I found out that there was another Wardlow Lane.

Given his northeast Texas constituency, Lane contrived to hide that he'd once been Phi Beta Kappa and Order of the Coif at the University of Texas. Instead, he regaled one and all with ribald stories, and picturesque tales of his spinster aunts, the Cox sisters, and his fast pink Thunderbird, and so on. About the last thing in the world he would have wanted was for anyone to dig up that he, once upon a time, had prevented lynchings or attacked privilege. But I succeeded nevertheless in piecing the stories together—from rumor, from yellowed newspaper clippings up in the files of the old Texas State Library, and from what my friend, old Charley Jones, a one-time senator himself but more recently the senate doorkeeper, would confide in me, sotto voce—and I will tell two of them.

Lane, while still in his twenties, had been a small-town East Texas prosecutor, when a young black male—a "nigger up-country"—was accused, in a grand jury presentment, of raping a white woman. That same night, an angry crowd gathered in front of the courthouse, some of them hooded, others bearing torches, and one holding a rope. They pulled the alleged rapist out of the courthouse jail, without much resistance from the sheriff, and onto the lawn in front, and they were fixing to dispense their own justice when Wardlow Lane appeared at the edge of the crowd.

With a drawn revolver, he worked his way through these self-styled knights, straddled the young black male who was prone on the ground, and told the crowd they'd have to kill him first before he'd let them hang their victim. Furthermore, if they wanted a lynching party bad enough to try, he'd take some of them with him into the fires of hell. Confronted in this way—by this young, short, but very determined prosecutor—the braves of the Klan backed off and disappeared into the night from whence they'd come, while Lane helped the accused black man to his feet and escorted him back to jail.

It really happened. And so did this second story:

A rich man's son, with more money than common sense, was racing his fast car down the backroads of Shelby County when he struck and killed a young woman. The driver blithely kept pedal to the metal and took refuge in neighboring Louisiana. His idea was to stay there until Texas's appetite for justice cooled off. Meanwhile his friends took care of things back home, so that when Lane, the young prosecutor, began to investigate, he ran into a kind of collective amnesia. Those he could find had seen nothing; those who might have seen something he couldn't find. But the perpetrator hadn't known whom he was going up against. Determined to bring Mr. "Born-with-a-silver-spoon-in-his-mouth" to justice, Lane packed a portable typewriter into his saddle bags and, strapping them to his horse, rode off alone along the creeks and hollows and into the piney woods that mark the Texas-Louisiana border. There he browbeat and cajoled several witnesses into signing notarized statements of what they'd seen, and when he was satisfied he'd built his case, he filed a formal demand through the governor of Texas for the fugitive to be extradited back to Shelby County. In due course, he was extradited, and in due course, he was convicted and incarcerated.

I took to watching Lane attentively. Far from being the caricature of the cartoonists or the know-nothing target of the "red-hots" (as the liberals in Texas politics were then called), he was smart, smarter than they were. Smart enough, I discovered, to hide his intelligence and cunning behind the slow drawl, the comfortable chuckle, and that monumental stubbornness against which the passions and tempers of his rivals beat with a signal lack of penetration. At the same time, I glimpsed the man's idealism at work time and again. There was a move on, at the time, sponsored by various ultra-right-wing groups, to curtail the Texas School Book Commission and its freedom to choose the books for our schools. Proclaiming his support for the idea loud and clear—how could we not afford the Lord's children every protection?—Lane nonetheless pigeonholed the measure, discreetly but efficaciously, every time it was brought up.

He was never one to be out-orated on the senate floor, and he had his constituents to worry about. But over and over again, the schemes, many of them harebrained, that I heard him champion in public failed to make it into legislation, and this because, once removed from the public eye, Senator Lane quietly killed them.

I only managed to speak to him a few times. Once, I had stopped him to offer congratulations on a lengthy and highly laudatory profile of him written by Robert Sherrill, a Pulitzer Prize–winning journalist for the *Texas Observer*.

The senator eyed me balefully as I said my piece.

"I don't see what was so good about it," he said gruffly when I was done.

I stared back at him, not getting it.

"Each of these fine people here," he went on, with a wave that encompassed the whole senate chamber, "thinks he's running things. How do you think they'll feel to read that *I'm* running them?" Then, turning to stomp off, he said, "Mr. Sherrill did me no good whatsoever."

He was hardly a role model in a literal sense—for one thing, his talent for deviousness and subterfuge was unmatched and probably unmatchable—but by the time I went north to Oklahoma to go to law school, I'd learned much from observing and studying him. About the price of one's convictions, for one. And the pleasures and risks of being a minority of one. And the need, for certain men in certain situations, to create a legend behind which maneuverability could be preserved. But, most importantly, about the values of courage and integrity and adherence to the law.

In a very real way, Wardlow Lane wouldn't let me say no to Judge Russell's offer.

As I said to Sherrel, that night in the library, "It's not that I *want* to do it. But I think I should."

And she said, "Well, Jonesy, if that's your decision, I'll support you without reservation."

And so, that night, we set about calling the children.

By Saturday morning, I'd reached them all, and a number of my clients too. Although ours was a litigation practice, there were certain clients with whom we had ongoing relationships, and I felt an obligation to consult with them. People like Lew Ward, Sheldon Elliott, Nancy Davies, and Bob Berry were friends and clients. Their opinions would be important to me. Although I didn't reach the governor directly, we talked through Tom Cole, his chief political adviser and Oklahoma secretary of state, who told me the governor was proud to have an Oklahoman do the job. Then, in the afternoon, I invited the other lawyers from the firm—Bob Wyatt, Mike Roberts, Jim Hankins, Julia Sims, and Jeremy Lowrey—out to the house. I told them what had happened. As senior partner, I knew the final decision would be mine—and so did they—but I wanted them to speak their minds, and they did.

That same day, I had a security expert, David Pritchett, come over, and I asked Tommy Freeman, a retired FBI agent, to join us. I wanted to know how much we were at risk, and they both felt the risk was considerable. The house, they pointed out, was in a very rural area, easily accessible from the highway but set back from it. We had no lights on the grounds, no electronic gate opener, but there were lots of windows, lots of doors. As Pritchett put it, somebody could be on our property and gone before we so much as knew about it—a prediction, unfortunately, that would prove accurate. The only safe solution, they felt, beyond the lights and the electronic devices, would be to have a security service guarding the premises, at least at night, and this, with the court authorizing the expense, we eventually did.

All that remained for me to do, then, was to call Judge Russell back.

"Your honor?" I said. Then, in lawyerly fashion, I repeated his words from the night before. "In response to your question—whether or not I would accept an appointment to represent one of the individuals charged in the Oklahoma bombing—if the offer were tendered to me, yes, I would accept it."

"Great!" he said enthusiastically. "Then I'm going to appoint you to represent Timothy McVeigh. Can you be in my chambers at 1:30 Monday?"

"Certainly I can," I answered. "But while I have your ear, may I raise some other subjects?"

He told me to fire away, and I did. One of those subjects was staffing; another had to do with money. As I've mentioned, I represented Roger Dale Stafford, the death row convicted killer, and the

Tenth Circuit (e.g., the United States Court of Appeals for the Tenth Circuit, the appellate court that includes, among other districts in western America, the Western Judicial District of Oklahoma) at this point owed me some $50,000 in back fees. I hadn't been able to collect a nickel in quite some time. The circuit hadn't even deigned to answer my dunning letters. I described the situation to Judge Russell, adding that I couldn't now take on McVeigh's defense without being assured that our statements would be processed promptly and that payment would be made within thirty days.

The money issue would come back, but at that honeymoon moment, Russell understood. He himself, he pointed out, would be reviewing our statements. No problem there. Furthermore, he promised to call Ted Lidz on Monday and get the arrears on Stafford taken care of. (As I recall, we had our check for the missing $50,000 the following Wednesday.)

Then the judge said, "Terry Nichols is going to be charged on Tuesday. He'll be brought down here from Wichita, and it's going to be up to me to find a lawyer for him too."

As for Nichols, all I really knew at the time was that the search for John Doe #1 had led the FBI first to Michigan, where James Nichols, Terry's brother, lived, and later back to Terry himself in Herington, Kansas. Terry Nichols had gone to the authorities voluntarily, in Herington, the same day McVeigh was led out of the Noble County Jail and had been interviewed for close to ten hours, after which he'd been ordered held as a material witness. Now he too was to be charged.

"One other thing," Judge Russell said. "I hope you realize it, but there's going to be enormous press interest in you. CNN and all the others are going to be camping on your doorstep, day and night."

I thought he was exaggerating, and I told him so. Tim McVeigh was the one the media wanted to know about, not me.

"Well, you're wrong," he said, "and you better start figuring out how you're going to handle it."

"Do you have any suggestions?"" I asked.

"No, I don't. But I want you to be ready for it."

I said maybe I could issue just one statement and that would satisfy all of them. I remember his reply: "Stephen, I know that however you handle it, you will do the right thing."

Having long since experienced the importance of the media in criminal cases, I still thought Judge Russell was exaggerating. Perhaps this only proved that I was nothing more, or less, than "a competent country lawyer," as a member of the media covering the case later called me (or a county-seat lawyer, as I often think of it), but ready or not, I was about to get a cram course in dealing with the media multitudes, from the New York City heavyweights—the Dan Rathers, the Barbara Walterses, the Diane Sawyerses—down to Mr. J. D. Cash, who wrote, very influentially, for the *McCurtain County Gazette* in Idabel, Oklahoma (population 6,500).

T hat same Saturday, after dinner, I went upstairs to my home office under the third-floor eaves. It's a large and very pleasant room. At least it was large originally. Now there are books everywhere you turn—stacked on the floor, on the available furniture, on the wall-to-ceiling shelves—because I'm an addicted book buyer, particularly in politics and history, and the overflow from home has long since filled the rooms of our offices downtown, and vice versa.

But there was still room for me up there, and yellow pads and pencils, and I still remember the first thing I wrote down that night:
"Why Murrah Building?"
Not why the bombing, but why this particular building.
And the second question, following immediately: "Why would two drifters, McVeigh and Nichols, one from upstate New York, one from upstate Michigan, bomb a federal building *in Oklahoma City?*"
I wasn't stating, obviously, that they *had* bombed the Murrah Building, but the government was claiming they had. It would be my task to prove the government wrong, or to convince a jury of it; but aside from who was right and who wrong, why Oklahoma? Why not New York City? Or Chicago, maybe? Or Los Angeles?
And something else. What ever happened to the FBI's first take on the case? Those two men of Middle East extraction whom witnesses claimed to have seen leaving the building just before the bombing? And the pickup they'd reportedly used to escape? And the Jordanian national who'd boarded a plane in Oklahoma City on his way to Rome, then had been detained by the FBI in Chicago, then had been arrested at London's Heathrow Airport and returned to the United

States? The idea that the bombing might have been of Middle East inspiration and execution hadn't seemed all that far-fetched at first. The massive explosion was reminiscent of anti-American bombings in Lebanon and at the World Trade Center. Then, too, Oklahoma City itself had that sizable population of Muslim fundamentalists.

But the moment the FBI found Tim McVeigh and "displayed" him like a trophy at the Noble County courthouse, we heard nothing further about the Middle East. Little did I know then—and the government would do its best to keep me from ever finding out—that even as the FBI was charging first McVeigh and then Nichols, the cable lines between our State Department and our embassy in Bonn were burning up concerning a German national I'd never heard of, one Andreas Strassmeir. Neither did I know that the government was outfitting a paid informant with a wire, a woman who had been warning the Bureau of Alcohol, Tobacco, and Firearms (ATF) since August 1994 about the bizarre and deadly plans of a group of white supremacists in a place called Elohim City, Oklahoma. Neither, needless to say, did I know anything about a phone call that had been placed, the night of the bombing, April 19, by a general in the Saudi Arabian intelligence service to a gentleman in Virginia who happened to be the CIA's former chief of operations for counterterrorism.

None of the above was leaked to the media. Not a word. As far as any of us knew—the media included—it was a "done deal": McVeigh and Nichols had done it, and maybe Nichols's brother, James, was involved, plus the ever-elusive John Doe #2. Not for another two weeks would I have an inkling that the government's case mightn't be as strong as its early posturing suggested, and it would be months before I began to understand why.

But during that weekend early in May, or what was left of it, I rushed to catch up. I read everything I could lay my hands on by way of newspaper and magazine coverage. The more I read, the more I realized the enormous authority that our federal government and its agencies carry in our land. This wasn't an entirely new discovery, and I'd long since stopped being daunted by it. Nevertheless, everywhere I turned, it was clear that in the eyes of the government, and therefore of the media, and therefore, presumably, of most of the nation, the case against my new client was overwhelming. He already stood convicted.

3

"MR. MCVEIGH, MY NAME IS STEPHEN JONES"

Fences had been put up all around the ruins of the Murrah Building, and there were police barricades at the entrances, and national guardsmen patrolled the perimeter. Police cars were everywhere. I didn't pause for long. It was Monday, May 8, and I was headed for the federal courthouse building across the plaza on Fourth Street, barely five hundred feet away. It hadn't escaped damage in the explosion—within a ten-block radius few buildings had—but by this time, some two and a half weeks later, it was functioning more or less normally.

U.S. marshals guarded the entrance, and there were metal detectors that had been in use for several years. Although the marshals knew me by sight, they searched me carefully—no one, I guess, was taking any chances—and I went up to Judge Russell's chambers.

"Come on in, Stephen," Judge Russell called out when he saw me in his doorway. He was in shirtsleeves. Magistrate Ron Howland was with him, and so were Susan Otto and John Coyle, and their mood was relaxed, almost light-hearted. We greeted each other. The judge was just putting the finishing touches to the order appointing me, and meanwhile he joked about how Susan and John couldn't wait to be discharged.

"I've arranged for you to go out and meet your client at El Reno this afternoon," he said. "John and Susan have agreed to help you every way they can."

They confirmed this. If I wanted them to, they said, they would drive out to El Reno ahead of me, tell Tim McVeigh I was coming, and hold the fort till I got there. I was greatly appreciative of this, needless to say, and we also arranged to meet the next morning so that they could brief me on what they'd done so far.

When we all got up, though, I said to Judge Russell, "Your honor, may I see you privately for a moment?"

"Well, yes, certainly," he replied.

The others left, closing the door behind me.

"I just want to thank you for your consideration of me," I said, "and for the appointment. To me, it's a mark of respect. I'm going to try to do a good job for you, but one consistent with my duties as McVeigh's lawyer. I'm not going to defend him with one arm tied behind my back. I may make some people unhappy, and that might include you."

He nodded. I think we both understood that our relationship was about to be very different. He stood up and came around to where I stood.

"Absolutely," he said, extending his hand. "I wouldn't want it any other way. That's exactly what we expect of you." We shook hands, and he looked me in the eye. "It's going to be rough, Stephen," he said. "Actually, I hope I haven't signed your death warrant."

To which, in a half-joking spirit, I replied, "Well, David, that makes two of us." This was the one and only time, since he became judge, that I used his Christian name.

In the coming months, as the handing-up of the indictments came closer and, with it, the assignment of the case to its own judge, our relations would indeed become strained. This was inevitable, I think, in that I was the advocate for "the most hated man in America," as the media dubbed McVeigh, and the chief judge was responsible for mediating between prosecution and defense teams that became more antagonistic toward each other as time passed. But I never lost my respect for David Russell, and I recognized that he was in a most awkward and difficult position. The stakes were very high—a man's life, on the one side, the government's integrity and trustworthiness on the other—and the attention focused on us all was intense and unrelenting.

That Monday morning, leaving Enid for Oklahoma City, I'd had the sharp premonition that my life was never going to be the same again. Now, as I left the courthouse building, it came again, an acute sense of having crossed some personal Rubicon. I was glad to have my colleagues, Bob Wyatt and Jim Hankins, along and also my daughter, Rachael, who'd come home from college the day before and wanted to be a part of the moment as much as she could. They hadn't been able to accompany me into the judge's chambers, and they'd have to wait for me too, once we got to El Reno, but I took comfort from their presence.

We'd come in two cars, and now we drove out of Oklahoma City, one following the other, then west on Interstate 40 some thirty miles to the dusty town of El Reno. Judge Russell had said he was going to file the order around three o'clock, which meant, as it turned out, that I had one more hour of traveling incognito. In El Reno, we took the 40-Business route through town, then out the other side onto old U.S. Route 66 till we came to the Federal Correctional Institution. At a glance, the facility resembles an army post more than a prison, with attractive, well-tended grounds and barrackslike buildings. In fact it had once been a federal reformatory. But then we turned in at the entrance, and I could see the blinking blue lights at the first checkpoint and the squat tower rising over it, and it came home to me that, right there, somewhere within those confines, was my new client.

Before I continue the story I need to caution the reader. Under the rules of attorney-client privilege, almost none of my conversations with Tim McVeigh—neither their actual words nor their substance—can be divulged in this book. I can't tell you if McVeigh told me he actually drove the Ryder truck to Oklahoma City and set off the bomb or bombs, or if he helped the person or persons who did, or if he had any knowledge of it. Moreover, I can't tell you whether or not I believed the things he told me, or if I sometimes did and sometimes didn't. I can't even tell you if I ever put questions like these to him. Communications between lawyer and client are—rightly—as protected in our system of justice as those between confessor and priest, or husband and wife.

In other words, if you, the reader, are reading this book to find out whether Tim McVeigh confessed to me, then I suggest you stop reading—right now—and let us go our separate ways. This isn't a book about what Tim told me about the Oklahoma City bombing, and it can't be. It isn't even a book about Timothy McVeigh, strictly speaking. It is, instead, the story of an ongoing American tragedy, in which the Oklahoma bombing is not the first chapter and, sadly, won't be the last, and of my efforts, as the accused's lawyer, to discover the facts and the reasons why our own government fought so long and so hard to keep so many of these facts from ever being aired.

To put it in a more succinct, if more cryptic way, when I met with Susan Otto and John Coyle the following day, in John's office, Susan's last words to me—and she is one I listen to carefully, for she chooses her words with care—were, "When you know everything I know, Stephen, and you will soon enough, you will never think of the United States of America again in the same way."

My prison escort and I came through the last of the airlock doors, turned to the right, and there, through a half-open door, I saw Susan and John seated at a table. They were chatting with McVeigh. They all stood as I entered, and I realized McVeigh was wearing shackles.

"Mr. McVeigh, my name is Stephen Jones," I said, holding out my hand. "I've been appointed by the court to represent you."

We shook hands firmly. We made and held eye contact. He was tall, a little taller than six feet, and thin. Clean-shaven and blue-eyed, he looked even younger than his twenty-seven years.

The prison officials closed the door behind me, and the four of us chatted for a few minutes. Then Susan and John left.

Symbolic as the moment may have been, it was short of drama, but even in that first brief visit, the enormous disparity struck me—between the demonized, most-hated-man-in-America image the media had begun to fabricate the moment McVeigh walked out of the Noble County Courthouse and the unassuming and seemingly intelligent young man I now represented.

We talked of nothing of substance that day. I gave Tim my business card, my various phone numbers, and told him a bit about me and my professional background. There were the usual caveats. He could call us collect, day or night, whenever he needed to, but he should never use the phone to discuss the case. The same went for anyone he met at the prison—not a word about the case—because anything he said could be used against him. Then I told him to get a good night's sleep, because I'd be back the next day and we'd get started.

And that we did. The first week, and on into the second, I saw McVeigh almost every day. Then, as the defense team expanded, we began to rotate our visits. One of us would be with him part of each day, including weekends, and it would be quite some time before we left him alone for more than twenty-four hours at a stretch. Much of this was practical—there was work to be done—but I had a psychological motive too. I thought it important for Tim to realize that there was a team of people working in his behalf, people who cared and who would never abandon him.

I was also worried about his safety. That was one concern the government clearly shared. Although I didn't learn it till later, one of the regular El Reno guards had lost his wife in the bombing, and the guards in Tim's immediate area belonged to a special detachment that had been brought in from Dallas–Ft. Worth. This, in turn, would make trouble for us in other ways. It was no coincidence, in my mind, that stories about McVeigh and El Reno always seemed to appear first in *The Dallas Morning News*, and I early got permission from the court to bring in a tape recorder so as to play background music during our meetings, this to keep us from being overheard by guards listening outside the door. Later on, the security issue would become serious enough that we filed a motion asking for the disclosure of electronic surveillance—(inevitably, the government, in reply, produced some low-level FBI staffer who testified that he'd swept the meeting room at El Reno and had found nothing)—but in the beginning my goal was simply to make sure our client was protected and reasonably comfortable.

I was still an unknown county-seat lawyer when we left the prison that Monday afternoon. That would shortly change. The media had a TV stakeout on the north shoulder of Route 66 directly across from the prison entrance (they could get no closer without an invitation or a pass), but they paid no mind to our two-car procession, either coming or going. On our way back to Oklahoma City, though, I called my office and asked them to get on to the press room at the State Capitol Building and tell them I'd stop by around 5 P.M. to answer any questions about my appointment. En route we had a small preview of what was about to happen.

That morning, when we'd gotten into our car, the wind was so strong that it had blown the car door smack into my daughter Rachael's forehead, and now she was complaining of a full-fledged headache. *You never know*, I thought, and I decided that before we met the media, we'd better have her checked out. Therefore, we stopped at Presbyterian Hospital and went into the emergency room. There were perhaps some thirty to forty people in the immediate area, staff and patients, none of them paying any attention to us.

I went up to the reception desk with Rachael, gave my name, started to explain what had happened. There was a TV just above our heads. It was tuned to CNN, and as we were standing there, the onscreen voice abruptly changed, and the new voice said, "We interrupt with breaking news on the Oklahoma City bombing case."

I heard that and stepped back a few feet, thinking I'd better pay attention. I looked up at the screen, and the first thing I saw was my own picture.

"CNN has just learned that the federal court has appointed a fifty-four-year-old Enid, Oklahoma, lawyer, Stephen Jones, to represent Timothy McVeigh."

And everything stopped in the emergency area—all movement, all conversation.

Dead silence. Either people had heard me give my name or they connected the onscreen face with the man standing under it. Or both.

They'd already taken Rachael back through the swinging doors. A young resident came out, and I explained to him who I was and why I had to leave. He reassured me. He didn't think anything was wrong with Rachael—he was right, as it turned out—but Jim Hankins volunteered to stay there until she was released, and so Bob Wyatt and I drove off for the Capitol.

I'd called ahead before we got to the hospital to tell the press room we were running late, maybe twenty minutes late or half an hour, and, in my naïveté, to ask whether anybody would still be around at 5:30. The legislature was in session, but not much usually happens there late on a Monday afternoon except for committee hearings. But the person who answered the phone had said, amid a lot of background noise, "I wouldn't worry if I were you, Mr. Jones. We'll be here."

I didn't get it. I still didn't get it when we got to the Capitol Building parking lot and saw the TV trucks. I even commented on it to Bob—Why were they there so late? I didn't see any activity around the trucks, though, and when we went inside and walked into the elevator, there was no one around.

I punched five. We rode up to the fifth floor. The door opened. And there they all were.

Some surprise party.

My first impression was of lights, a thousand dazzling lights. And noise. Dozens of voices shouting at once. And people walking backwards, away from us as we came toward them, as though they were subjects to some oriental potentate, while others at the sides crowded forward, arms reaching out. And tripping over each other, jockeying and jostling for position, yelling the whole time, while pole mikes bobbed up and down over our heads.

A chaos of TV cameras, bright lights, and clamor.

I thought, *Well, I'm going to have to get used to it*. But I'm not sure I ever did, altogether.

Finally, somehow, they subsided. I'd prepared a brief and unmemorable statement that I read aloud. Then I said I would field a few questions, and they came at me in staccato bursts of noise, left, right, and center, the trivial and the serious in random sequence.

Who was I? How had I been chosen? How did I spell Stephen? What qualified me to defend McVeigh? How many other lawyers had turned down the job? How could I, an Oklahoman, bring myself to defend McVeigh? Had I met McVeigh yet? Had he confessed to me? Were we considering a plea bargain?

Some of these people I already knew, mind you—the local crowd, people from the *Daily Oklahoman*, the TV and radio stations, Tony Clark, who was an Oklahoma City native and now a reporter and producer for CNN, and so on—but it was already clear that our relationship would be on a different plane. The next night, I would be on *Larry King Live*, and the other TV news and interview shows would follow. From that moment on, I, together with the other members of the defense team as it grew, would be like fish in the fishbowl, and that fishbowl, thanks to the media, would stay in full view of the public for the next two years.

I spent that Monday night in Oklahoma City. My usual lodging, the Waterford, was full—another sign of what happens when a high-profile case hits home—and I stayed a couple of miles away at the Governor's Inn. This was a good thing too. No one knew I was there, and I had a special appointment the next morning at 6:30 A.M. Meanwhile, as I found out, our phones in Enid, at home and in the office, had been ringing off the hook.

It was barely dawn when I returned to the federal courthouse building. I wanted to tour the Murrah Building myself, see the devastation with my own eyes.

My escort was waiting for me, an employee of the General Services Administration. I presented my credentials and was outfitted with a badge and a hardhat and we went on over, inside the perimeter fence and across the esplanade to the 5th Street side, on a motor scooter like a modified golf cart.

By this time—the following day, a Wednesday, would mark the three-week anniversary of the bombing—I had a pretty fair grasp of what had happened, according to the official version.

I knew all this, and God knows I had seen dozens, probably hundreds, of images of it, photographs and videos, and listened to the first-person accounts. But nothing, nothing I knew or had heard, had prepared me for the experience of the building itself. At this point, some three weeks after the event, the decision had been made to implode the building, and all the rescue and salvage work that could be done before then had long since been completed. My escort pointed out orange paint to me, marking those areas where there were still several bodies that could not yet be recovered. Only afterward, once the building was imploded, would those human remains be sifted from the rubble.

Our first fight with the prosecution would be over the implosion issue. We wanted it delayed so that we could have our own people examine the wreckage, and the court decided in our favor. But that first morning, in my dismay, I could only think of the incredible havoc we human beings can and do wreak upon ourselves. The presence and the literal smell of death were all around me, all-pervasive, and at least for that moment, at the edge of the cavernous ruins of the building, I was overwhelmed by the task before me.

There were, of course, practical reasons too why I should have felt that way. I was three weeks behind. In the three weeks following the bombing and the almost three weeks since Tim McVeigh's staged parade at the Perry courthouse, the government had had free rein not only in gathering evidence, interviewing witnesses, and harnessing its enormous resources to the investigation but also in convincing the media of its version of the story, which it quickly did. And through the media, it had also convinced the public.

By "the government" I mean principally the FBI. The Murrah Building was federal property, among the victims were federal employees, and, although the state troopers, the Oklahoma Bureau of Investigation, the Oklahoma City Police Department, and the Oklahoma County Sheriff's Office performed valuable services early, particularly with regard to the site itself, the local and state authorities were quickly brushed aside. Similarly, the Bureau of Alcohol, Tobacco, and Firearms stepped almost immediately, and probably thankfully, into the shadows. In addition to having played the fall guy for two previous government law-enforcement fiascoes—I'm referring to Waco and Ruby Ridge—ATF's own offices in the Murrah Building had been nearly empty at the time of the explosion. This had led, on the one hand, to persistent rumors of prior warning—had the ATF somehow known what was coming?—and, on the other, to a concocted story of two ATF employees who'd allegedly experienced a free fall of five stories in a building elevator and lived to tell about it, when in fact, according to the elevator engineers, who were among the very first people to arrive at the scene after the explosion, none of the elevators had fallen.

The two bureaus—ATF and the FBI—had collided before over questions of jurisdiction. That two such agencies exist, and that the ATF reports to the Treasury Department and the FBI to the Department of Justice, is a historical anomaly (and, today, a costly one), but in our case, any friction between the two was decided quickly in Washington, with the ATF genuflecting to the FBI.

In the days immediately following the bombing, FBI agents poured into Oklahoma City, into Kansas to the north, and wherever else in the country—Arizona, Michigan, upstate New York, Florida—there were leads to be followed up. Although we never ascertained how many agents were actively involved, we knew later, from documents that were finally handed over after a series of bitter struggles, that at least 30,000 interviews were conducted by the FBI.

The FBI's head start and superior resources might become less important in the longer scheme of things—Tim McVeigh's trial was not to begin for almost another two years—but it took us a long time to catch up, and in some respects we never did. For one thing, key witnesses were loath even to talk to our investigators once we began our own work. Hadn't they already told the FBI—and the media—all they knew? Besides, wasn't McVeigh guilty as sin?

This was the popular perception we ran into over and over again, and in good part it had come about because major elements in the government's circumstantial case were known early and widely publicized. In outline form, these claims included the following:

- Tim McVeigh was "John Doe #1," the composite character drawn by FBI artists from the first eyewitnesses.

- On April 14, in Junction City, Kansas, using cash and his own name, McVeigh had bought the "getaway car," the beat-up yellow Mercury Marquis without license plates that he was driving when he was arrested, the morning of April 19, near Perry, an hour and a half after the bombing.

- Also on April 14, McVeigh checked into the Dreamland Motel in Junction City.

- On April 17, using cash and a false driver's license issued to a Robert Kling, McVeigh had rented the Ryder truck at Elliott's

Body Shop in Junction City, Kansas, the same truck that four
days later exploded at the entrance to the Murrah Building.

♦ A Ryder truck, presumably the same one, was seen parked outside Terry Nichols's house in Herington, Kansas (twenty-four
miles from Junction City), on the evening of April 17.

♦ On April 18, several witnesses claimed to have seen a Ryder
truck parked by the lake at Geary State Fishing Lake, between
Junction City and Herington, where the government believed
the bomb was constructed.

♦ The bomb was a mixture of ammonium nitrate and fuel oil
(ANFO). Blasting caps and other suspicious items had been
discovered in Terry Nichols's home, as well as a receipt bearing
McVeigh's latent fingerprint, for the purchase, the previous
September, by one Mike Havens of forty fifty-pound bags of
ammonium nitrate at the Mid-Kansas Co-op in McPherson,
Kansas.

♦ The morning of April 19, several witnesses put McVeigh (John
Doe #1) and the Ryder truck at or near the Murrah Building.

♦ Bomb residue was found on the clothes that McVeigh was
wearing when he was arrested near Perry.

Much later, after finally forcing the government to disclose the
relevant witness statements, we would learn that there were major
inconsistencies in each of these claims, but at the time they constituted a coherent, if circumstantial, version of what had happened. In
addition, the FBI was still hot on the trail of John Doe #2, the second man identified by many of the eyewitnesses who had seen John
Doe #1, and also other men who, though no composites had been
made for them, were included in many of the eyewitness accounts
and fit the description neither of John Doe #1 nor of John Doe #2.
The government also had Terry Nichols, although he remained a
shadowy figure (partly, as we shall see, through his own efforts). But
at this early stage—and this would never change in the government's version—McVeigh remained the detonator of the bomb, the
centerpiece of the charges. As such, and as though to bolster the
case against him, he was at various times labeled a racist, a skinhead,

and a neo-Nazi in the media, although there was no evidence in support of these, and he was accused in the media, based upon calculated leaks and innuendoes from law enforcement, of involvement in additional crimes: armed robbery in Arkansas, the murder of a two-year-old child in Michigan, multiple bank robberies in Kansas and other Great Plains states, and lesser offenses such as credit card fraud, possession of stolen weapons, concealing stolen property, and violation of the tax law and banking regulations.

I had two goals in mind right from the beginning. They were interconnected. The first was to conduct my own investigation into what had happened; the second was to make sure my client got a fair trial.

Part of the lawyer's creed is to investigate the facts of a case independently and thoroughly. It is not enough, under this rule, for the lawyer to take the client's word for what happened—he must find out for himself—and my experience over the years has confirmed the wisdom of this counsel. The obligation of the prosecution to share the results of its discovery with the defense may have been the law in the United States for almost forty years, but as I will show it has never been so abused as in the Oklahoma bombing case. If we had relied on the government to disclose its findings, Tim McVeigh would have been totally defenseless.

The goal of a fair trial may sound strangely limited. After all, in an adversary system such as ours, isn't the defense lawyer's primary objective to get his client off? Yes—and no. I am not clairvoyant. It was impossible for me to predict with any degree of certainty, in the spring of 1995, what a jury might decide down the road in a court of law. But the prevailing atmosphere that spring was of a witch-hunt, and that is what I had to change.

My first order of business on both counts—the independent investigation and the fair trial—was to start building a defense team. Judge Russell, who was responsible for appointing two lawyers each for McVeigh and Nichols, had given me the résumé of one Richard Burr, whom he'd already met and whom Ted Lidz highly recommended. Burr had wanted the number-one position, but Judge Russell, even though he was impressed by Burr's work with the Texas

Resource Center and his apparent skills as a researcher, could hardly appoint someone with no experience as a trial lawyer.

State resource centers had been funded by the federal government in order to assure death-row inmates of proper counsel in their federal habeas corpus appeals. But the Republican-controlled Congress was in the process of eliminating them, and Dick Burr, having, as the Judge put it, "gotten crosswise" with Sen. Phil Gramm of Texas, was about to lose his job.

I called Burr and arranged for him to fly up from Houston. At the same time, I also sounded out an old friend of mine, D. C. Thomas, a thoroughly excellent and well-respected criminal defense lawyer of the old school, who had a number of forensic victories to his credit. D. C. was probably my closest friend in the Oklahoma bar, outside the lawyers in my own firm. I went to visit him in his offices in Oklahoma City, and we discussed the case at length.

"Partner," I said to him, "I'd like to have you along on this ride if you'd like to come. I don't know where it's going to lead, or how long it'll last, but apparently they'll pay us and I need you."

In the end, though, D. C. turned me down. He didn't want to get involved. For him, as for others, the bombing was just too close to home.

Dick Burr and I met later in the week. By then, I'd heard more favorable things about him. He was a fairly disheveled sort physically, a gentle soul with wild blond hair. I had my reservations—for one thing, I felt he was a "cause" lawyer, not a "case" lawyer—and there was a certain awkwardness between us. After all, he'd have much preferred my job, whereas I, to be honest, hadn't liked the idea of having him "wished" on me by Ted Lidz. Still, I found on that first day that I could speak my mind to him on the very question. I told him that there could only be one captain on the team, and that I was that captain. I even trotted out the old story about Abraham Lincoln's cabinet meeting, when every member voted yea on an issue except for Lincoln himself, whereupon the president announced, "The nays have it."

Dick said he had no problem with it. No legal defense team, he opined, could function democratically. He also understood, on another issue, that there was no way he could work on the case from Houston, and he agreed to move up to Enid.

He did—for a time.

Then he asked me if he could move back to Houston. I acqui-esced, somewhat against my better judgment. It turned out he wanted to be with Mandy Welch, a lawyer he'd worked with who was also his significant other. Later on he asked me to hire Mandy and I did that too.

They were both cause lawyers, decidedly, and their attraction to the McVeigh defense was the death penalty. (They weren't alone in this either. Randy Coyne, a professor at the University of Oklahoma Law School, joined us in the summer for the same reason.) A "case" lawyer, in contrast, approaches a legal proceeding from the stand-point of representing a client and, causes aside, utilizes whatever he can to his client's advantage. He is married to no particular cause.

All that first week, I had what seemed to be a running conversa-tion with Ted Lidz. Lidz, as I've mentioned, was the administrative director of the Federal Defender's Service in Washington, within the administrative office of the federal courts. If Judge Russell was, technically speaking, my paymaster, Lidz controlled the in's and out's of the money. I had to find out from him how we got paid, whom we could hire, what we could have authorized in front, and what required special applications—what the mechanics were, in sum. The money, of course, came originally from Congress, appro-priated to the Administrative Office. It was up to us to file vouchers with the court, which would review and approve them, subject to what had been authorized in advance. We would want to file a motion, Lidz suggested, for interim compensation, which would be granted, so that we could be paid every month. We would have to file applications for any experts we wanted to hire, get travel autho-rization above and beyond such standing travel authorizations as the court would agree to, and, in principle, obtain approval in advance for any individual expenditure exceeding $300.

All of this was the bureaucracy at work. But there was an aspect of it that troubled me, something I wanted to make sure both he and David Russell understood.

"You know, Ted," I said to him, "this is going to be a massive undertaking. I don't see it any other way. It already is, on the gov-ernment's side—hell, I read the papers too—and if we're going to do this thing right, it's going to take a lot more than two lawyers. So how do I go about staffing up?"

The issue, in other words, was money—the government's money, taxpayers' money—and paying for McVeigh's constitutional right to counsel.

Ted Lidz was a careful man, perhaps because he worked with the judges and served essentially at their pleasure.

"I'll tell you this much," he said. "You were Judge Russell's first choice, and his only one. You have incredible standing with him."

"That's very nice, Ted," I said, "but if I was his only choice, what took him so long?"

"For one thing, he was swamped with candidates. And everybody else had one, he had to interview them all. But finally—it was last Friday—he told me emphatically, 'I'm going to call Stephen Jones. It's what I should have done two weeks ago.'"

I didn't, at first, see the point of his telling me this. But then he made it clear.

"Whatever you need, Stephen," Lidz said, "go for it. Go for it now. That's my advice to you. Go for it right now, and you'll get it."

And so we did.

We worked up our organizational plan. It included Dick Burr, the associates in my office, another lawyer's slot for someone I already had in mind, two private investigators from Oklahoma City, Marty Reed and Wilma Sparks, whom I'd used successfully many times before, the first of several experts we thought we would need, and Ann Bradley, whom I'd also used before and whom I wanted as a researcher and aide-de-camp. A native of Enid and graduate of the University of Texas, Ann had, among other things, once dated my son and had helped me on several special assignments that had required goodly measures of analytical and literary skill.

The five other lawyers in my office were all brought on board. Bob Wyatt was (and is still) a remarkable and tireless detail person. An Oklahoma Democrat from short-grass country in the southwestern part of the state, he has what I call a "gnat's eye" approach to mastering the facts of a case. He would shortly take over the drafting of documents—and, as will be seen, there would be mountains of them—for the discovery of nonclassified information, the so-called Rule 16 discovery motions, and exculpatory evidence (meaning evidence the government had that might negate McVeigh's guilt). Ultimately, although it hardly seemed possible in the beginning, Bob would oversee our work to impeach the FBI Laboratory.

Mike Roberts had practiced no criminal law whatsoever, and initially I intended to keep him off the case, because we badly needed someone to take care of our other clients. But Mike, in due course, wanted in too, and he took on several critical responsibilities, including monitoring evidence and exhibits from the FBI. Once we succeeded, with the court's help, in prying that loose, it came in floods of material. In late 1996, when the McVeigh defense moved up to Denver, Mike became administrative manager for our whole operation.

Jim Hankins stayed with us until almost the end of the trial, performing myriad duties, investigative and legal, and though Jeremy Lowrey and Julia Sims, two able young lawyers, dropped out sooner, they were part of the nucleus in the hectic early days and performed valuable services.

By the time of the trial we had grown to thirty-five people, each appointed with the approval of the court, and the expense of the defense to American taxpayers was immense, although nowhere near what the government's case cost it. But the money—the cost of *United States v. McVeigh*—is the price we must pay, as a society, for a system that on the one hand casts prosecution and defense as adversaries while demanding, on the other, that the prosecution share its evidence and information. The two requirements are in obvious conflict. Whether it is too much to expect the powers that be in the Justice Department to keep them in balance is a question well worth debating, but the tilt, in *United States v. McVeigh*, always came down on the side of winning. As a result, in addition to our immediate staff and the investigators we employed in the field, we also, over time, had to call on a variety of experts, some of whom charged more than we lawyers, ranging from explosives and trace analysis specialists to a psychiatrist to an architect to an anthropologist.

In fact, even as I worried about staff, we had our first two experts already on the scene. One was Sid Woodcock, a bomb expert who had spent years working for the CIA and the FBI; the other was an architect named Frank Davies. The federal government, in its wisdom, had decided to implode what was left of the Murrah Building immediately. After all, it was their property, and the experts said it was too dangerous to leave standing. All we wanted was the chance to examine it beforehand. There would, obviously, be many issues that would come to rise in McVeigh's trial to which the wrecked building might offer clues, among them: the claim that a single bomb in a Ryder truck had done all the damage (when, from the very beginning, there were stories and rumors of other bombs, as well as the question of the second shock, registered seconds after the first, at the seismic center in Norman); or that that one bomb was in fact composed of what the government said it was (the question of whether the two-ton ANFO bomb the government described could bring down half a building); as well as clues in the rubble, like the unidentified leg about which we learned only later.

In the government's view, though, there was no need to delay the implosion. They'd already examined the wreckage thoroughly, and since they were legally required and honor-bound to share all their data with us anyway, what was our problem?

Our problem was simply that we wanted to see for ourselves. We ended up filing a motion with Magistrate Ronald Howland—the first of many motions aimed at compelling the prosecution to do what it was legally supposed to do—at which, before Magistrate Howland could decide against them, the government relented. They agreed to a ten-day delay in implosion and granted us access, subject to a series of ground rules and conditions that in substance allowed us to come and look—but not to touch.

Sid Woodcock, having been through similar exercises many times before, was highly skeptical about what we would find.

"They're going to have the place clean as a whistle," he predicted. "We won't find a scrap of anything of evidentiary value. What we really need, though, is the crater, access to the crater. We want the exact dimensions—the circumference, the depth, take our own pictures and so forth. But I'll bet you my last dollar they'll have it covered over by the time we get there."

Unfortunately, Sid won his bet. I stayed away from the building myself, hoping to minimize the attention our presence might attract, but Bob Wyatt, who accompanied our experts, reported that the media were there in force, as was the FBI, and the FBI was overtly hostile. They refused to answer any questions—"We're not

here to give you a tour," one of them told Bob contemptuously—
and furthermore, Bob and the others spotted microphones everywhere they turned, relics perhaps from the first days when the
search for victims was still ongoing but perhaps still in use to overhear anything we might say.

And, yes, the crater was covered. Our hosts refused to uncover it
for us or to let us do it ourselves. It was not the first, and it would be
far from the last, time that I found myself wondering what was so
dangerous about letting us take a look at something related to the
case. If the government was so certain with regard to its theory of
what happened, what did they have to fear from uncovering the
crater for us? What possibly could be buried that they might not
want us to find? It was our first hint that the government would hide
evidence from us and it would be the taxpayers who would pay—
millions of dollars—for this delay and obstruction.

The Murrah Building was imploded on May 23. The last three
bodies were recovered six days later as the rubble was sifted and
removed, piece by piece, to warehouses several blocks away. There,
under similar restrictions, we were again permitted to review it.

If I make much of the episode, it is because it illustrates perfectly
the adversarial situation we found ourselves in from the very beginning of the case—it would never end—and explains one reason why
McVeigh's defense, that the right to trial and counsel provided for in
the Sixth Amendment to the U.S. Constitution, would become so
costly.

W ith one significant omission, and a couple of minor ones,
the nucleus of our defense team was already in place by
the end of my first week on the case. I submitted the plan to Judge
Russell. Ted Lidz was right: With the exception of one expert on
eyewitness identification—the judge thought we should wait on
that—he signed off on everything we asked for.

During that next weekend—my first full weekend on the job—I
had an important meeting in the parking lot of a Holiday Inn in
Salina, Kansas. I'd driven up there with Sherrel that Sunday to visit
our son, Edward, at his school, St. John's, but before we left Enid I'd
put in a call to a good friend and former colleague, Rob Nigh, who

was then in charge of the federal public defender's office in Lincoln, Nebraska.

Rob Nigh—or "Mr. Rob," as I've always called him—had walked into my office in the early eighties looking for work while he was in his last year at the University of Oklahoma Law School, and I hired him on the spot. He was a small man physically, unassuming in manner, with large glasses and slicked-back hair, a chain-smoker who never lost his cool and was easy to get along with. In 1984, he'd virtually put together the Sue Caton defense for me, organizing the case and furnishing superb material for my cross-examination of the state's leading witness. After that, I'd given him his first criminal case to try completely on his own. He won it too. We were very close—when he and his wife married, Sherrel and I gave them a trip to Europe for a wedding present—but the day still came, as inevitable as it was upsetting, when he announced he was going to leave the firm. "If I stay in Enid, Boss," he said ("Boss" being what he's always called me), "I'll always be under your shadow." Selfishly—for I knew in my heart he was right—I tried to talk him out of it using money as well as persuasion, but to no avail. His mind was made up. Instead, he asked my help in getting the job he was after in the state public defender's office in Tulsa. It would be terrific experience for a young lawyer, I had to admit, and I did help him, and off he went. I'd followed his career as a trial lawyer since with a strong rooting interest and great pride.

Now I wanted him back.

So we met—in the Holiday Inn parking lot, because I'd already become cautious about whom I talked to where—and we chatted for about an hour, leaning against a couple of cars, and I frankly—and very honestly—told him I needed his help.

In the end, he agreed to come if I could fix it. The next morning I was on the phone to Ted Lidz, telling him I wanted Rob Nigh. With some reluctance, he called the federal public defender in Omaha, who was Rob's boss and who, predictably, tried to talk Ted out of it. Rob was involved in a couple of cases, and why did I want him anyway when there were others more qualified in the Federal Defenders Service? But I stood my ground—I wanted Nigh and no one else—and Ted, with a sigh, got it done.

Rob was assigned to the Oklahoma City office of the Federal Defenders Service and then reassigned to us. Before the next week was out, he was on the premises in Enid, in the additional space we'd leased (with the court's approval) on the tenth floor of Broadway Tower.

Allowing for people leaving and being replaced, and with major additions once we moved to Denver and prepared for trial, the core legal group was now in place. And we went to work. One of the first things we had to do was find out more about Timothy McVeigh.

4

ARMAGEDDON
AT MOUNT CARMEL

T im always faced two trials, one in the court of public opinion and the other in the court of law. No fact or pattern of facts concerning his youth, none of the entries on his report cards from school, or the comments of his teachers and his contemporaries culled by the investigators, or even his own reminiscences, disturbed the impression of a boy-next-door ordinariness. The McVeighs weren't well off, but they lived decently in a small-town, Rust Belt, middle-class environment some twenty-five miles northeast of Buffalo, New York. Tim was a good student in high school but hardly a brilliant one. His parents separated definitively in 1984, when he was sixteen, and his mother moved to Florida—"Aha!" the experts in "psychological profiling" all said, the divorced child, the broken family—but neither in Tim's own public version nor in any of the outward signs studied by the investigators did this seem to have affected him adversely. Having excelled in computers in high school, he won a small Regent's scholarship, which he used in 1987 to attend a local business college. Then, six months later, disillusioned by the "I'm-better-than-you-because-I've-got-more-money" attitude that he saw in the world around him, he enlisted in the United States Army. He was attracted most of all, he later remembered, by the commercial line, "We do more before 9 A.M. than most people do all day."

McVeigh seemed made for the army, the army for McVeigh. He took easily to the life of discipline, regimentation, and spit-and-polish rigor. He had "discovered" firearms even before the army, as friends from his youth attested, but now he became an expert marksman and later a "top gun" at Ft. Riley, that is, the best shot of all the gunners in his battalion. According to all his military records, he was a model soldier, and he rose rapidly to become sergeant before heading off to the Gulf War as a gunner on a Bradley fighting vehicle. There he was decorated for valor and performance with a Bronze Star and an Army Commendation Medal upgraded for valor. He and his unit were chosen to serve as honor guard to Gen. Norman Schwartzkopf when he negotiated the cease-fire with the Iraqi military command at a desert rendezvous, and McVeigh was photographed shaking hands with the illustrious general.

Much was made by the experts of his failure to make Special Forces (known popularly as the Green Berets), the elite combat unit to which he aspired. For a time, the media reported that he had failed the psychological tests given on entry. According to *The New York Times*, "Military officials said that preliminary psychological screening had shown him to be unfit." This was simply not true, and the source that leaked the story turned out to be an FBI agent, not a military official. The truth was that McVeigh, and another veteran who was also just back from the Persian Gulf, simply couldn't hack the physical stress and demands. Tim had lost weight in combat, was out of shape, and, as he later told David Hackworth of *Newsweek*, "If you develop blisters on your feet on the second day, you know you're not going to make it."

Not long afterward, he quit the army. Again, some experts wanted to make much of this. Tim, himself, never agreed with them. Citing the very high dropout rate from Special Forces training, he claimed (to David Hackworth), "It wasn't the straw that broke anything."

Of course, the experts could then say he was in denial!

After he quit the army, he worked for more than a year for Burns Security in upstate New York (where he also had a good job rating from his superiors). Beginning in early 1993, when he quit Burns, he took up a marginal and drifting way of life that saw him crisscross the country numerous times, with extended stopoffs in places like Decker, Michigan (at James Nichols's farm), and, in 1993 and again in 1994, Kingman, Arizona, where Michael and Lori Fortier lived and where Tim had several different jobs.

What I wanted to get across to the world, though, more than anything, was that our client couldn't be classified or pigeonholed as some kind of archetypal terrorist and that none of the details of his life—before, during, or after his military experience—supported the demonized image. Many of our youths, whether we like it or not, take up seemingly purposeless, drifting lives in their twenties. Many of our youths, too, are susceptible to extremist ideas and propaganda, be they of the left or the right, and anyone who has ever served in the military will recognize the prevalence of certain right-wing attitudes among many professional soldiers. Tim McVeigh was all of twenty-six when he was arrested. And the facts—that he'd led a marginal, quasinomadic existence, working here and there, traveling back and forth across the country, and that under whatever influences or combination of influences he had come to speak and write menacingly of the violent revolution(s) to come and the "big things" that were going to happen—none of these facts, alone or in combination, made him a bomber.

The federal grand jury in the Oklahoma City bombing case began hearing evidence almost immediately after the disaster. For reasons of security and secrecy, it met at Tinker Air Force Base in Midwest City, several miles east of downtown Oklahoma City. Its mission, as provided for under the Fifth Amendment to the U.S. Constitution, was to consider the government's charges, and such evidence and testimony as the government brought in support of them, and to determine whether there was "probable cause" sufficient to issue indictments.

If the trial-by-jury system of criminal justice is designed to allow two sides, prosecution and defense, to present conflicting and adversarial versions of the facts, a grand jury proceeding is strictly a prosecution show-and-tell, conducted in secrecy without the participation of the defense. Evidence is presented—including hearsay evidence—witnesses are examined and heard without legal counsel of their own, and the jury is left to weigh what is put before it in the absence of any cross-examination or rebuttal. Furthermore, "probable cause"—the standard a prosecutor must meet in a grand jury proceeding—is a much softer criterion, much easier for the prosecution to demonstrate than "beyond a reasonable doubt," the standard necessary to convince a trial jury to convict.

In the normal run of cases, in which there is little or no public interest, the grand jury system may indeed serve as a screening process and, along with the other provisions of the Fifth Amendment, protect the putative accused. But as a practical matter, there have been precious few instances when a grand jury has refused to indict. On the contrary, there's an old saying among lawyers that a grand jury would indict a ham sandwich if the prosecution wanted it to. Furthermore, in a high-profile case, where the public's interest is keen and the slightest morsel of leak, fact, rumor, or gossip becomes a lead-in sound bite on the evening news, the proceeding has become a kind of trial-before-the-trial, in which the accused is unable to defend himself and indictments, once they are handed up, serve only to reinforce the public's presumption of guilt. Defending a client becomes even more difficult when the prosecution attempts to frame a case as particularly black-and-white. We all know that life is what goes on in the gray areas, and never was this truer than in the Oklahoma City bombing. For example, we quickly realized that the story didn't begin and end on April 19, 1995. In fact, it didn't even begin in Oklahoma City. The government later decided, arbitrarily, that "the conspiracy" was launched in September 1994, but by their own logic, as expressed at the trial, it could as well have begun on another April 19, outside a medium-sized city in Texas. That city was Waco.

O n April 19, 1993, a small army of FBI agents, using CS gas (Orthochlorobenzalmalononitrile) and Bradley fighting vehicles furnished by the Texas National Guard and under direct orders from the U.S. attorney general, launched a final assault on the Branch Davidian settlement at Mount Carmel near Waco. The buildings of the settlement caught fire, and seventy-four people, women and children among them, were immolated in the ensuing holocaust. Some died from gunshots that might or might not have been self-inflicted, more from burning and smoke inhalation.

On the previous February 28, the Bureau of Alcohol, Tobacco, and Firearms, claiming various weapons and drugs infractions, had launched a first raid against the settlement. ATF was strongly influenced by former members of the sect, who for reasons of their own testified to horror stories about life within the compound—tales of child abuse, sexual orgy and enthrallment, enslavement, brainwashing, and drug abuse. The drug aspect was key. Three months before the raid, under the pretext that the Branch Davidians were dealing drugs, ATF had requested, and received, military assistance from the Texas National Guard, including specialized training and aerial reconnaissance of the site. Without the drug connection, federal law would have prohibited that federal-state collaboration. But ATF affirmed there was a drug problem and that the Branch Davidians were armed and dangerous, and the Texas National Guard thereupon helped formulate and execute ATF's planned attack.

In a classic case of the escalating and self-fulfilling paranoia that all too often afflicts law enforcement, ATF first convinced itself that the Branch Davidians could not be talked to or negotiated with, then that they were a threat not only to its authority but also to law and order in general. The agency took it upon itself to raid the settlement and in the process created exactly what it had feared. The vaunted raid was supposed to be a surprise. It wasn't. It met with stubborn armed resistance from the settlement, and by the time the assailants retreated and took up siege positions around the compound, four ATF agents and six inhabitants lay dead.

This "surgical strike"—one can almost hear the echo of Vietnam rhetoric—became a standoff, and ATF's failure now brought the FBI to the rescue. This, in turn, elevated Attorney General Janet Reno to battlefield command.

In the ensuing two months, an all-too-familiar process took place. The media, drawn like sharks to the confrontation but largely kept from contact with the besieged, were themselves manipulated by law enforcement agencies. They justified the siege by demonizing the Branch Davidians, particularly their leader, David Koresh. To Americans who get their news from TV, Koresh became a mesmerizer, a brainwasher, a polygamist, and a torturer of children—a Satan in every respect except in name.

The attorney general herself helped by expressing her grave concern about child abuse inside the besieged settlement—even though local authorities, who had already investigated the same charges before the initial raid, found the allegations baseless. Most important, we Americans were told repeatedly that every effort had been made to negotiate with Koresh but that talking to him proved impossible. There was just no reasoning with this man. All the FBI had gotten from him—in the FBI's very own words—was "Bible babble." Steadily, during weeks of siege, we were sensitized—actually, desensitized—to the inevitable that was to come.

The underlying causes of the Waco massacre were many, and they have been the subject of numerous studies since the disaster, among them an excellent group effort, *Armageddon in Waco*, edited by sociologist Stuart A. Wright, and *No More Wacos* by David B. Kopel and Paul H. Blackman. Certainly our national fear of cults— that is, of religious groups perceived by us "normal" Americans as different and outlandish and dangerous—played an important role. This might seem odd in a society founded on religious tolerance and freedom, but *cult* to many Americans means crazies and brings with it echoes of Jim Jones's Peoples Temple and the mass suicide at Jonestown, Guyana, or the Moonies of the Unification Church and lurid tales of young people being held captive against their will. We even have an organization in America called the Cult Awareness Network (CAN), which helped fuel the ATF conviction that the Branch Davidians could only be subdued by force of arms.

But if in fact the Branch Davidians at Mount Carmel were dangerous to anyone, it was only to themselves. Their essential harmlessness was as obvious to people who knew them before the siege, including local law enforcement people, as it was to those who studied them afterward, including experts appointed by the Department of Justice itself to analyze what had gone wrong. Founded in 1929 by dissident members of the Seventh Day Adventists, the Davidian sect, so called because its members believe that the Kingdom of David will be reestablished after the second coming of Jesus Christ, had become the Branch Davidians in the 1950s, when Ben Roden and his family had taken over leadership from the founding Houteff clan. Ever since, they had managed to scratch out a meager existence in the poor soil of their Texas settlement and to worship as their chosen way.

One awful consequence of the siege—one that besiegers certainly should have been aware of—was that it proved to the Branch Davidians their most apocalyptic beliefs. They believed—David Koresh had long preached it, as did other Christian groups—that the Tribulation prophesied in the Book of Revelations, that the time of catastrophes, natural and manmade, that would precede the second coming and the long-awaited millennium was now at hand. Whether law enforcement people actually intended it or not, their conduct during the ghastly siege only strengthened the convictions of the besieged. Law enforcers cut off electricity and water. Every night, they lit up the settlement with mounted floodlights. Every dawn, to their own eternal shame, they woke up the inhabitants with loudspeakers blaring weird cacophonies of sounds and messages—of rabbits screaming at their slaughter and Nancy Sinatra singing "These Boots Were Made for Walking"—all designed, presumably, to unhinge the Branch Davidians and encourage them to surrender. Instead they had the opposite effect: The loudspeakers were evidence of the Tribulation.

This, mind you, was an episode of Americans dealing with Americans.

But law enforcers don't like standoffs. Stalemates. The longer they last, the more they tend to diminish—at least in the eyes of the enforcers—officials' aura of authority, their legitimacy, their decisiveness, even their manliness. But then again, prior to the Waco siege the federal law enforcement agencies, notably ATF, had had spotty records in dealing with groups of extremists and religious sects. Branch Davidians are hardly neo-Nazis or white-supremacist Christian militants—although in the aftermath of the tragedy they would be championed by such groups—yet all tended to be lumped together by law enforcement, and law enforcement had fared poorly in its efforts to bring the truly dangerous among them to trial and conviction.

On the successful end of the spectrum, the FBI could point to its tracking down of Robert Mathews and his Bruders Schweigen (Silent Brotherhood, also known as The Order), the white-supremacist outlaw gang that had committed a number of armored-car and bank robberies on the West Coast and had murdered Allan Berg, the Denver talk-show host, in 1984. Mathews himself was incinerated when an FBI helicopter set fire to the house he was holed up in at Whidbey Island in Puget Sound, Washington, but many of his followers were tried before the same judge who would later preside at the trials of Timothy McVeigh and Terry Nichols.

But on the other end of the spectrum was a 1988 sedition trial in Fort Smith, Arkansas, in which Louis Beam, former head of the Texas Ku Klux Klan, and others were acquitted. More notorious is the 1992 shootout and siege involving ATF, FBI agents, and U.S. marshals, on one side, and Randy Weaver and his family on the other in remote, rugged country in the Idaho Panhandle at a place called Ruby Ridge. Ruby Ridge is as prime an example of overreaction as exists in the annals of federal law enforcement. It involved hundreds of federal agents, millions of dollars' worth of equipment. This time there were four deaths. One of them was a U.S. marshal. Another was Randy Weaver's wife, Vicki, who was shot in the head by a sniper as she stood in the doorway of her own cabin, holding her ten-month-old daughter in her arms. The last two were the Weavers' fourteen-year-old son, Sammy, and their Labrador dog, Striker. And what was the cause of it all? It was Randy Weaver's refusal to answer charges stemming from a sting operation in which he was allegedly caught selling sawed-off shotguns. When Weaver finally gave himself up, he was incarcerated pending trial. When he was eventually acquitted of murder, a lot of people started talking about overkill on the part of the federal government.

By the time of Waco, therefore, the two bureaus—ATF and the FBI—were badly in need of a win.

Two Congressional subcommittees subsequently investigated the Waco tragedy and joined together in issuing a final report. Here is a quote from it:

> Many citizens no doubt would be surprised and concerned to learn that components of the same forces the United States used in Operation Desert Storm, Somalia and Bosnia [i.e., the Texas National Guard], also can be used against them in the United States. The Waco and Ruby Ridge incidents epitomize civilian law enforcement's growing acceptance and use of military-type tactics. . . . When ATF

faced the option of conducting a regulatory inspection or a tactical operation, it chose the tactical operation. When ATF had to decide between arresting Koresh away from the Branch Davidian residence or a direct confrontation, it chose direct confrontation. ATF also decided to conduct a dynamic entry as opposed to a siege.

The report may have been nuanced in its condemnation by its own bureaucratic language—"dynamic entry" is hardly what most of us would call armed and violent assault—but there was no mincing of words in its conclusion: "The subcommittees find this trend unacceptable."

Surely any reasonably informed citizen would have agreed. Surely any reasonably informed citizen would have been outraged.

And yet?

Two ATF agents had already been punished by dismissal for their role at Waco. They had, according to ATF's own internal investigation, made gross errors in judgment and given false or misleading statements to superiors. Yet once the attention of the public—and the media—had been diverted elsewhere, the two men successfully appealed and were quietly reinstated, with full back pay and benefits. Their legal fees were paid. Their personnel records were sanitized.

Where were we? Where were our watchful media? Where were our political leaders?

Well, the Department of Justice, determined to find some way of proving itself right, was busily pursuing eleven Branch Davidian survivors in criminal proceedings! (All eleven were acquitted of the most serious charges against them—conspiracy to commit murder and aiding and abetting murder. Five of them were in fact convicted of aiding and abetting voluntary manslaughter. Four were acquitted on all charges.) In fact the biggest insult to national honor had already taken place. At the very height of the Waco tragedy, the cabinet member most responsible for the fiasco went on national television and indeed took "full responsibility" for what had happened. I'm talking about Attorney General Reno. In most civilized countries of the modern world, the official "fully responsible" would have then—logically and normally—have resigned, and that resignation would have been promptly accepted by the chief of state. But Janet Reno survived Waco—to preside over *United States v. McVeigh*.

Although the Oklahoma City bombing shocked the world when it happened, it scarcely came as a total surprise to those of us who knew about Waco. The coincidence of the dates obviously made us think either that the bombing was a payback or that someone wanted it to seem that way, and it came out early that Tim McVeigh himself had visited the site during the siege and had even been interviewed and photographed by a college newspaper's reporting team. It couldn't have been an accident either that the target was a federal building, one housing ATF offices. According to Michael Fortier—a friend of McVeigh and, as we shall see, hardly the most reliable of sources—Tim McVeigh had told him that the Waco assault was ordered from the Murrah Building offices. (It wasn't—regional ATF headquarters was in Dallas—and it seems far-fetched that McVeigh might have thought so.) But the violence of Waco—its official violence, its gratuitous and grossly unnecessary violence—could well have inspired someone else to rageful revenge. Anyone who has lived in the twentieth century understands that violence tends to beget violence.

But why Oklahoma?

Why the American heartland?

There was another source of anger loose in the land, one that suggested not only that a federal building would be targeted but also precisely that it be one right here, in the farming states of our Great Plains. Perhaps the best way to explain this reference is through President Clinton's televised State of the Union speech in January 1998. That speech, it will be remembered, was considered a good, upbeat, and well-wrought speech, one celebratory of our economic success, with some measure of vision to it, all the more remarkable because it was delivered amid the Monica Lewinsky scandal.

Probably a lot of Americans watched that night in the expectation that the president would say something about Monica. If so, he disappointed them. But there was another, much more significant omission that went largely unnoticed.

For the first time in living memory (with the exception of southeastern tobacco farmers, who President Clinton mollified to compensate for the federal antismoking campaign), a State of the Union speech contained not one single reference to the American farmer.

The message from this most political of presidents was clear: The American farmer, whatever his plight, whatever his virtues, was no longer worth mentioning. Or, to paraphrase historian David Danborn, the farmer had apparently passed from being a majority to being a minority to being nothing more than a curiosity.

This has been an amazing transformation. Our republic, needless to say, was based on "embattled farmers," and as recently as a hundred years ago, William Jennings Bryan, extolling the importance of farmers in his famous "Cross of Gold" speech, was very nearly elected president. Neither was the lesson—that of the farmer's political power and his solidarity with the voting bloc to which he belonged—lost on successions of politicians across the century. Before the age of television, national political candidates beat the hustings of farming America, and afterward the Iowa caucuses brought forth primary hopefuls every four years, fawning and genuflecting before the "rugged individualism" of our rural society.

But no more.

Nowhere has this phenomenon been more evident than in the Great Plains. The story has been documented in several detailed studies—among them Joel Dyer's *Harvest of Rage* and Raymond D. North's *Night Came to the Farms of the Great Plains*—how successive federal regimes, dating back to the 1970s, Republicans and Democrats alike, systematically decimated the farming population of the heartland, first with easy money, then with wildly inflated land values, finally with grain embargoes and foreclosures when the bad times came.

The villains of the story were the policymakers in Washington and the bureaucrats of the federal land banks and the Farmers Home Administration (FHA) who served them. Whether it was deliberate or came about through bungling, the effect of their work was to take farming out of the hands of the many and give it systematically to the few, to those companies who control what we now call agribusiness. If this was their intent all along, the way they went about it cost the American taxpayer untold billions of dollars. But the cost to those directly affected was still greater, and they constituted a large segment of American society.

Sources give the statistics: how many families lost their farms, the average size of a Great Plains farm today compared to twenty years ago, the diminished numbers of farm owners and operators today compared to twenty years ago, and so on. Other sources describe, more dramatically and vividly than I am able, the effect of these policies on a proud, hardworking, and God-fearing people, and the abandoned farm buildings, and the depressed small towns, up and down the Great Plains states from the Dakotas to Texas, that today give testament to what happened to them. Some of them went quietly. Some were ready-made candidates for extremist groups. A few tried to fight back, however futilely, like Gordon Kahl, a desperate North Dakota farmer who killed a U.S. marshal and a county sheriff when they came to arrest him in 1983, and Arthur Kirk, a Nebraska farmer who was gunned down the following year by a state SWAT team in his own barnyard. But one dry assertion—from Raymond North's book, referring to the year 1991—brings it home: "Death by farm accidents is no longer the leading cause of a violent end among Oklahoma farmers. Suicide is now the leading cause."

This isn't to suggest—obviously—that the perpetrators of the Oklahoma City bombing had to have been enraged farmers. But the desperate and despairing rural population of the 1980s and 1990s nonetheless offered prime and fertile ground to a variety of militant antigovernment groups. This has often been the case in America, going back to the farmers in the eighteenth century who took up arms against the Crown and those in the young republic who joined Shays' Rebellion in Massachusetts and the Whisky Rebellion in Kentucky. Vigilantism is a parallel theme in our rural and frontier history, echoed today in the self-styled militias that have sprung up in various, largely rural areas of the country. The common denominators in rural discontent have always been distrust of faraway forces, on the one hand—be they the federal government and its tax collectors in Washington or the absentee landowners and bankers of the eastern cities—and, on the other, reliance on the small and the local and, more recently, the literal words of the U.S. Constitution, which have been endowed, by some, with a quasisacred resonance.

Although human history offers numerous cases in which the terrorists of one era become heroes to the next—for example, were the perpetrators of the Boston Tea Party heroes or terrorists?—it is hard not to condemn most of the self-styled antigovernment groups that have sprouted in the backwaters of America, particularly in the more rugged parts of Idaho and Montana and the Ozarks of Arkansas and the Appalachians and Smokies of the East, where land is cheap and there are few inhabitants of "non-Aryan" race. According to the *Intelligence Report* of the Southern Poverty Law Center, which monitors so-called hate groups, 474 are currently active across America. (As other observers note, some bear startling resemblance to the extreme left-wing groups of the 1960s and 1970s, those who championed Karl Marx and communal living and at their most radical practiced a similar brand of terrorism against "the Establishment," complete with bank robberies—always to fund "the Movement"—and the planting of bombs.) Today's survivalist-radicals divide into two primary groups—neo-Nazi and so-called Christian Identity. Neo-Nazis are sometimes Odinists (that is, they worship the old Teutonic and Nordic pantheon of gods that became icons of fascism in Nazi Germany). Both groups lead white-separatist lifestyles, and both are white supremacist and virulently anti-Semitic and antiblack in their convictions. They are as conspiratorial in their practices as they are in their worldviews. To them, the Establishment, so hated in the 1960s, has become "ZOG," the Zionist Occupation Government. ZOG comprises a clandestine, international cabal of Freemasons and Jewish bankers, plus the Rockefellers, who seek world domination (and may already have achieved it) through the United Nations, the Trilateral Commission, the Federal Reserve, and assorted other instruments of oppression.

The Christians among them have organized into groups with names like Aryan Nation; Posse Comitatus; the Covenant, the Sword, and the Arm of the Lord (CSA); the Minutemen; there are doubtless others we have yet to hear of but one day will. Many belong to the Christian Identity movement. Christian Identity was founded, benignly enough, in early-nineteenth-century England by believers who held that Anglo-Saxons were the true Israelites, that is, the lost tribes of the Bible, and that therefore, at least in theory, they were the long-lost brothers and sisters of the Jews. But in the contemporary American version, Christian Identity membership has been expanded to include all Aryans, whereas Jews have become none other than children of Satan. Meanwhile, all other people—that is, those who are black, brown, yellow—are considered subhumans, "mud people" born outside the Garden of Eden and doomed to perpetual inferiority.

Among the required reading of these groups, it should be pointed out, aside from the Bible itself, are such texts as *The Protocols of the Elders of Zion* (the famous anti-Semitic tract dating from nineteenth-century Poland), Adolf Hitler's *Mein Kampf*, the United States Constitution, Louis Beam's *Essays of a Klansman*, and *The Turner Diaries* by William Pierce, a fictionalized tract, originally self-published in the 1970s, that describes the outbreak of revolution by a secret white-supremacist organization. The last-named book would become such a big part of the government's circumstantial case against Timothy McVeigh.

I n any highly circumstantial case, the question of motive becomes paramount. In the case of the Oklahoma City bombing, it was self-evident that the crime had been committed, and the government would have little trouble proving that it had been committed willfully and purposefully. But the "murder weapon" had literally gone up in the blast, and nobody had actually seen Tim McVeigh or anyone else ignite or otherwise trigger it. The evidence against the alleged conspirators was entirely circumstantial, and strong as it may have seemed at first exposure, it would fail to convince a jury beyond a reasonable doubt if the accused men could be shown to have been peaceable individuals with no special grievance against anyone.

This is why the government, from the beginning, placed so much emphasis on motive and why they harnessed the media to help create, in McVeigh, the image of a marginal radical "obsessed" by the federal government, against which he and Nichols had allegedly declared war. *The Turner Diaries* was one weapon in the prosecutors' arsenal, for it described the bombing of FBI headquarters in Washington by means of a truck bomb. Photocopies of pages from the book were found in McVeigh's car, and a copy of a sequel, *Hunter*, was found in Nichols's house. McVeigh was discovered to have sold copies of the book at gun shows and to have urged his friends to read it.

And then there was Waco—the Waco "incident," as the government insisted on calling it, the "Texas massacre" as it came to be known in right-wing circles. McVeigh, as I've mentioned, had visited the site during the Waco siege out of solidarity with the Branch Davidians and had even been interviewed by a student reporter accompanied by a cameraman from Southern Methodist University's *Daily Campus*, Michelle Rauch. According to Michael Fortier, he and McVeigh had visited Waco a second time, in December 1994, on their way to Oklahoma City. The government also knew, from Tim's correspondence with his sister, Jennifer, and others, as well as from the Fortiers, how strongly he felt about Waco. The bombing, in the government's theory, became a direct and deliberate act of revenge, Waco becoming an integral part of the demonic, obsessive portrait that the government and the media were methodically constructing for my client.

As McVeigh's lawyer, obviously enough—but also as a citizen of the Great Plains—I saw it differently. The fact that my client felt so strongly about Waco made him one among . . . how many thousands of people? In other words, it proved nothing. But the campaign of which it formed a part—to convict Tim in the media and thereby create a poster-boy monster—was highly and immediately effective. Our own investigators, Marty Reed and Wilma Sparks, ran into it the minute they hit the road. One of their first assignments was to interview the principal witnesses in Junction City, Kansas, all of whom had either appeared before the grand jury or shortly would. Among them were Eldon Elliott, Tom Kessinger, and Vicki Beemer at Elliott's Body Shop (the Ryder truck rental outlet in Junction City) and Lea McGown, manager of the Dreamland Motel. Lea McGown in particular had been vocal about the case, giving interviews not only to the government investigators but also to every news outlet that showed up on her doorstep. But in Kansas Marty and Wilma ran into a stone wall. Not a one of these people, as soon as they realized who we were, would talk to us. This was partly the FBI's doing. The employees at Elliott's told us that an FBI agent named R. Scott Crabtree had specifically directed the employees not to talk to us. Crabtree denied this, and the employees later retracted their statements. (The same thing happened when Marty tried to talk to Charlie Hanger, the state trooper who had arrested Tim on Route 35. The FBI had asked the Oklahoma Department of Public Safety not to make him available to us.) But part of it was also that McVeigh's guilt was a foregone conclusion in the minds of many people, and they didn't want to be seen consorting with "the enemy."

I ran into another version of the same phenomenon in my daily life—in the way people I'd never seen before looked askance or turned away when they realized who I was. How could I be defending McVeigh, the most hated man in America? We got anonymous phone calls at home—one caller threatened to drive a truck bomb into *our* house—and my son Edward ran into the anger in an Enid movie theater, where he faced down a woman who'd just called me a "money-hungry prick" behind my back. Although there were also expressions of support that bolstered us, there was a sense in which all of us on the defense team felt almost as ostracized from "polite society" as did our client.

May 26, the beginning of Memorial Day weekend. I met Ann Bradley at Dallas–Ft. Worth International Airport. As I mentioned before, Ann had worked for me off and on in a variety of capacities, and I wanted her on the defense team. I had tracked her down in Haiti of all places, where she was working under contract to the State Department, and she flew up from Port-au-Prince for an interview.

I also wanted to see Waco for myself, and so while we talked we continued south from the airport about a hundred miles, into the heart of conservative Southern Baptist country.

It was a particularly warm day. In our part of the world, the summertime thermometer routinely tops 100 degrees Fahrenheit, and although it was yet spring, the dry, treeless Texas prairie already danced and shimmered under a dazzling sun.

We had a great deal of trouble finding the exact site of the Branch Davidian settlement. The descriptions I'd read had been blurry, and for obvious reasons it wasn't marked on any "Welcome to Texas" map. Furthermore, when it came to asking for directions, we found the good citizens of the region wary—understandably so—about their recent and unwanted claim to notoriety. As a result, we drove up and down in the heat on backroads that seemed to lead nowhere, until finally, with the help of a friendly Texaco clerk, we found ourselves there.

It was midafternoon by the time we drove off the farm road and onto the grounds. This wasn't the first time I'd come across the remains of human settlement on the Great Plains. They're here in abundance, from Texas on up to the Dakotas and eastern Montana—in sagging farmhouses and huddled building clusters that have long since been abandoned, in whole towns that are overgrown by weeds and devoid of humanity. The railroads were responsible for much of this. In the early part of the century they invented and proclaimed brand-new communities along their rights of way— towns without logic or reasons for being except that they bordered the railroad—and the companies advertised widely, in the eastern cities and even across the ocean, to induce people to come live in them. Many of their ruins are still there to be discovered, half-submerged in the earth like the wrecks of ships.

What we found here, at Mount Carmel, was a ghostly scene all its own. We saw the burned-out carapace of what had once been the main building, with rusty spikes of rebar protruding from the concrete. We saw a scorched school bus, other abandoned vehicles, the wrecks of them long since stripped of anything useful. There were a sprinkling of people there, five or six perhaps—tourists, we assumed—and we also encountered one member of the sect. She was disheveled and shabbily dressed, a woman of indeterminate age who said she was the daughter-in-law of Ben and Lois Roden, one-time leaders of the Branch Davidians. Her husband, George Roden, now dead, had once waged a bitter and losing struggle with David Koresh for control, and she didn't have much good to say about Koresh or his followers. Ironically, though, she had ended up in charge of the property, having, she said, been named a trustee by the court, and she appeared to live in a sort of hut or shack on the edge of the settlement. At least that was where she kept her literature. There were also several old mongrel dogs sniffing and hovering around her, and they accompanied us on the brief tour she gave us.

Without her, we would probably have missed the crosses, because they were beyond the ruins, away from the road. They were in rows, maybe six or eight rows in all, plain, unpainted wooden crosses weathering in the Texas sun, and they would one day, perhaps, be shaded by the still-young trees that had been planted nearby in memory of the victims. I don't know if the crosses marked actual graves, but they made a crude memorial, and they reminded me, in miniature, of the fields of crosses I'd seen touring war cemeteries in France and Belgium and how someone who happened upon them without foreknowledge wouldn't be able to imagine what human catastrophe, or "incident," they commemorated.

This, then, was what was left of the settlement, two years later. Standing there, surveying the bleak landscape of the central Texas plain, it was very hard for us to imagine that anyone who'd lived there could have posed that much of a threat to the U.S. government. Hard to imagine the blaring loudspeakers, the cries, the gunshots, the gas, the flames, as America's law enforcers went berserk.

How could it have happened? Were the demons let loose there, that terrible day in April, ever to be exorcised? The bombing of the Murrah Building hadn't done it. Would the trial and execution of Timothy James McVeigh?

5

"Did Knowingly, Intentionally, Willfully, and Maliciously Conspire"

From the very beginning of the case, I set out consciously to cultivate members of the media and to let myself be cultivated in return. This wasn't a role I took to naturally—Rick Serrano of the *Los Angeles Times* dubbed me "Mr. Accessibility"—but as Judge Richard G. Matsch himself later observed, Tim always faced two trials, one in the court of public opinion and the other in the court of law. He was in the forefront from the beginning—the arch-villain, UnSub #1—and I felt it crucial, in getting him a full and fair trial, that the public begin to see a different Tim McVeigh—not the "Killer! Baby killer!" of that first "perp-walk" moment, April 21, at the Noble County Courthouse, but the personable and articulate young man we saw almost every day at El Reno. This was not going to be easy. I was, after all, seeking to do this in a community in which tens of thousands of people had had their lives ruined forever by an act he was charged with committing. To a limited extent I could help simply by being what I was—a county-seat lawyer seeking to represent his infamous client with competence, responsibility, and professionalism. But it became clear early on that in order to counteract the demonic public image of him manufactured by the government and the media, we would have to turn to Tim himself.

We decided to accomplish this, in part, with images of our own. With Judge Russell's approval, we brought in our own photographer. We hired our own expert in military matters to review McVeigh's exemplary record, because we wanted to disseminate it ourselves. But I also had it in mind to pick one member of the media, out of all those who had been clamoring for an interview with Tim, and invite him or her to do a one-on-one exclusive.

The question was who. And one obstacle to the scheme was the client himself.

It wasn't that Tim was averse to the idea of talking about himself. On the contrary! But he was naturally apprehensive after the probably millions of words that had already been written about him. So, admittedly, was I. We reviewed numerous possibilities that May and June of 1995, only to discard them, and I was therefore a little surprised when out of the blue, during a visit to El Reno, he handed me a letter he'd received and, while I was reading it, said: "I could talk to him. I wouldn't mind that."

The letter in question was a request for an interview. It was on *Newsweek* stationery. It had come from a David H. Hackworth, along with a copy of Hackworth's book.

"Why him?" I asked Tim.

Then he filled me in on Hackworth. He was a highly decorated soldier—a "grunt," as Tim put it—who had risen from the enlisted ranks in the United States Army to become an officer but had remained a grunt at heart. He had served with great distinction in Vietnam, where he'd made colonel. Then he'd abruptly resigned from the service and turned outspoken critic of the war, one who publicly castigated the politicians and the top brass for the way it had been waged and its destructive consequences for the armed services. His memoir, *About Face*, was one of the best first-hand accounts of modern warfare, with specific reference to Korea and Vietnam, and it had been a national best-seller.

Hackworth was by now a contributing editor to *Newsweek*, specializing in military subjects. As he later put it, "The idea to interview Tim McVeigh hit me during a morning hike in the Montana woods. I'd make a simple request—soldier to soldier." That is what he'd done in the letter, and clearly he had struck a responsive chord.

I called Peter Annin, the *Newsweek* reporter assigned to the Oklahoma City bombing. I told him my client wanted to do an interview with David Hackworth and, further, that I was willing to let it happen provided we could agree to terms. I wanted Tim on the cover. I would be present during the interview and would record it. Most of all, I wanted him to guarantee fairness.

"What do you mean by fairness?" Annin asked me.

"I mean, in the first place, that you can't misquote him. And what I don't want is for you to get your interview and then go off and write a story that says, 'It makes no difference what McVeigh says, the evidence against him is overwhelming, he's still a baby killer, case closed.'"

"I don't think that's a problem," Annin replied, "but I can't promise you the cover, unless we can get our photographer in there too."

The photographer he had in mind was Eddie Adams, whose name even I recognized, from one indelible image. I'm talking about the picture in the Saigon streets of the chief of police shooting a Vietcong sympathizer in the head. It won Adams a Pulitzer Prize. I knew Tim would like that, and he did.

Because the *Newsweek* incident caused quite a ruckus afterward, I should point out that the first time I'd met the warden at El Reno he'd explained to me who could get in to see Tim and how it would work. If we—McVeigh's lawyers—had any visitors we wanted to get in, all we had to do was write a letter giving their names, social security numbers, and dates of birth too, I believe, and as long as we vouched for them they were in. No special proviso was mentioned, then or later, about photographers or journalists or anyone else.

On the appointed day in June 1995, Annin and Hackworth flew to Oklahoma City, and Julia Sims and I drove down to meet them in El Reno at the local Braum's. Julia escorted them in. (Braum's is an ice-cream parlor chain in our part of the country, and we used the one in El Reno as a meeting place, at least until we found out, later, that the FBI had it staked out.) The interview lasted a little more than an hour, and it went wonderfully well. Of course, we had prepared, reviewing with Tim the kinds of questions we thought they would ask and those he should avoid. There was a great deal at stake, and he'd never before faced the media, but once he got past the first, inevitably nervous moments, he responded easily and with good humor. (Equally inevitably, this led *Newsweek* to characterize him as "savvy, world-weary and very media-wise.")

Hackworth's participation undeniably helped. As he wrote later in a separate *Newsweek* column, "When we talked about the military, a change came over him. McVeigh suddenly sat straight in his chair. 'The army,' he said, 'teaches you to discover yourself. It teaches you who you are.' I know what he means. To warriors, the military is like a religious order. It's not a job. It's a calling."

At the same time, Tim was, happily, able to correct a number of errors, misconceptions, and outright lies that had been spread by the authorities and media. The alleged psychic scars of his childhood, for instance. He claimed he had none and that his parents' divorce had had no lasting negative effects. He also got to deny that he'd ever called himself a "prisoner of war" when he was first arrested, and no, he'd never been a member or gone to meetings of the Michigan militia, and no, he'd never "confessed" to people in jail, which no less an authority than *The New York Times* had implied early in May.

As we'd agreed beforehand, Tim ducked questions about *The Turner Diaries* and his political views in general, as well as ammonium nitrates and what he knew about chemicals. But he answered most things forthrightly, and the most telling exchange, with a small intervention from me, went like this:

> NEWSWEEK: This is the question that everybody wants to know—
>   Did you do it?
> McVEIGH: The only way we can really answer that is that we are
>   going to plead not guilty.
> JONES: And we're going to go to trial.
> NEWSWEEK: But you've got a chance right now to say, "Hell no!"
> McVEIGH: We can't do that.
> JONES: And if he says, "Hell no," the government isn't going to
>   just say, "Well, okay, that settles that."

In fact I got a lot of grief later for Tim's answer, but the Local Rules of Procedure for the U.S. District Court for the Western District of Oklahoma, which we were obliged to obey, explicitly forbid lawyer and client from arguing about the facts of the case in public statements or proclaiming the client's innocence. In answering that he would plead not guilty, Tim wasn't trying to dodge the question. He was simply obeying the court's strictures, as we had outlined them to him in case this very question was asked.

NEWSWEEK: What do you think the outcome of the case will be?

McVEIGH: I can't really speculate on that. Time will tell. But I think this is one of the largest media-coverage events in a long time and that it will be very difficult to get a fair trial anywhere.

NEWSWEEK: Are you concerned that the ultimate punishment will be the death penalty?

McVEIGH: Yeah, I think that's a concern, and I think with anybody it would be.

NEWSWEEK: How will you handle that?

McVEIGH: I guess as anybody else would—one day at a time, see what develops.

The overall effect of the *Newsweek* coverage was extremely positive, particularly compared to the reams that had been written about McVeigh before. As the magazine put it in its lead-in, "With his stockinged feet propped up, his jumpsuit sleeves tied casually around his waist, he seemed a lot more like a typical Gen Xer than a deranged loner, much less a terrorist."

Thank you, *Newsweek*. That was exactly what we'd had in mind. And, as we say in criminal defense, it had the additional advantage of being the truth.

The issue hit the stands a few days later. At virtually the same time, I called a press conference to present and distribute Tim's exemplary military record, a set of stills of Tim, and a video we'd made of him. For example, we disclosed that Tim had ranked in the 96th percentile on the Iowa Basic Skills Test (that is, the top 4 percent in the country), that he'd been promoted ahead of time, and that his efficiency reports were highly complimentary, including this comment from one of his commanding officers: "McVeigh displayed all the skills, knowledge and attributes of an excellent leader throughout the program of instruction. Good marks academically, well-delivered instructional assignments and good use of all resources all point to an outstanding noncommissioned officer." Another evaluator called him "honest and truthful in word and deed" and said he "maintains high standards of personal conduct off and on duty," and yet another described him as "an inspiration to young soldiers who is willing to learn and grow and accept criticism."

Needless to say, this gave quite a different sense of McVeigh than the "psychological profiles" that had appeared in the major media. And so did his school records, which we released all the way back to the sixth grade.

"Excellent student."

"Making excellent progress."

"Effort is outstanding."

"An outstanding student."

And, repeated several times, the refrain: "I will miss him."

So much for the introverted, paranoid, aloof loner.

This double-pronged event—the *Newsweek* interview and the press conference—constituted a turning point in how Tim was perceived. In their lemminglike style, once they'd gotten over having been scooped by *Newsweek*, the media heavyweights from New York began to court us—all of them wanted access to Tim—and the process of "dedemonization" was under way. Confirmation also came from a totally unexpected force.

The Tuesday after the *Newsweek* issue appeared, I received a formal letter from our friend, the hapless warden of El Reno, accusing us of having sneaked in the journalists under false pretenses and threatening me with all kinds of dire consequences, including having broken the law. I'd broken no law, and the warden knew it, but just to make sure I reminded him, in my answer, of the *Newsweek* letterhead letters that were already in his files. You didn't have to be a rocket scientist, though, to figure out what had happened. The moment the magazine appeared, the questions had gone up one chain of command at the Justice Department—"How in hell did we ever let this happen?"—and down the other, through the Bureau of Prisons, to land on the warden's head.

We had quite a nice skirmish afterward, including a hearing before Judge Russell and even an inquiry (required by law, once the complaint had been made) by the Oklahoma Bar Association. It amounted to nothing—the complaint was dismissed—but I'd have taken far worse in exchange for what we'd gotten.

Score one for the defense.

Although our grand jury's secret deliberations wouldn't conclude until August, we already knew the substance of the government's case against McVeigh and Nichols. It was predicated on the fact that the pair had been friends ever since they'd enlisted in the army in 1988, serving first at Fort Benning, Georgia, then at Fort Riley, Kansas. In fact, during the early going in its investigation, the FBI concentrated on the military connection. Not only could it link McVeigh and Nichols, but it had Michael Fortier and his wife, Lori, both early targets of the investigation. The FBI also pursued current or former GIs it thought could be connected. One was still in the service and an AWOL from Fort Riley. The FBI tracked him down and, for a time, had him held in California, then let him go. Then there was Roger Barnett, a former member of McVeigh's company who bore a striking resemblance to John Doe #2 and, coincidentally, lived right across the Arkansas line from Oklahoma. He was closely questioned by the FBI but ultimately cleared following a polygraph test. John Kelso, another army buddy of McVeigh's, also bore a striking resemblance to John Doe #2, but on the day of the bombing, he was serving as an engineer, somewhere in western Nebraska, on a Union Pacific freight train.

Before the grand jury, the prosecutors would try to prove that both McVeigh and Nichols were vocally, and violently, antigovernment. They had samples of Tim's correspondence, public and private, and a very valuable potential witness in Tim's younger sister, Jennifer. For several years, Jennifer had been shuttling between her divorced parents, father near Buffalo, mother in Pensacola, Florida. The FBI had caught up with her in Florida and flown her back to Buffalo, all within days after Tim's arrest. When Rob Nigh and Dick Burr later went to upstate New York, in part to interview Jennifer, they also met with Joel Daniels, a top-flight criminal defense lawyer in Buffalo whom Jennifer had retained. I learned that before Daniels came onto the scene the FBI had grilled her for several days, quite literally, in a room decorated with poster-sized pictures of herself and Tim, captioned below with a list of charges and penalties, including "Death Penalty." Despite FBI threats of criminal proceedings, Jennifer had refused to give a statement, but in the end, after the FBI flew in her mother, Mickey Frazer, from Florida to help convince her, they'd worn her down. What she told the FBI then, some of which she would repeat two years later in a Denver courtroom, contributed to the portrait it wanted to create—of an angry, disillusioned young man with a passion for weaponry who'd confided his hatred of the government to his sister.

Terry Nichols was more than a decade older than Tim, already married, divorced, a father. It was on this last count—to take care of his son—that he got a hardship discharge from the army in 1989. By the time Tim got out of the army, Terry was already remarried.

In some ways, Terry Nichols fit the profile of the terrorist better than Tim did. Whereas Tim was outgoing and extroverted, Nichols was quiet and withdrawn. Having suffered a series of family and economic reversals, he had traveled all the way to the Philippines, or so he said, to find a sixteen-year-old Filipino bride. Then, while Marife Nichols waited in the Philippines for a visa to the United States, she became pregnant by another man. Terry took the child as his own, and after a stay in Nevada, the couple moved to James Nichols's farm in Decker, Michigan. There they had a second baby, a girl, but in 1993 their young son, Jason, died of suffocation in a plastic-bag accident.

I myself began to wonder, early on, if Nichols's trips to the Philippines—and there were a number of them—had been to look for a wife or whether there had been a more sinister motive. (It took me the better part of a year to begin to find the answer.) As for Marife, when she testified in Nichols's defense at the trial in 1997, she couldn't even remember the date they were married, and even though he and first wife Lana Padilla had divorced, he seemed closer to her than his current wife.

Terry had already demonstrated his hatred and distrust of the federal government back when McVeigh was still in high school. And he had joined the army at thirty-three—an anomalous age for a recruit. When we learned, early in the investigation, that Louis Beam and others had actively recruited new members to the white-supremacist cause among military personnel, I couldn't but wonder

whether Nichols himself might not have been enlisted on a scouting
mission. There was also Terry's brother, James, who had his own
disturbed ideas—among them, according to FBI interviews, that the
U.S. government was behind the downing of Pan Am 103. Our discovery that Dennis Mahon, a former imperial wizard of the Ku Klux
Klan and a key figure in our investigation, had lived but a hundred
miles away from Nichols in upstate Michigan, where, among other
things, Mahon had experimented with blowing up a vehicle loaded
with ammonium nitrate, added inevitable grist to our speculations
about the Nichols brothers.

Like McVeigh, Terry Nichols was interested in firearms and
explosives, and the two men had worked the gun-show circuit
together, dealing in weapons and military paraphernalia and consorting with a variety of arms dealers and right-wingers. Like
McVeigh, Nichols was outspoken about his political convictions.
But Terry Nichols had taken it a step further. After a series of failed
plans and moneymaking schemes that led them from Michigan to
Utah to Las Vegas, the Nicholses broke up. Marife and their daughter returned for a time to the Philippines, and Terry moved first to
Marion, Kansas, where he worked as a farmhand, then to a little
house in Herington, a poor town in the central part of the state,
some seventy miles north of Wichita, where Marife and their
daughter rejoined him. Whatever Terry's state of mind beforehand,
by the time he got to Kansas he was so strongly antigovernment that
in March 1994 he walked into the courthouse in Marion and formally renounced his U.S. citizenship.

T erry Nichols and Tim McVeigh, though, weren't the first
people to be indicted in connection with the Oklahoma City
bombing. On May 11, 1995, a full two months before the Oklahoma City grand jury pronounced itself, another federal grand jury,
sitting in the Eastern District of Michigan, Southern Division,
returned an indictment against James Nichols, Terry's older
brother, as follows:

That, from approximately 1988 to and including April 21, 1995,
defendant JAMES NICHOLS did knowingly, willfully, and inten-

tionally combine, conspire, confederate, and agree with Terry Nichols, Timothy McVeigh, and other persons, whose names are both known and unknown to the grand jury, to possess firearms, specifically destructive devices, not registered to any of the co-conspirators in the National Firearms Registration and Transfer Record.

It was part of the unlawful conspiracy that the co-conspirators would experiment with various materials to manufacture destructive devices and detonate them on the Nichols farm, located at 3616 North Van Dyke Road, Decker, Michigan.

In furtherance of the unlawful conspiracy, and to effect the objectives thereof, the co-conspirators committed at least one of the following overt acts, among others:

1. In approximately 1988, Terry Nichols and at least one other person constructed homemade bombs made out of diesel fuel.

2. In approximately 1992, JAMES NICHOLS, Terry Nichols, and Timothy McVeigh experimented in the manufacture and detonation of destructive devices made up of readily available materials such as brake fluid and diesel fuel.

3. In approximately 1994, JAMES NICHOLS and Terry Nichols made and stored grenades.

4. On April 21, 1995, JAMES NICHOLS possessed components of improvised explosive devices.

The "components" referred to in the last paragraph above were discovered by the FBI when it searched James Nichols's farm over the weekend of April 21 to April 24. In one barn they found twenty-eight fifty-pound bags of ammonium nitrate, a fifty-five-gallon drum containing fuel oil, large quantities of 35 percent solution of hydrogen peroxide, and a half-pint of aluminum powder. They found large fuel tanks at the farm containing diesel fuel, and in James Nichols's farmhouse they came across a supply of nonelectric plastic caps, pyrodex, and safety fuse. According to the FBI there were metal fragments in an adjoining field that appeared to be shrapnel from explosions.

James Nichols was a year older than Terry. After the divorce of their parents, when, as part of the separation settlement, the boys' mother took control of the farm, James, in the tradition of older sons generally, worked the farm while Terry took up a semi-vagabond life. The two men, though, remained close, at least outwardly. Their political views certainly remained very close. Although he denied having been a member of the Michigan Militia, James admitted to the FBI to having gone routinely to their meetings and later to meetings of the Patriots, a more radical splinter group. Witnesses who knew him said he was vocal in his antigovernment positions and talked of renouncing his citizenship and refusing to pay taxes. Waco had hit everybody hard, he said in an FBI interview. At the same time he admitted to having made bottle bombs with McVeigh and Terry and, on his own, small explosive devices using prescription bottles, pyrodex, blasting caps, and safety fuse, but he denied that he'd ever purchased ammonium nitrate and claimed he had no personal knowledge of either McVeigh or Terry doing the same. He stated that his brother owned "survival" books containing information about ammonium nitrate bombs and—a very typical Nichols pronouncement—that Tim McVeigh had the knowledge to manufacture a bomb. But he hadn't seen Tim for several months prior, and his last contact had been a letter, about a month before, from "somewhere in Arizona."

Of all the people interviewed by the FBI about James Nichols, by far the most intriguing was a former seed salesman who, during a three-year period from 1987 to 1990, had sold seed up and down the so-called thumb of Michigan. James Nichols had been his customer. The FBI (who promised the man it would not reveal his name) interviewed the salesman on five different occasions, and he had passed a polygraph test.

The salesman—he had asked that his identity be protected—recalled several different visits to the Nichols farm. During one, in 1988, he remembered a very strong odor of diesel fuel in Nichols's machine shed and James telling him that his brother and an army buddy had been there during the weekend making bombs. (He thought it was McVeigh, but it couldn't have been, because Tim wasn't in Michigan in 1988.) James also kept a perennial stockpile of urea fertilizer, a nitrogen source used to fertilize wheat—approximately fifty fifty-pound bags, the salesman estimated. (Urea fertilizer can also be used in explosives. It is believed to have been used in the World Trade Center bombing. It is, however, distinct from ammonium nitrate.) In his thirteen years of selling seed, the salesman said he'd never seen a farmer stockpile such an amount.

Most of all, the salesman recalled during several interviews a conversation about bombs and buildings he'd had with James Nichols in the machine shed in 1989. Nichols explained that there was a simple formula to calculate the force required to shear the front and middle support columns of a high-rise and, beyond that, that you would have to know the composition and density of the columns—for instance, steel I-beams surrounded by reinforced concrete—before you could choose your explosives. To illustrate the point, James Nichols went rummaging for a newspaper clipping amid piles of clippings that he kept in drawers near his workbench. Unable to find it, he started to draw on a scratch pad, and what he drew was the sketch of a building. Subsequently, he did find the clipping. The clipping made mention of the same building Nichols had drawn and had identified for the salesman. It was the federal building in Oklahoma City—the Alfred P. Murrah Federal Building.

James Nichols spent a month in federal prison. Then, on May 22 in Detroit, a federal judge released him on bail, holding that the prosecutors had failed to produce any evidence directly connecting him to the bombing, and on August 10 the government dropped the charges entirely. Perhaps the date was a coincidence, but on that same August 10 the other federal grand jury, the one in Oklahoma City, finally pronounced itself. The government, as we shall see, totally lost interest in any other potential conspirators, and James Nichols, insofar as this case was concerned, sank further back into the shadows behind the already shadowy figure of his younger brother. The seed salesman, who had passed the polygraph test on whether James Nichols had shown him a picture of the Murrah Building while talking about blowing it up, was quietly forgotten.

The prosecution dated the conspiracy from the fall of 1994, when—so the theory went—McVeigh and Nichols and associates began to put into action plans to destroy the Murrah Building by assembling the materials necessary to build a truck bomb. In September, one Shawn Rivers rented a unit at the Mini-Storage Shed in Herington and then another, at Clark Lumber, also in Herington. Rivers, the government would claim, was McVeigh. In October, another storage shed was rented to one Joe Kyle in Council Grove, Kansas, another in November to one Ted Parker. Joe Kyle and Ted Parker, the government said, were Terry Nichols. There were other units as well, in Kingman, Arizona, and Las Vegas, Nevada, which were supposedly used in the conspiracy, but the Kansas ones, according to the government, were the sites where components of the ANFO bomb had been stashed.

On September 30, 1994, one Mike Havens purchased, for cash, forty fifty-pound sacks of ammonium nitrate at the Mid-Kansas Co-op in McPherson, Kansas. On October 18, the same Mike Havens returned to the Co-op and purchased another forty bags, for cash. According to a witness at the Co-op, the fertilizer was loaded onto a trailer constructed from a pickup bed and pulled by a dark-blue or dark-green pickup with a camper shell. Mike Havens was an alias Nichols was alleged to have used on other occasions. Mike Havens was accompanied at the Co-op by another man, who was not Timothy McVeigh, but on a receipt it discovered in searching Nichols's house for the first purchase at the Mid-Kansas Co-op, the FBI claimed to have identified McVeigh's fingerprint.

All the storage sheds and the aliases weren't per se incriminating. After all, Nichols had left many unsatisfied creditors behind him in Michigan, including judgments against him, and he may plausibly have feared that if he stored household belongings and other property under his own name they could be traced and attached by creditors. The two purchases at the Co-op constituted some of the strongest evidence, as we would later learn, that Nichols could very well have been guilty and McVeigh not and that there were others, including at least one person who nearly resembled Tim and could well have been part of the conspiracy. Frederick Schlender, manager at the Co-op, affirmed this to the FBI. The person who accompanied Nichols on these two occasions, Schlender said, was definitely not Tim McVeigh, although he may have somewhat resembled him. Therefore, if Terry Nichols was involved in the bombing and the purchase of four thousand pounds of ammonium nitrate, the largest purchase in the history of the Co-op, and if he was a terrorist building a bomb, *why on earth would he have kept the receipt?* Why didn't he simply destroy it? Unless, perchance, he wanted McVeigh's fingerprints on it? In fact, there were no fingerprints on the receipt *other* than McVeigh's. But McVeigh, according to the eyewitnesses, had never been at the Co-op in McPherson with Nichols.

That wasn't everything. The FBI also claimed to have linked McVeigh and Nichols to two thefts. There was a burglary of a quarry in Marion, Kansas, from which nonelectric plastic caps and other materials were stolen, and a robbery, on November 5, of firearms, ammunition, coins, and other valuables from an Arkansas arms dealer McVeigh knew named Roger Moore. The government's theory was that the proceeds from this second robbery had been used to finance the bomb. The circumstances of the robbery itself were strange. According to Moore, he was coming out of his house at 9:00 or 9:30 A.M. to feed his animals and was surprised by a man wearing a black ski mask and holding a gun on him. The man allegedly forced Moore to crawl back into his house, then, still holding the gun on him, tied him up with duct tape and rope. Michael Fortier claimed that McVeigh gave him a detailed account of the Moore robbery, but when later asked during cross-examination how one man could bind another with duct tape and rope while holding a gun, Fortier simply said that's what McVeigh had told him. There were other inconsistencies, beginning with the fact that a gun owner and dealer like Moore would have had quite a security setup in and around his house and that a single man, even an armed man, would most likely have a tough time robbing him. In addition, there was the question of Terry's glasses. If Terry was wearing a ski mask, where were his glasses? Nichols saw poorly without them and he didn't own contact lenses. And though Nichols never did account for his whereabouts that night, the FBI learned that McVeigh had been at a gun show in Kent, Ohio, hundreds of miles away—an airtight alibi.

Given all this, why would the FBI insist that McVeigh and Nichols had robbed Moore? Perhaps because they needed to fit these two suspects, and only these two suspects, into its version of the story. In fact, the government's argument that the robberies were carried out to finance the Oklahoma City bombing seemed to

fly in the face of its separate claim that the elements of the bomb
had already been purchased by the date the robbery took place. In
the case of *United States v. McVeigh*, it often seemed as though the
government not only could have it both ways but also that it actually
preferred to.

The same can be said of the fuel that was mixed with ammonium
nitrate to make the ANFO bomb. At trial, the prosecution would
produce a witness, one Glenn Tipton, a salesman for VP Racing
Fuels, who was "90 percent" certain Tim McVeigh had approached
him in October 1994 at the Sears Craftsman Drag Race in Topeka,
looking to buy anhydrous hydrazine, a high-powered racing fuel.
(Tipton was less certain earlier, but he had spent hours with prosecutors preparing his testimony, and with the help of that preparation his memory somehow improved.) But the prosecution's very
own explosives experts, who also testified, didn't believe anhydrous
hydrazine had been used in the bomb!

True, there were some circumstantial links between Roger
Moore and the suspects. Moore later claimed that some of the
weapons that had been found in Arizona and at Nichols's house
belonged to him, and Nichols had a key to Moore's safety deposit
box in his possession. But that didn't prove robbery. Later, at
Nichols's trial, Moore's girlfriend produced a list of weapons that
she said had been stolen from Moore, but on that list was one that
beyond dispute had been purchased by Nichols at a gun show several years before the robbery. In fact, Moore's neighbors (and the
local sheriff) were of the belief that there'd been no robbery. And in
the end whatever actually happened among Moore, Nichols, and
McVeigh—and whether there actually was a robbery—is lost to
conjecture, because McVeigh had an airtight alibi, Moore himself
wasn't on trial, and Nichols never took the stand at his own trial.
The truth remained, as was so often the case, in the shadows.

For the days immediately preceding the bombing, the government had uncovered the events in and around Junction City that
I've already described: Tim's purchase of the "getaway car" on April
14 (from Manning at Firestone) and his alleged rental, as Robert
Kling, of the Ryder truck (at Elliott's Body Shop), the witnesses
who'd identified him at the Dreamland Motel, and those who had
seen a Ryder truck parked at the Geary State Fishing Lake during

the day of April 18. As for the morning of April 19, witnesses claimed to have seen the truck and various combinations of John Does at or near the building just prior to the explosion, and then there was Trooper Hanger, who'd arrested Tim in the yellow Mercury Marquis up on Route 35.

But early on, I'd started asking myself what exactly the case against Tim actually consisted of. So he didn't like the federal government, was antigovernment, distrusted the government, even had expressed threatening and violent thoughts regarding the government. So what? He was scarcely alone in harboring such convictions, for they could have been those of any typical Pat Buchanan supporter. He was said to have been a fervent reader of *The Turner Diaries*, which, the government claimed, was a "blueprint" for the bombing. But more than 200,000 copies of *The Turner Diaries* had been sold. Was Tim McVeigh the only one of the 200,000-plus readers to see it as a plan? And a plan for what? *The Turner Diaries* describes the blowing-up of the FBI building in Washington, D.C., by parking a bomb-laden truck in the underground bowels of the building. The motive was to destroy a nationwide passport computer system. The bomb used was akin to the one that blew up the World Trade Center, not the Murrah Building. The Murrah Building didn't even house the FBI, and if *The Turner Diaries* had been the guide for building the bomb, the building would still be standing. The book was—and is—a fictional tract, not a blueprint for anything, but because of its virulently antiblack and anti-Semitic themes and language, it could easily be used by the government to demonize McVeigh. (I suppose that if the government had found a copy of William Faulkner's *Sanctuary* in McVeigh's car, they'd have said that he, like Popeye, believed in raping women by instrumentality.) Were there similarities between *The Turner Diaries* and the Oklahoma City bombing? Of course. And is *The Turner Diaries* an offensive, racist book held in high esteem by the extreme right and racist fringe? It is. But none of that necessarily meant Timothy McVeigh was, unlike the hundreds of thousands of others who read the book, guilty of carrying out the attack.

Then there was the bomb itself. Clearly it was a large, deadly instrument, and its construction, in the opinion of every expert we talked to, required clever, indeed sophisticated engineering. Nothing in McVeigh's or Nichols's background or education or training, in the army or elsewhere, equipped them to construct such a device—unless, of course, they themselves had had help from professionals. Furthermore, as experts from two continents testified two years later after reviewing all the forensic evidence that had been collected at the site and subsequently examined in the FBI Laboratory, they could only speculate as to the bomb's precise makeup. From other sources—for instance, the purchases at the Mid-Kansas Co-op—they might surmise that it had contained four thousand pounds of ANFO mix. But the experts could not determine whether the main charge—the ANFO itself—was exploded through a three- or four-step explosive train, or by using an electric or a nonelectric blasting cap, or as a "booster," PETN (pentaerythritol tetranitrate) or TNT (trinitrotoluene).

And then there was the question of the "John Does." Tim had been identified as John Doe #1, but Junction City, where the Ryder truck had been rented, was the veritable backdoor of Fort Riley, and Fort Riley was a large military installation where there were hundreds of GIs taller than six feet, slender, of military bearing, with light-colored, close-cropped crewcuts—in other words, hundreds of Tim McVeigh look-alikes. Yes, there was a picture that had been taken of Tim by a security camera at a McDonald's more than a mile downhill from Elliott's Body Shop, about twenty minutes before he supposedly had arrived at Elliott's to pick up the Ryder truck. But the clothes he was wearing in the McDonald's image were not those described by the witnesses at Elliott's. Furthermore, there was evidence that it was raining, and though he might barely have had time to walk the mile in the interval, he wasn't wet once he arrived. So how had he gotten to Elliott's? By taxi? There was no record of one. (The government checked.) Well, possibly John Doe #2 had driven him. And possibly McVeigh could have changed clothes in the backseat.

John Doe #2, according to the first FBI sketch released on April 20, 1995, had full lips, a square jaw and broad face, black hair, an intense look, and a thick and muscular neck. The FBI described him as five-nine or -ten, a white male around thirty, 175–180 pounds, with a snake tattoo on his left upper arm. A second sketch, released five days later, depicted him wearing a baseball cap, and there was also a profile drawing of the same suspect. These sketches were published in newspapers all over the country and shown countless times on television. Hotlines were set up that were deluged with calls, and hundreds, probably thousands, of federal and state law enforcement agents tracked down leads. Reports popped up nationwide of FBI agents descending on hot suspects, sometimes with guns drawn, and with the media descending right on their heels, only to find out that a mistake had been made. As *Time* put it in its May 15, 1995, issue, "For a while it seemed as if there were as many potential John Doe #2's as clowns tumbling out of a circus car."

The circus imagery was apt enough. To cite one of the more intriguing examples, on May 2, 1995, FBI agents descended on a motel in Carthage, Missouri, and arrested two drifters, Robert Earl Jacks and Gary Land—apparently (if disingenuously) for no other reason than they had lived in a motel in Kingman, Arizona, from December to April, when McVeigh lived five blocks away, and second, because they had been registered in a motel in Perry, Oklahoma, the day of the bombing. The arrest was televised. The two suspects were interrogated and quickly released. Then a realtor in another small Missouri town who saw pictures of the arrest on the news realized that the FBI had the "wrong" Robert Jacks. As the realtor and two other witnesses subsequently told the FBI, the previous November Terry Nichols and Tim McVeigh had visited his office, inquiring about an isolated piece of property that his agency had advertised; the two men were accompanied by a third, short, dark, muscular man who had introduced himself as Robert Jacks. Only this Robert Jacks had mentioned that he spelled his name differently.

Jacques? Jocques? Possibly Jacquez?

There was, however, at least one other reason the FBI could have been looking for Jacks, in addition to the motel registers in Kingman and Perry. Marife Nichols, Terry's wife, had kept an address book, and on a blank page the name "Jacks" had been written four times, each time with a different spelling, as though the writer, be it Marife or someone else, hadn't known how to spell it. And there were more coincidences—if that's what they were—involving this man. A convicted Kingman drug dealer told the FBI in June 1995 that Michael Fortier and Jim Rosencrans, two of McVeigh's buddies in Kingman, had had another friend, "Bob," who matched the description the Missouri realtor and his cowitnesses had given them of the mysterious Jacks. And later still, after the trail had gone cold, Denver's *Rocky Mountain News* would discover that during 1996 this same Jim Rosencrans, who had moved in the interim to Odessa, Texas, was sharing a post office box with a man who had boasted of being an undercover drug agent and whose name, it turned out, was Robert Jacquez!

In the early days of the case, when we had an abundance of John Doe #2's, I used to ask myself, half in jest: Suppose they never find him? What will happen then? Will they try to claim McVeigh did it all by himself, since Nichols could prove he was nowhere near Oklahoma City on April 19? It was a bad joke, but two years later, that is exactly what happened.

T here was a time in 1995, during the heyday of the John Doe #2 sightings, when the FBI thought Pvt. Todd Bunting, stationed at Fort Riley, might have been the man they were after. He certainly resembled John Doe #2, and he owned a Carolina Panthers cap like the one in the sketches. The only trouble was that Bunting had an alibi for Monday, April 17, when Robert Kling had rented the truck at Elliott's Body Shop, and another alibi for the morning of Wednesday, April 19, when the truck exploded in Oklahoma City.

Nevertheless, Todd Bunting was just what the government needed. It turned out that on Tuesday, April 18—the day after Robert Kling's rental—Private Bunting *had* been at Elliott's Body Shop, renting a truck with his sergeant from Fort Riley. The rest was easy as pie—particularly for a group of government prosecutors who switched versions of the bombing with the ease and aplomb of a gang of quick-change artists. At a pretrial hearing before Judge Matsch in January 1997, they reformulated their theory of the case and announced that John Doe #2 had never existed. All three witnesses at Elliott's had been mistaken. The man they thought they'd seen with Robert Kling on Monday had really been Todd Bunting on Tuesday, and when they remembered it Wednesday for the FBI's sketch artists they'd simply gotten it all bollixed up. Now the story was that Tim McVeigh had walked up the hill alone from McDonald's on Monday afternoon (in a light drizzle), arrived at Elliott's alone, rented the truck alone, driven off alone, and destroyed the Murrah Building . . . alone.

I am tempted to call it the pigs-have-wings theory. But the absurdity of the government's change of heart, almost two years after the event, should not diminish its seriousness. Over and over again, witnesses shifted earlier testimony either to support the government's theory of the case or, more frequently, to justify shifts in the theory necessitated by facts that otherwise failed to fit. Typically, this happened when government prosecutors took over questioning from FBI agents. In some cases, I've no doubt, witnesses were pressured. Others, I know, came to believe they had a chance at all or part of the $2 million reward posted by the government. (In this they were wrong; the reward has never been awarded, in whole or in part.) Still others, I'm sure, wanted to "do the right thing" and help the FBI convict the most hated man in America. The Fortiers, as we shall see, were the most important of anybody who changed stories, but a classic example was the testimony of Tom Manning, the manager of the Firestone shop in Junction City.

On the morning of Good Friday, April 14, 1995, McVeigh, according to Manning's statements, drove his battered Pontiac station wagon into the Firestone parking lot. Its head gasket had blown. The two men had known each other from McVeigh's army days at nearby Fort Riley. Now McVeigh wanted a new car, cheap, and Manning was able to unload the 1977 Mercury Marquis on him for $250 plus the Pontiac.

That morning, while McVeigh was at Firestone, Robert Kling made his first call to Elliott's Body Shop, inquiring about renting a Ryder truck. The government believed the call had been made on a telephone debit card and, originally, that it had been placed at 8:30 A.M., although they later changed this to just before 10 A.M. If the call was made shortly before 10:00 A.M., though, they had a major problem. In the early weeks of the investigation, Tom Manning was interviewed no less than nine times by the FBI, who took him over that morning's events step by step. Not once did he mention that McVeigh had left the premises during the transaction or while the Mercury was being readied for delivery. McVeigh hadn't asked to use the telephone, either. It was more than a year later, when interrogated by Larry Mackey, the second-in-command on the prosecution team, that Manning suddenly "remembered" that, oh yes, McVeigh had left the store once, briefly. Lo and behold, there was a pay phone one block away. That's where he must have called Elliott's from, the government now decided, and he'd used the so-called Daryl Bridges telephone debit card—a card that, as I'll explain later, would be spuriously used again and again by the government to tie McVeigh to the crime.

Unfortunately, the "solution" to one problem sometimes creates new problems. In this instance there were two. When the defense asked Tom Manning during cross-examination when exactly McVeigh had left the store and when he'd come back, he answered it was *after* the time the government said the call had been placed. In addition, the prosecutors could produce no direct, objective evidence that this particular call had in fact been made on the Daryl Bridges card. This, in turn, required yet another modification on their part. Now, we were told, there had been a "computer glitch" in the telephone system—at the precise moment the call had been placed. But for that glitch, the government said, the call would have been entered automatically on the Daryl Bridges records.

By the time of Terry Nichols's preliminary hearing on May 18, 1995, I had studied the affidavit the FBI had filed to hold him as a material witness—this after the nine-and-a-half-hour interview he'd given them on April 21 and the subsequent affidavit, some ten days later, that supported the request for his arrest as a conspirator. What they had on Nichols was physical, as well as circumstantial, evidence. They claimed to have found blasting caps at his house in Herington and a fuel meter, guns and ammunition, and a rocket launcher. There was also ammonium nitrate and fuel oil. Either the government had found it or planted it, but even as skeptical as I was about them, I didn't believe they'd have gone to such lengths.

Unlike McVeigh's preliminary hearing, which had been held at the El Reno prison before I joined the case, Nichols's took place, by mutual agreement, at El Reno. A general visitor's room was converted into a makeshift courtroom complete with American flag, judicial bench, a witness chair, and three tables, one for the government, one for Michael Tigar and Ron Woods (Nichols's counsel), and one for McVeigh's counsel, which was allowed to observe. Rob Nigh and I attended. The media—there may have been fifteen present, no more—were admitted based on a pool and lottery arrangement.

The rules of evidence at a preliminary hearing are, if not nonexistent, then very relaxed. Usually, as was the case here, the prosecution will offer a "fall down" witness, not the FBI agent who signed the original affidavit of complaint but another one who knows relatively little about the case. The reason for this is one of what-you-don't-know-won't-hurt-you. In other words, the threshold of probable cause at a preliminary hearing is sufficiently low that a relatively uninformed witness can do the job, whereas a highly informed one might, under cross-examination, be obliged to give away prosecution secrets.

I was the only one in the courtroom who had ever actually worked with Mike Tigar. I thought I knew what he would do, and he didn't disappoint me. Merrick Garland presented the government's case. He was the third-ranking official in the Department of Justice hierarchy, preceded only by the attorney general herself and Jamie Gorelick, her deputy. No sooner had Garland finished with his witness than Tigar, on his feet, was all over him. For every last one of the alleged facts the government had brought out that suggested guilty involvement, Tigar's line of cross-examination educed—from the witness himself—a reluctant, but utterly innocent, alternative explanation. And each time, even though Tigar was asking the questions and the FBI agent was answering, it was as though you could hear Terry Nichols giving voice to a compendium of excuses and rationales.

The FBI, for example, had found a fuel meter in Nichols's possession, and the testifying agent contended that it had been used in measuring out the precise dosage of fuel oil needed in the ANFO bomb. But according to Nichols, the meter was broken. Besides, he'd only had it because he was trying to sell it.

Well?

Well (the hapless FBI agent had to admit), when the FBI found the fuel meter, it *did* appear to be broken, or was at least disassembled as if someone was trying to fix it. Lo and behold, the same Wednesday as the bombing, a classified ad *had* appeared in the local giveaway paper, offering it for sale.

The same went for blue plastic fuel barrels also found on the premises, and the rocket launcher, and the guns and ammunition, and the detonator cords. For everything incriminating there was an explanation. When it came to traces of ammonium nitrate, the FBI agent admitted that, yes, ammonium nitrate was commonly used to blow up tree stumps on land-clearing projects on farms. In addition, hadn't Terry Nichols readily admitted to having ammonium nitrate around in order to sell five-pound bags of it at gun shows? Sure enough, five-pound bags were found, along with a kitchen grinder that had been used to grind the nitrate.

And then there were the questions about Nichols's exact whereabouts on certain key days.

The day of the bombing, Wednesday, he hadn't been anywhere near Oklahoma City. Could he prove it? Yes, there were alibi witnesses galore.

What about Tuesday, the day the bomb was built? He'd been at Fort Riley, attending a sale. (And sure enough, there was a sign-in sheet showing that Terry Nichols had indeed signed in at the Ft. Riley sale at 1:30 P.M.)

But what of the Sunday before the bombing, when Nichols had admittedly been in Oklahoma City? Nichols explained that he'd only gone down there because Tim had called him. McVeigh was driving from Arizona to New York, but he'd had car trouble in Oklahoma City and asked Terry to come get him. Plus Tim had Terry's TV in his trunk, which he wanted for his son, Josh.

And sure enough, when Josh Nichols woke up the next day, he'd found the TV set in his living room.

And on and on, coincidence piling onto coincidence.

Why, after all, had Nichols waited till Friday, two days after the bombing, to go to the authorities, knowing what he knew?

Because he hadn't even known about the bombing on Wednesday or Thursday.

But how could that be?

Because his cable-TV wasn't hooked up till Friday.

And—wouldn't you know?—the cable company's records showed this to be true.

It was, in sum, a bravura performance on Tigar's part—or Nichols's part—and when it was over, even Merrick Garland begrudgingly came over and shook Tigar's hand, saying, "I was told I would be impressed, and I am."

The only trouble was that Terry Nichols was lying.

McVeigh couldn't have called him from Oklahoma City that Sunday, April 16, because McVeigh wasn't in Oklahoma City at the time. It had already been established that he was up in Junction City, twenty-odd miles from Herington, registered under his own name at the Dreamland Motel. When he'd arrived in Junction City the previous Thursday, he'd driven to the Firestone store, where he bought the yellow Mercury Marquis. His old car had broken down. There, in the presence and under the gaze of Firestone employees, he emptied everything out of his old car and loaded it into the Mercury, and guess what?

Nobody saw a television set. There wasn't any.

Unless we were to assume that Tim had stopped his car on the outskirts of town and buried the television set he was bringing to Terry in the tall prairie grass so that the Firestone people wouldn't see it, then Terry's tale was just that, a fabrication. The fact he had a TV, somewhere, that he could introduce into his living room that week offered him yet another of those convenient corroborations. Furthermore, Terry had to know full well that Tim was in Junction City, not en route from Arizona to New York, because there was a record of Tim having called his house in Herington from the Dreamland Motel.

But why? Why would someone feel compelled to invent a parallel version of events—complete with the detail of the TV set? The only answer I could come up with was that the truth, if Nichols had admitted to it, would have been far more damaging to him than the lie. Maybe, for all any of us knew, he needed it in order to manufacture an excuse for a trip to Oklahoma City. Maybe he'd gone to Oklahoma City that Sunday—but not to see Tim McVeigh or to bring him back. After all, the only "evidence" that Tim was in Oklahoma City that Sunday afternoon came from Terry himself.

Knowing this, I began to look at everything Nichols had said in a different light, and the more I looked, the more it appeared that Nichols, with Tigar as his advocate, was going to try to save his skin at Tim McVeigh's expense. Not that I could blame him for that, but from there it was but a short jump to a second deduction. Surely it had occurred to me before—it is part of any lawyer's training to conjure up dozens of possibilities and hypotheses to fit a set of facts—but this time, it hit me right between the eyes. Now I had to consider the possibility that the Oklahoma City bombing could have been a very clever, well-executed conspiracy. Could it have been designed to protect and shelter everyone involved? Everyone, that is, except my client—who may or may not have been involved but whose role, if he had a role, would have been the designated patsy?

I found myself focusing, for example, on Nichols's whereabouts the morning of the bombing. In one of their very early versions of what had happened, the government speculated (for and with the media) that Nichols himself was John Doe #2 and that he had driven the bomb truck from Herington to Oklahoma City. But Terry had so many alibis for that day, people who had seen him in Herington, three hundred miles from the bombing, that you got the impression he'd spent the daylight hours parading up and down the streets of the town, carrying a sandwich board that said, "TERRY NICHOLS IS HERE, NOT THERE."

Why would he have done that—unless he'd anticipated coming under suspicion? By contrast, he had been like a wraith in the days immediately preceding and following April 19—understandably, because he had no need of alibis for those days. How could it be that on the day of the bombing so many people saw Terry, but on the two days afterward he was so isolated that he never heard a single word about or saw a single image of the explosion? And none of the people who saw him on April 19 so much as mentioned the bombing, when the whole state was talking about it?

There were also some strange aspects to the events of Friday, April 21. Tim had been all over television, in the Noble County Courthouse walk-out, and the Nichols brothers had been mentioned too. The way Terry told it, once he heard the news he'd simply driven to the Herington police station, walked inside, and said, "Gee, I understand you guys are looking for me."

This was true. He did do that. But—typical Terry—before he did, he'd also been calling a travel agency, inquiring about quick tickets back to the Philippines, and there was some evidence, never quite proven, that he was driving *out* of town and that he changed direction and headed *toward* the police station only when he realized he was being tailed by FBI cars. He had also called his brother, James.

Once inside the police station, Terry quickly distanced himself from his old buddy, Tim. Whereas Tim, en route to El Reno prison that same day, kept his own counsel, Terry talked and talked and talked.

He talked for nine and a half hours.

As I said, who could blame him? The accused were fighting for their own lives. In such situations, you do what you have to do. But my revelation about Terry's and Mike's strategy reinforced my convictions, if I'd had any doubts before, on two crucial counts:

First, we—my colleagues and I—had to conduct a completely independent investigation, separate and distinct from what Terry Nichols said and what our own client had told us, in order to try to piece together exactly what had happened and what had not. And second, we would have to fight like a steer to get a severance—in other words, to get a separate trial for our client.

I knew right away that severance would mean a legal battle, for the government was equally determined to link the two cases and try them together, and in fact the decision on the severance issue wouldn't be handed down until 1996. Our own investigation was almost as slow to get under way. As I've said, few people that spring and summer would talk to us. Meanwhile, despite court orders and admonitions to the contrary, the government diddled and ducked and delayed on the issue of discovery—their legal obligation to share their findings with us—so as to leave us largely in the dark.

Which is exactly where they wanted us.

And then there were the Fortiers, Michael and Lori.

From the beginning, their fingerprints, so to speak, were all over the case. Almost immediately after Tim's identification as John Doe #1, the FBI descended in force on Kingman, Arizona, and the media descended after them. The young, hippyesque Kingman couple, Michael and Lori Fortier, became familiar targets of television cameras and reporters. Mike gave one interview on CNN and talked to the *Los Angeles Times*, and on a couple of occasions he answered questions while sitting in his pickup, but most of the TV footage was simply photo-ops taken of him leaving or entering his house or walking to his truck. The thrust of what the Fortiers told the world was that Tim was innocent. They themselves professed to know nothing about the bombing, and they were sure their friend couldn't have been involved. A few days after Tim's arrest, Michael told the media, "I hope he [Tim] sticks to his guns. If what they're saying on TV is right, he's a political prisoner." In a statement he and Lori drafted and handed out, Mike wrote, "I would like to say, to everyone, that Timothy McVeigh is a close friend of my family's and mine. He stands accused of the bombing of the Alfred P. Murrah Building, but from knowing him I believe in no way he was responsible for this crime."

The Fortiers—she was still Lori Hart then—had been friends of Tim's ever since Fort Riley, and Tim was best man at their wedding. In 1993, after he left upstate New York and after a detour to Michigan to the Nicholses', Tim settled in Kingman, the first of several stays. Kingman is a good-sized town that straddles Interstate 40 in northwest Arizona, some ninety miles south of Las Vegas, Nevada. It is a known center of right-wing sentiment and activity. Tim worked for a security company there, and later, in early 1994, thanks to Mike's introduction, he worked for True Value Hardware. They—Mike and Tim—had traveled together on several occasions, notably in December 1994, when, the government would allege, they had taken possession in Kansas of the firearms stolen from Roger Moore in Arkansas and moved them to Kingman.

Fortier readily admitted that he shared Tim's antigovernment views and his fascination with weapons, and he flew a "Don't Tread On Me" flag on his flagpole. (According to Jo Thomas of *The New York Times*, an unidentified ATF agent reported having seen him and McVeigh taking part in a paramilitary training exercise in the northern Arizona desert.) Fortier too had been shaken by Waco. But he also, it turned out, had a fascination with drugs, and at the time the FBI began to harass him he was already under suspicion for trafficking in amphetamines.

The FBI kept the couple under intense pressure. At the height of the FBI investigation, an estimated one hundred agents were assigned to the Kingman command post—later on, local retailers took to selling T-shirts that said, "I survived the FBI"—and to the Fortiers it must have seemed that every last one of them was watching their every move. Armed with a search warrant as well as shotguns and automatic weapons, some twenty FBI agents went over their mobile home with a fine-tooth comb and, while they were at it, installed hidden microphones and a phone tap. They questioned the Fortiers on numerous occasions, promising to help them if they cooperated, at the same time threatening them with other charges in addition to the bombing, including drug charges, if they didn't. According to Fortier, one FBI agent called him a baby killer.

The Fortiers tried to fight back. On April 27, eight days after the bombing and six after Tim's arrest, Mike and Lori gave a long interview to Sean Calebs of CNN. It was held in a small park near their home in Kingman. In addition to defending Tim, Mike accused the FBI of fabricating evidence against him, even of altering their drawing of John Doe #2. "I believe that's happening right now," he said in the interview. "I get the impression that that sketch is being modified to fit my face." But at the same time, Fortier couldn't miss the fact that just about everything that was being said of Terry Nichols could be applied to him:

McVeigh and Nichols had been friends for a long time?

So had McVeigh and Fortier.

McVeigh and Nichols had gone through basic training together and served in the same company?

So had McVeigh and Fortier.

McVeigh and Nichols had sometimes shared a house?

So had McVeigh and Fortier.

Ammonium nitrate fertilizer was found at Nichols's house?

It was at Fortier's too.

Nichols had guns and antigovernment literature at his house?

So did Fortier at his. Plus blasting caps (electric and nonelectric), Kinestiks explosives, and primadet detonators, among other objects of destruction.

There were the phone calls too. A key element in the government's case, as I have mentioned, was the Daryl Bridges phone card, a *Spotlight* calling card issued by the right-wing Liberty Lobby in the name of Daryl Bridges. It had been bought in October 1993 on an application filled out allegedly by Nichols and paid for by a money order that allegedly bore McVeigh's fingerprint. It was a debit card, where the user prepaid a specific amount and then was charged twenty-five cents per minute for calls within the United

States. The initial deposit had been renewed from time to time by subsequent money orders, and both McVeigh and Nichols—and others—had made calls on the account. In tracing all the phone records, the government identified, for instance, a number of calls made to suppliers who dealt in items that could have been used in the building of an ANFO bomb. But as we would learn from our own telephone experts, tracing the activity on the debit card was neither simple nor foolproof, a good case in point being the previously mentioned call on the morning of April 14, 1995, to Elliott's. Meanwhile, the Daryl Bridges debit card records showed that there had been more phone calls to and from the Fortiers' number in Kingman than to virtually any other source.

The FBI, somewhat chillingly, took advantage of another of the Fortiers' weaknesses. Michael was unemployed. Their plans to open a tanning salon (in the desert no less!) had come to nothing. They had even been reduced to selling guns to satisfy their dope habits, and FBI bugs had picked up a series of conversations in which they talked about changing their story in order to make millions of dollars. At the same time, as the FBI well knew, their violations of the federal drug laws exposed them to greater prison liability than the crimes for which Michael ultimately pleaded guilty.

Once they have identified their quarry and have begun to work them, FBI field agents can be utterly relentless, and after several weeks the Fortiers broke. On May 17, they drove from Kingman to Oklahoma City. It was the day before Terry's preliminary hearing. In Oklahoma City, they checked into a Motel 6, and from there they called the FBI, asking for a meeting in order to "correct" their previous statements.

At first, the Fortiers asked for immunity, which the government categorically refused. Then, as time went on, they made a series of "proffers" through their lawyers, that is, statements about what their testimony *might* be in court in exchange for an acceptable deal. The government, however, kept insisting on more. It would not be until August that the two sides finally cut a deal, but long before then the substance of their "corrections" became known:

- All their earlier statements to the FBI were lies. They were now telling the truth.

- ◆ Tim and Terry had done it.

- ◆ Long before the bombing, Tim had told them the Murrah Building was their target. He'd described in detail the bomb they intended to build. He'd even demonstrated with soup cans, on their living-room floor, what the bomb would do to the building.

- ◆ On the trip they'd taken in December 1994 to collect the weapons stolen from the Roger Moore robbery, Tim had taken Mike on a detour to Oklahoma City to inspect the Murrah Building.

- ◆ On the same trip, Tim had taken Mike to view the rented storage sheds in Kansas, where components of the bomb had already been stashed, and to the Geary State Fishing Lake, where, Mike said, Tim and Terry planned to build it.

- ◆ All during this trip, Mike Fortier said, Tim pressed him to participate in the deed itself, but he—of course—had refused.

The government's problem, all during the negotiations, was that it had little concrete evidence tying the Fortiers to the bombing itself. Then, too, Lori was clearly smarter than Michael. She hadn't given the interviews or appeared on CNN. She'd been content to stand to one side, the attractive young wife in the tight white sweater with her brunette hair blowing in the wind and her child hugged to her hip. Michael, meanwhile, looked like what he was—a desert rat.

None of this escaped their lawyer. Lori Fortier might have come across to some as a dumb brunette, but in that motel room in Oklahoma City, when her husband invited her to "correct" her statement first for FBI Agent Floyd Zims, she replied, "No, you go first, Michael." By her statements, she'd helped Tim make a false ID card, had wrapped packages containing materials stolen from the Kansas quarry, and had gone with Mike and Tim to watch Tim detonate a small bomb in the desert—all of which legally made her a conspirator—but without those statements, and her later testimony corroborating them, the government had nothing against her. Beyond that, could they really seek the death penalty for her—

which is what Janet Reno had committed them to? And if they did, wouldn't that have weakened the case against the others?

With Michael, it was different. The government liked to say later that Mike and Lori weren't involved in the conspiracy, but Mike was hardly an innocent bystander. The government, in its most extreme position, could brandish the death-penalty threat; Mike's lawyer, in his, could threaten no cooperation at all. Somewhere between those extremes, somewhere short of total immunity, lay the basis for an agreement. So the Fortiers, through their attorneys, kept making their proffers, and the government kept rejecting them.

Just days before the grand jury was due to conclude its deliberations, the deal was finally struck. Although Michael was uneasy about it, and supposedly threatened to walk at the eleventh hour, the Fortiers testified on August 8, 1995.

In exchange, the government agreed to the following:

+ Lori Fortier would be granted "use" immunity. Technically, this is less than full immunity. Nothing she said before the grand jury could be used against her, since, under the law, a husband can't testify against his wife. Finally, the prosecution had no other evidence to present that implicated Lori, and so the idea that her immunity was "limited" was but a fiction to save face for the government.

+ Michael Fortier would plead guilty to several charges, including possession and interstate transport of stolen goods (from the Roger Moore robbery) and lying under oath.

+ Any drug charges that could have been brought against him were forgotten altogether. So would all other charges relating to the conspiracy and the bombing.

When the Fortiers gave the FBI their "corrected" statements on May 17 at the Motel 6, they had something else on their minds. We didn't find out about it until the following January, because till then the government had kept us from getting our hands on the Fortiers' 302s. (A 302 is the report form an FBI agent fills out covering his interrogation of a witness or suspect.)

But there it was. One of the Fortiers' demands, in exchange for changing their statements, was protection.

Protection from what? the agents asked.

From the Aryan Nation, the Fortiers answered. They'd kill us if they knew what we were saying.

Aryan Nation was Richard Butler's Christian Identity group based in Hayden Lake, Idaho, otherwise known as Church of Jesus Christ Christian, which had spawned, among other splinter groups, Robert Mathews's murderous Bruders Schweigen. Richard Butler himself had been a defendant in a sedition trial in 1988 but was acquitted. In any case, if curious readers want to know what else the Fortiers might have told the FBI about the involvement of Aryan Nation in the Oklahoma City bombing, or what the FBI might have found out in further investigations, then ask the FBI. We were unable to learn anything more.

The Fortiers' change of heart that May obviously cost us ground in the media's rush to judgment, but it troubled me less in terms of the overall case. There is nothing that makes a trial lawyer rub his hands more than the prospect of cross-examining a key witness who has changed his or her statements and admits to having lied. If a witness lied once, what (the jury is bound to ask itself) is to prevent him or her from lying again? Particularly if being charged with a death-penalty felony was the alternative? As the details of the Fortiers' "corrections" became known, we were able to demonstrate that every last one of them, every item, every detail, had already been aired in the media, specifically in local Arizona newspapers that the Fortiers were known to have read. In other words, by the time they checked into the Motel 6 in Oklahoma City on May 17, they had had ample time to adapt their new version of the truth to versions already published and, with the subsequent prodding and massaging and coaching of the prosecution, to perfect it and sculpt it to the government's theories.

Two years later, in a Denver courtroom, this was exactly the thrust of my cross-examination of the Fortiers, and I believe it greatly diminished their effectiveness as witnesses. Even Joe Hartzler, the government's chief prosecutor, admitted as much in public when he said that as important as the Fortiers' testimony was the prosecution's case against McVeigh and Nichols was more than strong enough without it. But if that was true—if the government's case was that strong without the Fortiers—then why, I began to ask

myself, were the FBI and prosecutors so keen on making a deal with
them that summer? After all, as they kept repeating to the world,
this was the worst act of terrorism in the two hundred years of the
republic. One hundred sixty-eight Americans had died, nineteen of
them children. All the resources of American law enforcement had
been committed to finding the perpetrators, and the FBI had vowed
not to rest until those involved—all those involved—were brought
to justice. If that were true, though, why deal with the Fortiers?
Why not simply charge them along with Tim and Terry and go for
the death penalty for all four?

I'm sure Hartzler would have answered that no case, as every
lawyer knows, is ever so strong that the lawyer will reject reinforc-
ing evidence or testimony. And that is true enough, as far as it goes.
But there was something else that occurred to me, as early as that
May. Maybe you could say that in those dark days for the defense I
was ready to grasp at any straw, but the idea, once it formulated in
my mind, wouldn't go away. On the contrary, as time wore on and
more of the evidence—and lack of evidence—came to light, it
gained in strength. The idea was simply this:

Possibly—just possibly—the prosecutors had to make a deal with
the Fortiers because beneath all the bravado the underlying case
they were developing had weaknesses. What if it *wasn't* as strong in
their own minds as they had led the world to believe? What if they
made the deal with the Fortiers because they *needed* them? What if
the theory of the case was simply wrong or mistaken or incomplete?

The maximum potential sentence under Michael Fortier's deal
with the government was twenty-three years. However, the prosecutors pledged to intercede with the court and file a motion for a lower
sentence if they were satisfied with his efforts at cooperation. Having
been in prison ever since his plea bargain, he was finally sentenced in
1998 to no more than twelve years. Meanwhile Lori, who by her own
admission might have prevented the deaths of 168 people just by
picking up the telephone, gets to sleep in her own bed at night.

The Fortiers were virtually the last witnesses the government
produced before the grand jury. Two days later, on August
10, 1995, the following indictment was returned:

- Count One: Conspiracy to use a weapon of mass destruction in violation of Title 18, United States Code, Section 2332a.

- Count Two: Use of a weapon of mass destruction in violation of Title 18, United States Code, Sections 2332a and 2(a) and (b).

- Count Three: Destruction by explosives in violation of Title 18, United States Code, Sections 844(f) and 2(a) and (b).

- Counts Four Through Eleven: First degree murder in violation of Title 18, United States Code, Sections 1114 and 1111 and 2(a) and (b); and Title 18, Code of Federal Regulations, Section 64.2(h).

If one had only read the indictments and what the media had reported about Tim and Terry, it would have seemed like a clear, open-and-shut case. But Count One of the indictment, conspiracy to use a weapon of mass destruction, began as follows:

The Grand Jury charges:

1. Beginning on or about September 13, 1994, and continuing thereafter until on or about April 19, 1995, at Oklahoma City, Oklahoma, in the Western District of Oklahoma and elsewhere,
TIMOTHY JAMES MCVEIGH
and
TERRY LYNN NICHOLS,
the defendants herein, did knowingly, intentionally, willfully and maliciously conspire, combine and agree together and with *others unknown* to the Grand Jury to use a weapon of mass destruction.

The italics are mine.

PART
II

6

THE FORCES AGAINST US

Just about everyone, in the first days, had declared the Murrah Building explosion to be the work of Middle East terrorists, a fact we kept coming back to. Government officials had said so themselves, something that was not to be taken lightly. After all, the prosecution had at its disposal the resources of every federal, state, and local agency in the United States to interrogate, arrest, and then prosecute and convict those that the grand jury charged with the bombing. The president of the United States pledged to send "the world's finest investigators to solve these murders." Within hours of the president's statement, the U.S. attorney general emphatically stated that "the FBI and the law enforcement community will pursue every lead and use every possible resource to bring these people responsible to justice."

The government began its search for suspects within minutes after the bombing. The White House Situation Room, the FBI Command Center, the CIA Watch Office, and other agencies' nerve centers established communications with personnel located at or near the scene in Oklahoma City. Government agencies throughout the United States were alerted to the potential for similar attacks. At the White House, a "crisis team" was convened in order to coordinate the intensive investigation. This team, under the direction of the Justice Department, consisted of personnel from ATF, FBI, the

U.S. Secret Service (USSS), CIA, the National Security Agency (NSA), and members of the National Security Council. According to media reports, the crisis team first met on the day of the bombing via teleconference in Washington and convened again the next morning at the White House. CIA spokesman David Christian verified to the media that the agency was involved in the Murrah bombing investigation. In addition, the investigative machinery of U.S. military intelligence agencies was used. It was reported that "the nation's intelligence community, the CIA and defense intelligence officials, also will contribute information, and send their own agents overseas to work digging up leads, according to the law enforcement experts."

That wasn't all. Civilian and military intelligence agencies were placed on the highest alert here in the United States, and similar warnings of impending attacks were forwarded to U.S. installations overseas. For example, the CIA's Directorate of Operations (DO) transmitted to stations and bases worldwide a high precedence cable instructing agency officers to query sources for information about the attack. The FBI's Counterterrorism Center issued a directive to all CIA stations to search their international sources for possible leads among foreign terrorist groups. Officers in the DO's six overseas divisions immediately began arranging meetings and conducting debriefing sessions. The domestic arm of the DO—the National Resources (NR) Division—also began combing contacts for leads concerning the bombing. The CIA's sources included individuals holding positions in governments, military services, corporations, universities, political parties, and terrorist groups. The agency's officers utilized unilateral assets—those who are cooperating with the United States unbeknownst to their superiors—as well as liaison relationships—formal contacts between the CIA and foreign law enforcement, intelligence, and security agencies.

In the immediate aftermath of the explosion, the CIA searched its databases for candidates who might have the means and motive to perpetrate the bombing. CIA databases were also used to verify the bona fides of sources providing leads, and the CIA's stations and bases submitted numerous "name traces" on individuals as a result of the bombing investigation. (These traces were requests for information on individuals, including those suspected of having knowledge of the bombing.) Technical assets, such as global, regional, and local communications intercepts and reconnaissance satellites, were also used to obtain or verify information about the bombing. The CIA's Counterterrorism Center was the focal point for all reports. The information gathered was then sent to government analysts and other official consumers, including the Justice Department.

Also in response to the attack, the NSA promptly supplemented its existing "watch list" for domestic terrorist threats related to the bombing, potential suspects, and suspect organizations. The watch list enabled NSA listening posts to key on specific words spoken in their global network of intercepted oral and electronic communications.

The number of government agencies and departments involved in the investigation was staggering. Procedures similar to those in the CIA and NSA for gathering information on the bombing were employed by foreign and domestic personnel, including the Department of Justice and its enforcement agencies—FBI, the Drug Enforcement Administration (DEA), the Immigration and Naturalization Service (INS), and the U.S. Marshals Service; the Department of State's Bureau of Diplomatic Security (DS); the Department of the Treasury's ATF, U.S. Customs Service (USCS), Internal Revenue Service (IRS), and USSS; the Postal Service's postal inspectors; the Department of Defense's Armed Services Defense Intelligence Agency (DIA), Naval Criminal Investigative Service, and Defense Investigative Service; the General Services Administration's Federal Protective Service; the Department of Transportation's Coast Guard; and even the Federal Aviation Administration (FAA). Other agencies, bureaus, and departments participated in the gathering of information as well. Personnel at all levels, suspecting the bombing to be a large scale terrorist attack resulting in numerous deaths, immediately mobilized all resources at the government's disposal. The result was a mammoth investigation without political or geographic limits.

News reports conclusively showed that the early FBI analysis and the judgment of other counterterrorism experts pointed toward foreign responsibility for the bombing. CBS News reported shortly after the bombing that the FBI had received claims of responsibility for the attack from at least eight organizations. Seven of the claimants were thought to have Middle East connections. Steven Emerson, an expert on Islamic Jihad, an Iranian-backed militant group, said: "There is no smoking gun. But the modus operandi and circumstantial evidence lead in the direction of Islamic terrorism." The government received calls from six people saying that they were from different Muslim sects and asserting that they were responsible for the bombing.

On April 20, 1995, *The New York Times* reported that federal authorities opened an intensive hunt for the perpetrators of the bombing on the theory that the bombing was a terrorist attack against the government. Some experts focused on the similarity of the attack to the February 1992 World Trade Center bombing, itself the work of Islamic militants. The FBI even went so far as to approach the Department of Defense about including Arabic speakers from the Pentagon on the investigative team. Oliver "Buck" Revell, a former FBI assistant director in charge of investigation and a counterterrorism expert, was quoted as saying, "I think what we've got is a bona fide terrorist attack." Mr. Revell went on to state, "I think it's most likely a Middle East terrorist. I think the modus operandi is similar. They have used this approach."

FBI officials in Washington, speaking anonymously, suggested strongly that their investigations were focusing on Middle East terrorists. Among the leads being investigated was a television report of three males of Middle East origin who rented a brown Chevrolet pickup at Dallas–Ft. Worth International Airport. Witnesses reported seeing three men driving away from the blast area in a similar pickup.

An FBI communiqué that was circulated on the day of the bombing read, "We are currently inclined to suspect the Islamic Jihad as the likely group," and suggested that the attack was carried out in retaliation for the prosecution of Muslim fundamentalists in the World Trade Center case. These were not the suspicions of small-town sheriffs or beat cops but of numerous government and law enforcement experts at the highest levels.

The evidence strongly suggests intelligence assets were being used in the bombing investigation. A Jordanian American suspect's luggage was searched in Italy, and the suspect was detained by British authorities and then forcibly returned to the United States. According to *The New York Times*, Abraham Ahmed was "caught in the dragnet that spread around the world after the bombing." The newspaper went on to state: "In his case, he was first singled out for attention in accordance with a general profile of possible suspects, including young men traveling alone to destinations like the Middle East. The FBI issued the profile to police agencies and airport authorities throughout the world."

Ahmed lives in Oklahoma. He checked into O'Hare International Airport in Chicago on Wednesday night for a flight to Rome, with connections for a flight to Amman, Jordan. In addition to fitting the suspect profile, he was dressed in a jogging suit similar to one that a witness in Oklahoma City had reported seeing worn by a man at the scene of the explosion.

Ahmed, initially held as a material witness, was never charged.

This initial focus on foreign terrorist connections was not limited to the Middle East. According to *The Sunday Times* (London) of February 4, 1996, senior FBI sources confirmed that the bureau was "also pursuing inquiries into a possible neo-Nazi link between the Oklahoma City bombers and British and German extremists." And because of Terry Nichols's ties to the Philippines, within days of the bombing U.S. and Philippine officials began reconstructing his movements there. A U.S. embassy legal attaché interviewed Marife Nichols's father, Eduardo Torres, and showed him sketches of the two original bombing suspects. Philippine intelligence agents briefly placed Mr. Torres under surveillance to make sure he was not involved with terrorism.

I shall come back to both Europe and the Philippines, but one of the first motions we filed with the court was based on the Classified Information Procedures Act, which requires the prosecution to provide classified exculpatory material from other government agencies. Time and again we'd ask for something we'd learned about from other sources, only to get the runaround. If we were told anything, it was that there was no need for us to see what we'd requested, or that it was irrelevant, or that letting us look would endanger national security, or, most often, what we were asking for didn't exist. Time and again we'd discover—often through our own efforts, sometimes when it was too late—that the information was extremely relevant, that looking at it in no way would have imperiled national security, and that—invariably—it damaged the government's case.

The process was extremely frustrating, but it was more than that. If convicted, Tim McVeigh would likely be executed. He would be labeled the worst mass murderer in American history. But by lying, hiding, and obstructing our investigation into what actually happened that terrible April morning, the government did more than violate his right to a fair trial and thorough defense. It violated the right of all Americans to know the truth about what happened and who exactly was responsible.

This isn't to say we never got anything we asked for, but when we did it usually took weeks, months even. For example, in June 1996 the government released to us a multitude of FBI 302s, including a sheet of paper stating that Serial #14838 (the FBI coding system) contained "classified material not associated with this case." One month later, we again received this same sheet of paper including Serial #14838, but now attached to it were two extremely important FBI 302s. Yet getting information—in any form—was better than the frequent alternative of getting nothing at all. For instance the prosecution informed us—and the court—that no intelligence agency possessed discoverable information because prosecutors had already sent letters to CIA, DIA, and NSA requesting relevant material and had been told there was nothing. Of course, they refused at the same time to provide us with their supposed letters of inquiry, so we were forced to take their word for it.

The crime, at the heart of the case, had been directed against the government; the prosecution was the government; the judge was government-appointed; and the evidence we needed was held by the government. The defense found itself, needless to say, in a Kafkaesque situation. And those who would criticize us for a lack of "good faith" in not accepting the government's word must ask themselves the question: Should I take someone's word on "good faith" if I knew, as Tim McVeigh did, that the person's mission was to obtain my execution?

I'd best explain more about the "government," this entity that causes me to rail on so throughout this book. Who was the "government"? Our visible adversaries were the prosecutors. Less visible were their bosses in Washington who were so clearly pulling the strings, all the way up to the attorney general herself. In the very beginning, that is, in May 1995, most of us had assumed Pat Ryan would be the lead government prosecutor. Ryan was an extroverted, good-looking Irishman with an infectious sense of humor, a New Democrat in the Clinton mode, and on the day the Murrah Building exploded he had already been named U.S. attorney for the Western District. (That district, one of three in Oklahoma, is relatively large, with some thirty to forty assistant U.S. attorneys [AUSAs], lawyers of high competence and experience.)

Although Ryan would participate in the case till the end, no sooner was he sworn in as U.S. attorney than the decision was made, in Washington, to push him out of the leadership role. The same thing had already happened on the investigative side, where the local FBI chief gave way to Weldon Kennedy, who was brought in from Arizona to take charge. Apparently Washington wanted its own people. (And of course, while a Department of Justice search committee looked for a special prosecutor to head the team, Merrick Garland, number three at Justice, prosecuted the preliminary hearings, first of McVeigh, then of Nichols.)

This decision to bring people in from the outside was not without cost. Although the lawyers for the government brought in from outside were capable, none was more capable or professional—and in some cases less so—than the assistant U.S. attorneys in Oklahoma City. As Arlene Joplin and her senior trial prosecutors in the Oklahoma City office were systematically dumped overboard, a resentful, if not mutinous mood was inevitably created. Then, too, of all the possible candidates for the top job, an obscure AUSA from Springfield, Illinois, seemed a most unlikely choice. Joseph Hartzler was totally unknown outside his home state. It later leaked out that the Justice Department search committee itself had picked Larry Mackey, an AUSA from Indianapolis. But when the appointments came down, it was Hartzler at the top and Mackey as number two, later to be joined by other appointees from Washington.

According to some, Hartzler was the protégé of a person high up at Justice, either Jamie Gorelick, who was number two to Janet Reno, or Merrick Garland. Others made noises about a political payoff of some kind. Contrarians maintained that Hartzler had no special ties whatsoever in Washington and that he'd been chosen because the real, behind-the-scenes prosecutor would be Garland.

Whatever the reasons, Hartzler was in charge by June, and I found him a redoubtable foe. He was tough, arrogant, and often rude behind his boyish, open countenance and as bent on thwarting the defense as any prosecutor I'd ever come up against. When he got off the plane for the first time in Oklahoma City, after his appointment, he announced, according to the press, that his mission was to send McVeigh straight to hell.

Although Hartzler gave few interviews, one reporter he did talk to shared a small, intimate insight with me. He'd asked Hartzler about the candidacy process, what it had been like, and specifically what was the toughest question his Justice Department interlocutors had put to him.

Hartzler replied, "They asked me if I would do what they told me to do without reservation."

"And what did you say?" the reporter asked him.

"I told them I would."

This came to mind much later, when Hartzler asked Judge Matsch to stay an order reflecting an adverse ruling for three days so that he could "check with Washington" first. And I remember, when we delivered our volumes of supporting newspaper clippings to the courthouse in huge and bulky blue binders as supporting documentation to our change of venue motion, how the FBI agent who took them complained mightily about how they were ever going to get them on the plane for Washington.

Merrick, it seemed, had to see everything, even the newspaper exhibits.

Regardless of who was ultimately responsible, from the start we encountered an arrogant, antagonistic stance on the part of the government that went well beyond our adversarial system. Actually, it was expressed not only toward us but even toward the court. Early on, we petitioned the court for help in getting the prosecution to release discovery material to us. Although they were technically within the law in not doing so—until there is an indictment prosecutors have no legal obligation to share with the defense—in the interest of a speedy trial we saw no reason the process couldn't begin. Judge Russell agreed with us and called a meeting in an effort to mediate.

This was a federal judge, mind you, a chief judge, calling lawyers to a meeting who, on both sides, were preparing a case that would be tried in his jurisdiction.

The government didn't even deign to show up; another obstruction that added to the defense costs borne by the taxpayers.

After the grand jury handed down its indictment in August 1995, Judge Wayne Alley was assigned, by lottery, to our case. Alley had had an illustrious career. A former one-star general and a Stanford law graduate, he had served on the Army Court of Military Review and had written the opinion upholding the conviction of Lieutenant William Calley for the My Lai massacre.

Just before Alley got the case, we'd filed a motion requesting that interrogatories be issued to all the eligible Western District—that is to say, Oklahoma judges. One judge had been to six or seven funerals of victims of the bombing, two of them had nearly been killed, and several, including Alley, had had their chambers hit, and in Alley's case his courtroom was heavily damaged. Fortunately Alley himself had been working at home the morning the Murrah Building exploded.

Judges had recused themselves for much less, including cases I'd been involved in myself, but Alley wouldn't. *United States v. McVeigh* was his case. All he would agree to was a change of trial location, but still in Oklahoma. In fact, even before we could deal with the recusal issue, we got a call from him announcing that he was going to move the trial to Lawton, Oklahoma, and that it would begin May 15, 1996. The reason for his advance call was to give us time to make our hotel reservation before the stampede!

Lawton is a small city, about twice the size of Enid, some ninety miles southwest of Oklahoma City. It also happened to be the home of Fort Sill, an enormous army base, which, coincidentally, was sure to offer better than adequate accommodations to a retired brigadier general who also happened to be a trial judge. In all other respects, though, Lawton would have been a nightmare.

For one thing, Lawton was very close to Oklahoma City. For another, the courthouse (built during World War I) was hopelessly inadequate for a major trial. Security was a factor. There was no safe approach to the courthouse and there was no acceptable facility to hold Tim, so the judge proposed to build a cell in the courthouse! All the hotels were typically two story affairs with the comings and goings of people clearly visible. Then, too, there was the trial date: May 1996. Joe Hartzler, afflicted with multiple sclerosis, a condition aggravated by heat, would be prosecuting a case where summer temperatures exceed 100 degrees almost every day. There was no convenient airport and no adequate office space.

Then to top it all off there were two other factors: As soon as Lawton was selected, the local coordinating committee dubbed itself "Task Force 169" (at that time it was thought 169 victims had died). Clearly this was not a city committed to giving the American people a fair trial. But the best was yet to come: Every weekday at 3 P.M. a large, and I do mean large, artillery round is fired at Fort Sill, site of the Army artillery school. The sound resembles, obviously, a large explosion and can be audibly heard downtown where the jury would be sitting. Alley, as a retired Army officer had to know this. When Judge Matsch heard the testimony at the change of venue hearing about the daily firing of "Big Bertha" his face went blank and he slowly turned around on the bench and looked in my direction with an expression that I read as "My God!" I was little surprised then when Judge Alley was recused. Whatever hope he had of keeping the case, which he could have moved anywhere in the country, was gone when the Court of Appeals read the implications in the order for a trial in Lawton.

The early concern of the Oklahoma federal judges in reviewing the defense's expenditures convinced me recusal was necessary. As the government poured in not hundreds, but thousands of FBI agents and dozens of prosecutors we got the impression the judges thought two, maybe three lawyers and a couple of defense investigators would be sufficient. They simply had no idea of the scope and breadth of what this case involved. Later, it would be obvious Judge Matsch did. But in fairness, I could understand the attitude in Oklahoma City. One or two of the local judges were nearly killed, and the courthouse staff had friends who were killed. The judges thought they were being fair, but it was too much to ask of them. Not just justice but the appearance of justice had to be accomplished. Needless to say all of our efforts to remove the judges and change the trial site did not make me popular.

So for once, an issue brought Mike Tigar and me together.

We aired our frustrations concerning Alley—for one thing, he alone among the Western District judges had no standing orders on discovery, meaning he had yet to move a finger to get the government to share the first bit of evidence with us—and Mike, gritting his teeth, said, "I'll tell you this, Stephen, this trial's *not* going to be held in Lawton, Oklahoma."

He was right too.

We moved that Judge Alley recuse himself. He denied our motion.

Mike Tigar and I were both infuriated. There was no question in our minds but that recusal was called for, and if Judge Alley was that adamant about holding onto the case, then we had no choice but to appeal his ruling to the Tenth Circuit.

If the Tenth Circuit had turned us down, we feared Alley would have made our lives a living hell. But the argument was clear: Adam Thurschwell, a colleague of Mike's, wrote a terrific brief in support of it, and in the end the appellate court removed Alley from the case entirely and assigned it to Judge Richard G. Matsch, a member of the federal bench in the District of Colorado.

For just a moment, when Matsch's appointment was first announced, I was a little dismayed. There is a volume we defense lawyers all use called the *Almanac of the Federal Judiciary*, and in Matsch's entry in the "Lawyers' Evaluation" section, he was given very high marks for intelligence, but there were also comments like, "He can be irascible and is easily miffed by things," and, "If you make a stupid argument in front of him, he will take your head off," and, "A lot of attorneys have gotten burned by him, and not always justifiably. If you don't know your case, he comes unglued."

Better the known devil, I asked myself?

But the more I learned about the man, and certainly this was confirmed when I met him myself, the more I realized that if he could be prickly or snappish and something of a tyrant in his own courtroom, it was simply because he didn't suffer fools gladly.

Nothing wrong with that.

Matsch was sixty-five, a Michigan law graduate, and had served as an AUSA and deputy city attorney in Denver, then as a bankruptcy judge, before being appointed to the federal bench in 1974 by President Nixon. Probably his highest profile federal jury trial had been the 1987 case I mentioned before against four former members of the Silent Brotherhood. In previous cases concerning Robert Mathews's group, beginning with a racketeering and conspiracy trial in Seattle in 1985, the government had batted 1.000, winning convictions across the board, but only two of the accused in Judge Matsch's court were convicted, the other two acquitted.

The judge turned out to be a small, bespectacled, precise man. As others had observed, he *was* easily irritated. He was also punctual to a fault. His court opened for business at 9 A.M. sharp. If you weren't there, you were in big trouble, and if you weren't prepared, well, God help you because Judge Matsch wouldn't. Even so, there was little pomp and circumstance and no rolling of drums in a Matsch courtroom. An American flag, yes, but no Great Seal of the United States. The bailiff simply said, "Please rise," when Judge Matsch came in, and that was it. The journalist Eric Sevaried's description of Gen. Vinegar Joe Stillwell as a soldier who had "an exalted concept of true soldiering and an impossible ideal of what a true soldier should be" was somewhat on point to Judge Matsch: Matsch had an exalted concept of true lawyering and an impossible ideal of what the true lawyer should be. But to be honest, it was a goal worth reaching for. Just to be in his courtroom made me proud to be a lawyer and I think I mentally squared my shoulders when I walked in the door.

His treatment of McVeigh won me over very early. Among other things, Tim had been under twenty-four-hour TV surveillance in his cell at El Reno, and though we thought we'd worked out a deal to give him some relief, the Bureau of Prisons had fudged on it. Judge Alley, typically, would do nothing about anything once his assignment to the case had been challenged.

Not long after Judge Matsch took over the case, we had a hearing on the subject, with Tim present. Tim spoke, and the Judge listened to him carefully.

"It's like this," Tim said. "I'm on this camera twenty-four hours a day, and I get absolutely no privacy. I'd like to have some. Not much, but I'd like to have some periods of the day when I'm not on camera. I'm not going to commit suicide and I'm not going to escape. At night, for example, when I have to go to the bathroom, the only guard on duty is a woman."

Matsch leaned forward and cocked his head at that.

"What?" he asked.

"That's right," Tim said. "At night, the guard is a woman, and if I have to sit on the toilet, there's a little barrier in front of me, but that's not much privacy."

Matsch blew his stack at this. I never saw him madder.

"Turn it off," his order went out. "Turn the camera *off*."

It was the same with the manacles. Tim's guards soon learned that they had to remove the manacles before they got anywhere near the judge's chambers. Clearly, in Matsch's courtroom, no accused was guilty until so proven, and every accused deserved to be treated as a human being.

Once in charge, the judge went quickly to work. There were a number of motions pending based on prior filings with Judge Alley, and Judge Matsch now tackled them one by one. I should illustrate two defense motions that were crucial to our case: a motion to change venue and a motion to sever McVeigh's trial from that of Terry Nichols. On December 6, he ordered a change of venue hearing (although we had gotten our new judge, the venue remained in the Western District until the court ordered otherwise). On December 7, we made a lengthy report to him on the government's failure to produce discoverable evidence, and on December 12, he called us together, defense and prosecution, for a conference on the issue of witness statements and other items "discoverable" by the defense.

The change of venue hearing was held in January, and we were extremely well prepared. We started off with Governor Keating himself. We'd given serious thought to subpoenaing him for the hearing, and Mike Tigar wanted to, but, having represented the governor on several personal and political matters as well as advising him on judicial appointments, I didn't feel it appropriate that I examine him myself. None of the other members of the defense team, in my judgment, was sufficiently well versed in Oklahoma history and politics to take him on, and I also felt, frankly, that given Mike Tigar's personality and tenacity, and Frank Keating's personality and tenacity, we would look as though we were picking a fight.

In the early days after the bombing, the governor, as the chief executive of the aggrieved state, had been the epitome of dignity, and he and his wife, Cathy, had been seen as caring and sympathetic Oklahomans. Cathy's friend, the wife of the governor of Illinois, had sent down a load of teddy bears to be given to the families of vic-

tims, and through that gesture the teddy bear became the quasioffi-
cial symbol of the Oklahoma City bombing.

But Frank Keating's background was in law enforcement, being a
former FBI agent and U.S. attorney, and he also, to the despair of his
political handlers and advisers, could never resist shooting from the
lip when it came to talking about subjects he cared deeply about. No
sooner were McVeigh and Nichols arrested than he referred to them
as "creeps." On the one hand, he proclaimed their obvious guilt,
while on the other insisting that Oklahomans could be fair and that
the trial should stay there. His message seemed to be: *First we're going
to give these creeps a fair trial, then we're going to take them out and hang
them*—good politics in Oklahoma, but poor justice anywhere. And
the more he spoke, the more we saved the transcripts and video clips.
Governor Keating, it might be said, became our Exhibit A.

At the hearing, we led off with a video we put together of the
governor, in living color, excoriating Judge Matsch for even enter-
taining the idea of a change of venue. The video was perfect for us.
We didn't have to call him and run the risk he would be tempted to
use the occasion for political purposes, and a video can't be cross-
examined or rehabilitated. I watched the judge's expression carefully. Keating, after all, was a member of the bar, a former U.S.
attorney and assistant attorney general. He had even been a Tenth
Circuit nominee of President Bush, in which capacity he might have
sat in judgment on Judge Matsch's own rulings!

Although we had other evidence to present of the deep prejudice
against the defendants in Oklahoma, and volumes of newspaper
clippings in support of it, I was confident, once we were done with
the governor, that the game was already won.

The following month, on February 20, Judge Matsch ordered a
change of venue to the District of Colorado.

This was a substantial victory, but a much knottier issue
awaited us, with a less certain ruling on the judge's part.
That was our motion for the severance of the two trials.

The statements Terry Nichols had made to FBI agents during his
marathon interview on April 21 were, we knew, highly prejudicial to
Tim. Nichols, as we have already seen, had taken the position that

McVeigh must have been the perpetrator. McVeigh was his friend, yes, and he may unwittingly have helped him, but he—Nichols— had been a largely innocent bystander.

The prosecution clearly intended to call Nichols's FBI interroga- tors to testify—there were four in all—because the statements Nichols had made were going to be a cornerstone of the case against him. The prosecution knew that he had lied at key junctures and could prove it. If that testimony was introduced in a courtroom where McVeigh was a codefendant, without our having a chance to cross-examine Terry himself on his statements, it would have a dev- astating effect on the jury.

Of course—as the prosecution would argue and the judge would acknowledge—in a joint trial, the jury would be instructed to "disre- gard" any such testimony as far as McVeigh was concerned. But that would be like telling someone to "disregard" a punch in the face because it had been aimed at someone else. There was simply no way, in what would be a key element in the case against Terry Nichols—one that would occupy center stage for a good amount of time and entail lengthy cross-examinations by Tigar and Woods— that the jury could ignore or overlook or disregard or pay no atten- tion to how it reflected on Tim McVeigh.

Furthermore, as the Nichols defense knew full well, the only way Terry could plead his innocence was by claiming that Tim had duped him. In other words, there were certain provable actions Terry had taken part in that he could "justify" only by saying Tim had asked him to and that he'd had no idea why. And, once again, if Nichols's own lawyers chose not to put him on the stand, then where was our chance for rebuttal?

There was only one solution: McVeigh and Nichols *had* to be tried separately. We *had* to obtain severance.

But it wasn't that simple.

A major element in the government's case, and in the grand jury indictment against the two defendants, was conspiracy. *Conspiracy* means that they had acted together, that they had *conspired* together, that they had planned and carried out the crime or crimes together. The prosecution argued, therefore, that they should be tried together, in the interest of speedy and economical justice, and that a jury of their peers would still be able to consider and weigh the cases against them fairly.

We could (and we would) move for severance under Rule 14 of the Federal Rules of Criminal Procedure, but people accused of conspiracy have often been tried together (as in the Silent Brotherhood case that had been tried in Matsch's own courtroom), and the U.S. Supreme Court has limited the bases for severance in conspiracy cases. Finger-pointing—that is, one defendant saying the other did it, and vice-versa—just isn't enough. Nor is antagonism, nor is potential prejudice. You have to be able to demonstrate the likelihood of actual prejudice to one defendant's rights in a joint trial, and the likelihood, therefore, that the jury will be unable to reach a fair and just verdict.

Both defense teams would move for severance in written motions that ran into the hundreds of pages each. But unlike the change of venue debate, where I thought the outcome seemed relatively certain (the only question being where: Tulsa or Denver), this pending decision, critical as it was to our chances, hung uncertainly over our heads throughout much of 1996.

Meanwhile, we moved steadily apart from Tigar, Woods, and their colleagues. It even happened in a purely physical sense, for almost immediately after Judge Matsch's change of venue ruling, the Nichols team moved up to Denver. Judge Matsch set a tentative trial date for March 1997, and we, in turn, decided to keep our base in Enid for the time being. There were two reasons for this. The first was money—lodging, per diem, and office space would have cost us an additional $100,000 a month (and later did). But I also wanted to keep us all out of the constant fishbowl scrutiny of the Denver media as long as possible.

In addition, Nichols's defense, it was now clear, would be based in good part on finger-pointing at Tim, and the more I studied the case, the more I became convinced that Terry Nichols was at, or close to, the heart of the plot. And it was this consideration, as well as some disturbing insights I'd gotten in March 1996 from two experts in Washington, that made the Philippines a very logical target of the McVeigh defense investigation.

7

"THE FARMER"

On my way home from London that January, a trip I will describe in due course, I made a quick detour to Washington, as there was someone I very much wanted to meet and possibly recruit for the defense team. His name was Vincent Cannistraro, former chief of operations and analysis of the CIA's counterterrorism center, and once upon a time he'd been a clandestine services officer for the CIA in Europe, the Middle East, and North Africa. He was now out of the government, at least officially, and had become an international security "consultant." His writings also appeared in print from time to time, notably in an article that ran in the *Boston Globe* in April 1995, comparing the Oklahoma City bombing with the World Trade Center disaster.

When I suggested he might come to work for us, Cannistraro turned me down. He'd already made a consultant deal with ABC News on the bombing and other matters as well. But in the course of our conversation that afternoon, he made some interesting observations and a recommendation that turned out to be very good for us.

The recommendation was that we hire Laurie Mylroie, a Harvard Ph.D. and an expert on Iraq and terrorism aimed at the United States from the Middle East. Mylroie was then a research analyst at the Foreign Policy Research Institute, which is part of the University of Pennsylvania, and not long after that she came on our payroll as a consultant. She and Cannistraro were both convinced that the

Iraqis, spearheaded by their intelligence service, were deeply committed to attacking the United States—*within* its borders. Cannistraro made the point that all federal buildings outside Washington, D.C., were "soft" targets in that they tended to lack security and had been built at a time when glass featured in the prevailing architecture. (And, of course, their theory about the targeting of American "soft" targets would be buttressed in 1998 by the catastrophic bombings of the American embassies in Kenya and Tanzania.)

Cannistraro further pointed out that the Murrah Building and the American embassy in Beirut, Lebanon, looked almost the same.

Was that a coincidence? Or that both had been attacked and destroyed by an ammonium nitrate vehicle bomb?

A key figure in the Iraqi effort, according to both Mylroie and Cannistraro, was one Ramzi Yousef, who along with two confederates would be convicted the following September of conspiring to blow up simultaneously eleven U.S. commercial jet planes and who, according to a federal indictment, had masterminded the World Trade bombing and who, according to Mylroie, was an Iraqi Intelligence operative. Cannistraro had written, in that *Boston Globe* article, "Yousef had carefully prepared his escape [from the World Trade Center], leaving from New York the evening of the bombing. He abandoned his comrades to the police. If the Oklahoma City bombing follows the same pattern, the foreign sponsors will have covered their trail carefully, leaving only the support cells of local adherents to face the prosecutor."

That afternoon in my hotel room, with Ann Bradley feverishly taking notes, Cannistraro explained to me in detail how the bombing of the World Trade Center appeared, or, should I say, had been made to appear. Some "drifters," local Arabs with a grudge against the United States, had rented a Ryder Truck in New Jersey, filled it with explosive nitrates, driven it to New York and detonated the explosion under the World Trade Center. They were so stupid—so he said it was thought—that they had actually gone back and tried to reclaim their deposit on the Ryder Truck, explaining that it had been stolen from them. In fact, Cannistraro went on, that's not what happened at all. Actually, the mastermind (or at least one of the masterminds) had flown out of New York the very day of the bombing, removing all traces of a more sophisticated scheme, and let the local boys hang out and get caught. The bombing of the World Trade Center, Cannistraro said, was a very skilled, complicated job that caused enormous property damage but didn't take many lives. But its real skill—at least at first—was leaving the impression it was the work of amateurs, but it wasn't. Now we know, three trials later, how correct Cannistraro was. Of course the parallels to Oklahoma City were obvious. Alleged "amateur" "drifters" who were "malcontents" with a "grudge" had supposedly rented a Ryder Truck (again) filled with nitrate (a different type of nitrate, but still nitrate), driven from one state to another (again), the bombers leave (again) and commit a stupid blunder (again), this time leaving the license plate off the getaway car. How many bales, not of cotton but of coincidences are you going to load on, Cannistraro asked me, before the weight collapses the wagon?

Cannistraro told me about a "wet test" Ramzi Yousef had carried out in December 1994 with the liquid components of explosives that he had managed to pass undetected, in separate containers, through airport security in Manila. Once aboard a Philippine Airlines flight bound for Japan, Ramzi mixed the components in the lavatory, set a detonator, then placed the bomb under his seat. He got off the plane at an intermediate stop. On the next leg of the flight, the bomb exploded, killing a Japanese businessman who had taken Yousef's seat.

I asked Cannistraro how this could tie into the Oklahoma bombing. If he were I, he said by way of an answer, he would check into some of Terry Nichols's associations in the Philippines, particularly Southwest College in Cebu City, which Nichols's wife, Marife, had attended. The Philippines, according to Cannistraro, was a hotbed of fundamentalist Muslim activity, and if Ramzi Yousef had used the Philippines as a base, and Terry Nichols had made numerous visits there, who knew who might have been recruited? Or who might have recruited whom?

I was impressed by how much Cannistraro knew for someone who had been out of the CIA for several years. (Indeed, I wasn't the only one who trusted his expertise and insight. When hundreds were killed in August 1998 by bombs exploded outside the U.S. embassies in Kenya and Tanzania, *The New York Times*—the "paper of record"—turned to Cannistraro multiple times for his assessment of who was responsible and what should be done.) I was also impressed with his summing-up of the case:

"The government just isn't interested in uncovering a foreign plot," he said. "It has its perpetrators, and it doesn't want anyone or anything complicating its case."

What Cannistraro said made sense to me, and we began to make those points in court and publicly. It didn't so much as occur to me in passing, that afternoon in Washington, that Cannistraro might be hiding something.

I n fact, there were things that didn't quite add up in Terry Nichols's Philippines connection. He had gone there first in 1990, which was after his divorce from Lana Padilla and his hardship discharge from the army, looking, so he always said, for a new wife with whom to start a new life. A friend, so he always said, had told him Filipinas made good wives. And—who knows?—maybe they do. Through an Arizona mail-order bride service, he found Marife Torres, a traffic policeman's daughter in Cebu City, the country's second-largest city, on the island of Cebu. Marife was sixteen, a little bit of a thing; Nichols was thirty-five, an American with no prospects. They married, and Terry left almost immediately for Michigan. While Marife waited for her visa, so the story went, another man made her pregnant. She gave birth to the child, a little boy named Jason, and when she joined Terry in Michigan in 1991 she brought him along. A few years later, after Jason died accidentally, the Nicholses had another child, a little girl named Nicole.

Over the next four years, Terry made numerous trips to the Philippines. Some of them were lengthy—thirty days or longer— others were quickies. Some were with Marife, some without. Some were just to visit her, for she went home periodically, once for as long as six months. The question occurred to me early—what did he do, all the time he was there? He claimed, at various times and to various people, that he was looking for "business opportunities." If he was, then none of them must have panned out, because in 1994 he was working as a farmhand in Kansas. Still, strange sums of money popped up unexpectedly.

Nichols's last trip to the Philippines started in November 1994. Marife had gone ahead in September and was taking some college classes with an eye, so she said, to becoming a physical therapist. She had rented a two-bedroom bungalow on a Cebu beach. According to an article in *The Dallas Morning News* that ran about a month after the bombing, Nichols had done nothing much during this visit except to hang out on the beach, take care of his little daughter, and cook pancakes for breakfast. He returned to the United States in mid-January. This would certainly have seemed a very strange idyll, and a long absence, for someone who had been planning the most violent terrorist act in American history. But it was vintage Terry Nichols, the same man who three months later made sure he was seen around town on April 19 yet claimed he knew nothing of the bombing in Oklahoma City because he didn't yet have cable-TV service.

It was in December, while Nichols was on Cebu, that Ramzi Yousef executed his "wet test" on Philippine Airlines flight 434, and in January, when the Pope arrived on a state visit, that an alleged plot to assassinate him was foiled, to which the Abu Sayyaf group was linked. Abu Sayyaf was a small army of some five hundred or more radical Muslim fighters based on the island of Mindanao, the second largest of the Philippines. Mindanao is largely Muslim in population and, for many years, has seen intermittent separatist uprisings. In addition to the plot against the Pope, moreover, Ramzi and his team, with Abu Sayyaf support, were allegedly planning to attack the U.S. embassy in Manila and other U.S. facilities throughout Asia.

This is not to suggest that Terry Nichols was in the Philippines *because* of these activities. But there were some strange and ominous goings-on surrounding this last trip. According to Terry's former wife, Lana Padilla, who lived in Las Vegas, Nichols had given her and their twelve-year-old son, Josh, the impression that he might not be coming back. He also had given Lana a mysterious package containing a letter from him, telling her to open it in the event of his death or if he hadn't returned in sixty days. Lana, however, opened it anyway and discovered, by the account in her own book (*By Blood Betrayed*, written with Ron Delpit and published in late 1995), a virtual treasure hunt, instructions to be followed in the event of Terry's death. These led her—for she didn't wait for the sixty days to elapse—to a stash of $20,000 in cash and a Las Vegas storage locker filled, so she said, with wigs, masks, gold bars, and precious stones. The package also contained a life insurance policy, with Marife as beneficiary, and a letter to Tim McVeigh (to be given him in the event Terry didn't come back) telling him he was on his own.

Why would a man who was supposedly about to spend a couple months lounging on a beach on Cebu face the trip with such foreboding? After all, he had been to the Philippines before, had even considered moving there, and he had married a Filipino woman who had two generations of policemen in her immediate family. What made him think he might even be killed? Unless, of course, he was doing something that put him at risk? Or—again—was trying to create a legend for the future, so that people, thinking he was dead, would never come looking for him? And what led, after he returned to the United States, and as a study of his phone records revealed, to almost manic barrages of telephone calls to the Philippines, many of them lengthy, made now on his own phone, now on the Darryl Bridges debit card?

By far the greatest number of these calls was made to a boarding house in Cebu City, owned by one Ernesto Malaluan, that catered to students studying at Southwest College, particularly to Muslim students from the island of Mindanao. It was known that Marife, after Terry had left for the United States in January, had moved into the boarding house (breaking the six-month lease on the beach house in the process). But why, after she herself had left, were there twelve more calls to that number from Terry? And why, all in all, were there *seventy-eight* phone calls in all placed to the boarding house from January 31 to March 14, 1995? Or was Terry, as he liked to say, simply pursuing new "business opportunities?"

Given the government's theory—that all the preparatory purchasing and stashing and quarry-robbing, plus the Roger Moore robbery, had been accomplished by November 1994—and the careful "Who me?" pattern of Terry's behavior during the week of the bombing itself, and, finally, Vincent Cannistraro's tip about Cebu City, the question kept bothering me: What was Terry's Philippines connection really all about?

In fact we weren't the only ones pondering the question. Terry's brother, James, for one, couldn't understand the connection either. In a manner reminiscent of Terry's own sly way of taking his distance from Tim McVeigh, James pointed out to an interviewer how his brother had gone to the Philippines and come back, gone again, gotten married, come back, and then again, picked Marife up, come back, and so on and so forth, going and coming, with Marife, without Marife, and who, James asked aloud, had paid for all the plane tickets?

The FBI wanted to know too. It had already been in the Philippines, interviewing Terry's in-laws, among others. We found out later that the FBI had enlisted Philippine National Police Intelligence to help. And now, with the court's approval for expenses we would incur, we set out to investigate on our own.

Both during and after the trial, some politicians and commentators said that the money spent for the defense of Tim McVeigh was outrageous. One senator said it was $50,000,000. Our trips abroad were criticized as "junkets" and our investigative expenses were said to be too high.

We went to the Philippines because the government went there, because Terry Nichols went there (six times), because he made over 200 phone calls there, because he took a book on how to make a bomb with him there, and because, as I'll explain shortly, he may have met with some particularly relevant people while there. We went to Israel, London, and Belfast because that's where experts on bomb trace analysis and bomb engineering are, because that's where ammonium nitrate bombs are set off, by the dozens. Our litigation support was modest compared to the elaborate government retrieval system available to the FBI and DOJ. We hired dozens of expert witnesses on subjects ranging from terrorism, Waco, tool marks, tire imprints, fingerprints, bomb trace analysis, eyewitness credibility, and analysis of news content to support a change of venue motion. Then there were more than three dozen motions filed for discovery request, almost all of which Judge Matsch granted or which the government conceded after the motion was filed (but not before). The government listed over five hundred names on their final witness list and, as I've said, there were over 30,000 government witness statements, over 100,000 photographs, hundreds of hours of video and audio tapes to review, 7,000 pounds of debris, and 156 million telephone records. This is what cost so much to sift through, analyze, study, and prepare to defend against.

Judge Matsch understood our needs. He trusted the integrity of our representations. Could the defense have cost less? Possibly, but those would have required an end to prosecution foot-dragging and discovery production. But once appointed, I was going to use every resource at my command to represent my client, and I did, with Judge Matsch's eagle eye on every affidavit and voucher that I filed.

F or most Americans, the Philippines are a very far-off place, known mostly because of Douglas MacArthur, Imelda Marcos, and the Bataan death march. How would a county-seat lawyer from Enid, Oklahoma, go about getting information about people and events that had taken place there?

Well, by calling Joe Linklater at Baker, McKenzie.

Baker, McKenzie is one of the largest law firms in the world. It is headquartered in Chicago, but it has offices in virtually every major city you can name, including Manila. I called on the firm for help, and through Baker, McKenzie's Manila office we came up with recommendations for two private investigators, one a former CIA man named Richard Post, who was based in Hong Kong; the other, also American, lived and worked in Manila.

Although Post did useful work for us on the fringes of the case, our Manila investigator, who has asked to remain nameless, got off on the wrong foot with us. What we wanted was evidence tying Nichols to the terrorists, but what he'd been giving us was a lot of smoke and mirrors and little of substance. Finally, after various members of our team had gone to Manila and gotten nowhere, I went myself.

Actually, I had another reason for going. A source of mine in Washington, who also wishes to remain anonymous, had arranged entrée for me with an official high up in a very key Philippines ministry.

That visit became very Graham Greene, as if "Our Man in Havana" had been transposed to the Far East. Ann Bradley and I went by taxi, the morning after I arrived in Manila, to the imposing Spanish-looking edifice that housed the ministry in question. A good thousand people seemed to be milling around outside, matched by another thousand inside. The official's office—I will call him the Director—was a vast space upstairs, where everything but a cockfight seemed to be going on and where four men in the sheerest shirts over white undershirts were playing cards at a corner table. Electric fans whirred, and through the partially open wooden shutters you could hear the din of the world.

The Director was seated at his desk, under a faded picture of President Ramos. After the introductions, he opened a drawer and pulled out a folder that I was reasonably certain had absolutely nothing in it. My first impression was that whichever Philippines law enforcement agencies had investigated for the FBI the Director's ministry had been left out of the loop. But as quickly became clear, he knew chapter and verse about Marife Torres Nichols and her family.

He knew about Terry Nichols too, but he grew circumspect when it came to terrorists in and around Cebu City and elsewhere in the Philippines. Either he was incapable of connecting the dots, or—as I now believe—he was unwilling to do so. My audience with him didn't last long, and even though, as we parted company, he said, "Have your associates here call me," I came away feeling I'd accomplished nothing.

In this I was wrong. Or, as it turned out, both right and wrong.

After I returned home, dribbles of information came our way. For instance, among the original 302s the FBI had gathered from their first investigations in the Philippines, there was one in which they'd interviewed the owner of a lumberyard in Cebu City, next door to where the Torres family lived. The Torreses habitually used his telephone. According to the lumberyard owner's 302, Marife's father had told him he'd seen a book in Terry Nichols's luggage about how to build explosives. When the FBI asked Marife's father about it, he categorically and emphatically denied having said it. Our investigator sent someone to interview him, and he denied it again. But then our man got the Philippine National Police to interview both men, first the lumberyard owner, who confirmed the story, then Marife's father, who admitted that it was in fact true.

Interesting, but hardly conclusive of anything, and on the larger assignments I gave him, our investigator failed to produce. Tim Kelsey of *The Sunday Times* (London) had told me that there had been, according to certain federal government documents he knew of, a go-between or a cutoff between Terry Nichols and Iraqi contacts in the Philippines. (Kelsey's source was an interesting character called William Northrup, of whom more later.) But we could never pin down the go-between. I also wanted to interview Edwin Angeles, an associate of Ramzi Yousef. Angeles had been arrested in the Philippines and was being held in "protective custody." Apparently he was telling some highly interesting stories. According to our investigator in the Philippines, though, this was a virtually impossible assignment. Angeles's captors, he said, knew they had a valuable prize, and they weren't about to let anyone near him.

The inconclusiveness of our efforts continued to gall me, the more so when I learned how my own government had reacted to news of my visit. Sometime after my departure, the FBI attaché from Tokyo and a Justice Department lawyer (whom I later came to believe was Larry Mackey) showed up in Manila. They demanded an audience with the minister himself—the Director's boss—and lodged a formal complaint. It was totally unacceptable to the United States, they charged, for an official of the Philippines government to give assistance to a lawyer (Stephen Jones, by name) who represented terrorists in America.

According to our man in Manila, the meeting turned stormy. In the course of it, the affronted minister apparently showed the Americans the door. They were insulting a sovereign nation, he told them, trying to interfere in its domestic affairs. Subsequently, though, and privately, he ordered the Director to shut down his contacts with us.

For some months, the Philippines file, so promising at first, had to be labeled "interesting but not conclusive." Meanwhile we had other leads to pursue.

C hasing pieces of the puzzle took me all over the world in 1996. In September I was in Israel, having gone with Sherrel through Frankfurt and on to Damascus, where we spent two days with Dr. Stanislaw Pawlak, an old friend who was then Polish ambassador to Syria and Jordan, before arriving in Israel by the "backdoor," that is, by tourist bus across the Allenby Bridge from Jordan.

I had two reasons to go to Israel. One was to meet Dr. Jehuda Yinon, a living legend in the field of bomb trace analysis, coauthor of the premier textbook in the field, and consultant to the Israeli National Police. I wanted him as an expert witness, and I got him.

The second was much trickier.

The Israelis are notably discreet when it comes to intelligence matters. They like to be seen as keeping arm's length from the intelligence services of other countries. So when rumors began that two Israeli experts had toured the Murrah Building site in the days immediately following the bombing, both sides professed not to know what anybody was talking about.

The rumors persisted. We'd even heard that the Israelis had done a report on the subject, but very typically, the prosecution denied its existence, and when we demanded copies of clearances of people who had been allowed into the wrecked building, no Israelis were among them. But then, through the good offices of the aforementioned William Northrup, I came upon someone who knew the truth.

Northrup lived part of the year in Scottsdale, Arizona, part in Tel Aviv. He was said to have been a friend of William Casey, head of the CIA, mentor to Oliver North, and architect, before his death, so it was always said, of Iran-contra. In the mid-1980s Northrop and eight others, including a retired Israeli general, had been accused of conspiring to sell sophisticated U.S. weaponry to Iran, but the charges were dropped on the grounds that the prosecution couldn't *disprove* the counterclaim that the defendants were acting with the complicity of the U.S. government.

Northrup told me about a man named Moshe Tal, a dual citizen of Israel and the United States and owner of a company in Oklahoma City called Tal Technologies. I got Mr. Tal on the phone, and fortunately, as I will explain, I taped our conversation. In Oklahoma, such surreptitious taping is legal so long as one party to the conversation consents, and as one of the parties, I consented.

Mr. Tal was chair of the Bricktown Association, a downtown Oklahoma City business group, and as such he said he'd organized members into a volunteer service to feed and supply the rescue workers at the bomb site. The bombing had been a nightmarish experience, he said, but he was very proud of what he'd done.

I told him what I wanted. With Judge Matsch's approval, I was fact-finding about the bombing—first off, if there'd been any prior warning to our government from Israel, then about bomb experts examining the site.

Mr. Tal knew nothing about the first, other than stories he'd heard on the news. But, a little reluctantly, he admitted that the two Israelis—Eilon and Yerushalmi were their names—were known to him. The first turned out to have been a security officer from the Israeli embassy in Washington, the second a civil engineer who had, per Tal, analyzed bomb damage to buildings in many parts of the world. Both had come to Tal's office at the Bricktown Association. After a fair amount of prying on my part, Tal admitted that he'd previously met both men in Israel, Eilon during his military service, Yerushalmi some ten or twelve years previously.

This was about the extent of my conversation with Tal. The two Israelis had come, he said, about two, possibly three weeks after the bombing, and ATF had shown them around. When I asked him if the two Israelis had written a report on their findings, he hesitated, saying he wasn't sure, but he knew they'd made recommendations for future prevention programs. He wasn't exactly evasive on the phone, but he wasn't forthcoming, either. And when I suggested I visit him in his office, he told me he traveled a lot.

It turned out, though, as I would shortly learn, that there was a lot more to Mr. Tal than he'd let on.

For one thing, he had been an interviewee, some years before, on Ted Koppel's popular ABC show *Nightline* in connection with an investigation into a Dr. Ihsan Barbouti. Dr. Barbouti was an Iraqi businessman who dealt arms and chemicals and had been described as the mastermind behind Pan Am flight 103. In the course of the interview, Tal admitted to Koppel that Israeli intelligence had asked him to obtain detailed information about Barbouti. He also told Koppel that he'd worked on a similar project for the CIA.

Furthermore, Tal had been contacted by the Israeli embassy before the two Israelis came to Oklahoma City. Originally he made it seem as if the two men had bumped into him by chance in Bricktown, but now it appeared he had received a specific phone call from the embassy. (My source for this and the following is an FBI 302 dated September 11, 1996, reporting on an interview with Tal.) The embassy, having already gotten approval from the ATF head in Dallas, Lester Martz, for its two visitors, had asked Tal to "ensure that they had access to the building, a car, and a place to stay." This he did. He also got them passes to the bomb site. Each day during their visit, he had breakfast with them, then drove them to meet the ATF agent who served as escort. At night he would pick them up. Eilon left the second day; Yerushalmi stayed on.

Several things should be noted at this point. First, as is and was well known, the United States and Israel had long since agreed to cooperate, sharing information and intelligence, in dealing with terrorism. Second, a "representative" of the Israeli embassy and a "private engineer" from Israel don't travel to Oklahoma City and show up at a bomb site on their own. Clearly they had come at the direction of the Israeli government. Mr. Tal was something more than just a public-spirited Oklahoma City businessman whom the Israeli embassy just happened to call. And equally clearly, Lester Martz, the ATF boss in Dallas, would not have authorized the two men to tour the Murrah Building site without instructions from Washington.

Furthermore, by the time the Israelis arrived, two weeks had passed since the bombing. McVeigh and Nichols were already under arrest. The grand jury was meeting. If, in the eyes of the American investigators, this monstrous crime had been perpetrated by just two old army buddies, with no ties to the Middle East, using a good-ol'-boy, home-brew device—and this is what they were saying publicly—would the Israelis have even been interested? Finally, although a few Oklahoma City officials knew about it, Eilon and Yerushalmi's visit had been a very well kept secret for a good year and a half.

Only now it was out.

Apparently, this fact—that I was aware of the story and that the media was too—brought the prosecution and the FBI to a state of near panic. Either that or Mr. Tal himself panicked and called the FBI. In any case, they—Tal and the government—"found" each other, for on September 10, as reflected in an FBI 302 dated September 11, Tal was interviewed jointly by Special Agent Carlisle of the FBI and Special Agent Harry Eberhardt of the ATF.

According to the 302 resulting from this interview, my phone conversation with Tal had gone like this: "JONES kept pushing TAL to the point where he began to threaten TAL. JONES made a number of assertions to TAL regarding his power and connections and what happens to people who don't help him. JONES told TAL he had a secret connection to Judge MATSCH. JONES said if he could get a statement from TAL, he could see the Judge privately without the prosecution knowing or being present. JONES wanted to file an in camera (i.e., private to the judge) motion with a statement from TAL about Arab or Iraqi terrorist involvement in the bombing."

There was more.

Tal claimed that Jim Hankins from my office, during my absence in Israel, had hounded him to get names and addresses in Israel for Eilon and Yerushalmi and also to get him to talk to ABC's Koppel and tell him there was Arab involvement in the bombing. Tal said further that Jayna Davis, a reporter for local Channel 4 who had been covering the case and particularly the possibility of an Arab-American connection, had told him I'd also boasted to her of my "special connection" to Judge Matsch and that I'd offered to take her with me on my trips, where we would "travel by first-class and stay in suites"! (The exclamation point is mine.)

Finally, Tal told the FBI that, yes, there had been a report of sorts on the Israelis' visit. That is, over lunch, the second day of his visit, Yerushalmi, the engineer, had apparently held forth about the bombing—and on "how the building could be reconstructed to make it a monument"! (Again, my exclamation point.) Tal said he himself had taken notes and had faxed them to the mayor of Oklahoma City and other city officials—five pages in all, including a cover page from Yerushalmi.

A likely story. Yerushalmi had come all the way to Oklahoma City just to tell local dignitaries how to turn the remains of the Murrah Building *into a museum*? And Tal, the "businessman," had simply served as his amanuensis?

No sooner had I returned from Israel than I found on my desk a government motion filed with Judge Matsch under seal that included Tal's 302 with his scurrilous allegations. Obviously the idea was to convert Tal's statement as the basis of a personal attack on me. I read it in disbelief, amazed first at Tal's naïveté in assuming I wouldn't have taken the elementary precaution of taping our conversation, then at the government's gullibility in using a 302 that could be so easily impeached. I had transcripts and tapes not only of my conversation with Tal but also of Jim Hankins's as well, which I presented to both the court and the government. I also had a statement from Jayna Davis denying everything Tal had attributed to her. Never had I proposed to her that we jet off anywhere together, first-class or any class.

Still, if I hadn't recorded Tal, it would have been his word against mine and Jayna Davis's. The FBI, I knew, wasn't any happier with her than they were with me, so they'd taken the chance. The more intriguing question was why Tal had told me anything in the first place. We didn't know each other, yet he'd told me enough over the phone to send me looking. Then, when I went to Israel and began to make additional inquiries, somebody must have called him and asked what in the hell he thought he was doing, telling Stephen Jones two of our men were there? In fact, he'd told not only me but also another reporter, Christy O'Connor of the CBS affiliate in Ft. Worth, who through her own sources had spent some time cultivating Tal. Tal had even given O'Connor a copy of one page of the Yerushalmi report on the bomb site.

The Israelis, meanwhile, had continued to pass off the visit as nothing more than casual, their inspection as superficial. While they were in the neighborhood, so to speak, Eilon and Yerushalmi had simply dropped in on their old army buddy, Tal, and had given him their ideas on converting the building into a monument to the victims.

But the one page of Yerushalmi's report had nothing to do with building a monument. It described the blast damage in engineering terms and pointed out that the close proximity of the Ryder truck to the building was a key to the building's collapse. Jayna Davis, meanwhile, told me she understood from another "reliable source" that the full report ran three pages and that Tal had told her, previously, that it attributed the bomb's design to Arab sources.

The truth was obvious enough. ATF, at least until it lost control of the investigation, hadn't discarded the idea of foreign or indeed Middle East participation in the bombing. The Israelis had come to Oklahoma City at its invitation. But without Tal's cooperation as a witness, and without Judge Matsch being willing to use the full power of the bench to demand classified information from other federal agencies, which became a kind of leitmotif to the case, we never got to see the other two pages of Yerushalmi's report. Nor could we ever determine who had instructed Tal to backtrack. Whether it was the FBI, the CIA, or Mossad (Israeli intelligence) is anyone's guess.

While I was in Israel, even though I had conversations with two people high up in Prime Minster Rabin's entourage, I'd essentially gotten nowhere beyond confirming what Tal had already told me. Polite though people were, no one was interested in helping Timothy McVeigh's defense counsel. The best I got was very much off the record and secondhand. I was able to read the memorandum of an interview with a high-ranking Israeli security figure, although I am pledged not to reveal either the interviewer or the interviewee. The memorandum stated, among other things, that shortly before the bombing, Israel had given the United States a general warning—a *general* warning, that is, nothing to do with any specific targets—of terrorist activity ahead of time and that after the bombing the United States approached Israel for consultation and advice. Although Israel thought the bombing was not "Islamically motivated," it believed it could have used "borrowed methods" and been "inspired" by Islamic actions. According to the memorandum, the source said that since the bombing an Israeli official had met regularly to "compare notes" with an American counterpart, the State Department's coordinator for terrorism.

But with regard to this general warning, I asked the question then that I ask still: What did the Israelis know that the U.S. government didn't? Or, perhaps I should say, what did the Israelis know that the U.S. government later *insisted* it didn't?

The questions remain. The answers were never given.

The Israeli warning was not the only one we discovered. On March 15, 1995, Eduardo Gonzalez, director of the U.S. Marshals Service, sent a memorandum to all U.S. marshals, alerting against possible future attacks. According to Gonzalez, an "informed source" had warned that a *fatwa*, an Islamic religious death sentence, had been issued against all service personnel as punishment for the marshals' role in dealing with World Trade Center bombing prisoners. "Possible targets," he wrote, "include the United States Courthouse and federal buildings, targeting as many victims as possible and drawing as much media coverage as possible." Gonzalez further advised, "We believe there is sufficient threat potential to request that a heightened level of security awareness and caution be implemented at all Marshals Service protected facilities nationwide. Particular attention should be given to screening persons and items entering court facilities and in and around judicial areas. Deputy marshals and court security officers should be encouraged to increase their vigilance at all times."

In Oklahoma City, the two most likely targets covered by the warning would have been the federal courthouse and the Alfred P. Murrah Building. But we were never able to ascertain if that "heightened level of security awareness and caution" had been implemented at either facility.

On September 30, 1996, with our own investigations now in full swing, we filed yet another mammoth motion with the court, entitled "Defendant McVeigh's Fourth Supplemental Specification of Materiality of Requested Classification." This included detailed documentation on many of our own findings, but its purpose—yet again—was to get the court to shake the information tree, or, as we put it in formal legalese, "This Specification of Materiality is submitted to the Court to supplement the previously filed Specifications of Materiality and further to support Defendant McVeigh's specific requests for information believed to be in the possession of the intelligence gathering agencies of the United States."

This was no fishing expedition on our part. We had seen enough to know there had to be more. The prosecution's protestations— that they knew of no evidence of foreign involvement—sounded increasingly hollow. In a case that had aroused the concern of the president of the United States himself, someone—if someone had wanted to—could certainly have breached the walls of jealousy that divide key Washington law enforcement agencies into impenetrable fiefdoms. But no one wanted to, obviously enough, and Judge Matsch proved unwilling—yet again—to take the next step, which would have been to *order* agencies like the CIA to disclose classified information. He preferred to rely on the representations of Beth Wilkinson, another sharp lawyer the Justice Department had sent out from Washington to deal with such matters, that neither the CIA nor NSA had any information relevant or exculpatory in the Oklahoma City bombing.

But the more critical event, even as we filed our "Specification of Materiality"—which sought to prove just the opposite of what

Wilkinson kept saying—was the hearing on severance in Judge Matsch's Denver courtroom.

As I've described, severance was absolutely crucial to McVeigh's chances, and our strategy had to be thought out to the nth degree. What we were up against was simple statistics: Many motions for severance are filed in federal courts, but the great majority are never granted. Legal experts for the media once again predicted we would lose.

Mike Tigar led off, but Terry Nichols didn't have persuasive grounds for severance. Only McVeigh did on grounds of the so-called confrontation issue. If, in a joint jury trial, the government introduced Terry's nine-and-a-half-hour statement, as they were bound to, Tim (or his defenders) would be barred from cross-examining his codefendant (i.e., Nichols) on its contents. This would be wildly prejudicial to McVeigh and would clearly deny him his Sixth Amendment right to confront his accusers.

Rob Nigh argued the motion during the second day, backed by an impressive brief complete with precedents from federal case law—and then the government decided to roll the dice.

We, and the Nichols defense, had already moved that the nine-and-a-half-hour statement be suppressed as evidence in the trial. The government now moved *in limine* (i.e., preliminarily), asking that the statement be admitted because the part McVeigh would challenge was self-evidently true. Specifically, Terry Nichols stated he made the trip to Oklahoma City the Sunday before the bombing for the purpose of picking up McVeigh, which could only be the truth because it was highly incriminating of Nichols himself. It had clearly happened. If it hadn't, why on earth would Terry Nichols have invented it?

The shift in argumentation was subtle. The government now sought to make truth the issue, not confrontation. It was good tactics. If Terry Nichols had self-evidently told the truth, thereby pointing the finger at himself, then the jury should hear that in a joint trial.

The government introduced a single witness at the hearing in support of its motion, an FBI special agent named Jablonski, but one was perhaps too many. On cross-examination, I led Jablonski to the admission that Nichols had lied on a number of points in the nine-and-a-half-hour statement, indeed so many times that it was impossible to tell where fact left off and fiction began. And when Judge Matsch intervened on that key issue of the trip to Oklahoma City—why *would* someone lie about it, if lying meant incriminating oneself?—I decided to roll the dice for our side.

"I agree, your honor," I said. "There's only one reason anyone would lie that way. And that would be if the truth were all the more incriminating."

The judge's eyebrows went up.

"How so, Mr. Jones?" he said.

"Well, your honor, I can imagine two possibilities. If you will look at these pages." I gave him the reference numbers to some FBI 302s, which showed that Terry Nichols had filled up the gas tank of his pickup twice within an eighteen-hour period that day:

> The government is going to contend that fuel oil was part of the bomb, and if they're right, that fuel had to have come from somewhere. They haven't yet told us where. But suppose Mr. Nichols had to have an explanation for why he'd filled up his truck twice in eighteen hours. His explanation would be that he'd had to make a round trip to Oklahoma City, some six hundred miles, but the truth could be that he'd siphoned off the gasoline and used it in making the bomb.

I saw Matsch studying the 302s carefully. The courtroom was still.

"But there's a second explanation too," I went on, slowly.

> Maybe Terry Nichols did go to Oklahoma City that Sunday, but not because Tim McVeigh had called him from down there, and not to meet McVeigh. Suppose he had another reason for being there and didn't want anybody to know about it. And what if somebody popped up and said they'd seen him while he was there. He had to invent a cover story, just in case, and the story he came up with was that he'd gone to pick up a TV set that was his from his old buddy, Tim McVeigh. If he could make that stick, then he had an explanation that was far more incriminating to McVeigh than it was to him.

I came away thinking the judge had to deny the government's *in limine* motion, and if he did, well, severance was a foregone conclusion. Still, as any lawyer knows, nothing is certain in a court of law. We were in court in Denver on October 2, 3, and 4, although the third day was devoted largely to arguments on other matters, then the McVeigh defense team retreated to Enid, while Judge Matsch deliberated. And deliberated.

Two tense weeks passed. An awful lot hung on the judge's decision. Then around ten o'clock one morning, the telephone rang. It was the clerk's office in Denver. We were told to turn on the fax machine, put the encryption device on, and be prepared to receive immediately an order from the court.

A few minutes later the fax machine, with groans and clanks, started spewing out the pages. We gathered around expectantly. The government's motion *in limine* had failed, and the judge, in his order, had quoted at length from my cross-examination of Agent Jablonski.

One week later, on October 25, we went through the same exercise. Severance had been granted!

In spite of ourselves, bedlam and jubilation broke out among us. Probably it is true in any profession, but for a team of lawyers who have worked long, hard hours—in the trenches, so to speak—a favorable decision on a crucial issue is almost as irresistible as the final verdict of a jury. So we celebrated, spontaneously and a little crazily, and to top it off, the story led off the evening news that night on all three networks.

S ome ten days later—it was Election Day night—I was at home in Enid when the phone rang.

It was our man in Manila.

"Stephen, I've got news for you," he said. "We've just interviewed Edwin Angeles. What's more, he claims that he met Terry Nichols. Or someone I think is Terry Nichols."

I all but fell out of my chair.

"Did he tell you this personally?" I managed to ask.

"Not personally. But he told it to the Philippine police."

"Then how did you get it?"

"We've got some friends in there," he said. "And your friend helped us out. They've got access to him, and we told them what to ask."

My "friend," as it turned out, was none other than the Director I'd called on during my visit.

I asked him to send me a transcript in English via Federal Express, not fax. Two days later it came. I then sent our man a letter back by the same method, not willing to entrust my message to the telephone lines. I told him I wanted him to send his Filipino cop friends back in to question Angeles again, only this time I wanted the interview videotaped, with, again, an English translation of the text.

In due course it came. And there it was.

Edwin Angeles had met "the Farmer."

That is, at a meeting in Davao, on the island of Mindanao, sometime in the early 1990s (Angeles recalled the date differently in different versions), he had met an American who introduced himself as the Farmer. Among those present at this meeting were Ramzi Yousef, then traveling under the name of Abdul Basit (which was in fact his real name), Abdul Hakim Murad, Yousef's friend since childhood, and one Wali Khan Amin Shah (who, we had reason to believe, had known Marife Torres Nichols and her sister through a mutual friend).

The subject of the meeting was terrorism. Angeles, in a written statement that accompanied the videotape, affirmed that three specific topics were discussed: bombing activities; providing firearms and ammunition; training in making and handling bombs.

Abdul Hakim Murad and Wali Khan would become codefendants, with Ramzi Yousef, as a result of the plot to blow up twelve U.S. jetliners. All three were convicted on September 5, 1996, and all three are now in American prisons. On April 19, 1995, Abdul Hakim Murad, already in his New York cell, told a guard that the Oklahoma City bombing was the work of the Liberation Army of the Philippines. Edwin Angeles was now quick to correct him. Angeles was specifically asked, "What was the identification of the 'liberation army' Murad had referred to?" Nothing to do with the Philippines, he said. It was the *Palestine* Liberation Army that Abdul Hakim was referring to, working with Islamic Jihad.

It was unclear whom Angeles meant. What was the Palestinian Liberation *Army*? But he was definite on the meeting, and he was also definite on the Farmer, to the extent of drawing us a pencil sketch of the man he'd met.

I studied the sketch. It was a remarkable likeness. Putting aside one detail—hair that, as drawn, appeared to be lighter in tone than the subject's—the man it depicted, the Farmer, was a dead ringer for Terry Lynn Nichols. But there was more, much more.

The Angeles interview had taken place at the Basilan Provincial Jail, and Angeles's interrogators were two Filipinos, one from the National Police and the other from the National Bureau of Investigation. Not only were his statements revealing, but many were in several ways verifiable, and the more I studied the tape, the more I became convinced we were onto something.Others maybe were less sanguine. They were less certain than I that the sketch was Terry Nichols. Or that the Farmer Angeles spoke of was Terry Nichols. Maybe there was someone else who called himself the Farmer. And how could I believe a character like Angeles anyway?

But why would Angeles have lied? I asked in return. Besides, he was a cooperating witness with the Philippine investigation into Ramzi Yousef, wasn't he? And wasn't there documentation indicating that he had been a cofounder and second-in-command of Abu Sayyaf?

There were any number of reasons why someone in protective custody in a third world country might lie, my colleagues replied. Or say what he thought people wanted him to say. Or what people prompted him to say.

But I trusted our man there, I said. He wouldn't have dared have set it up.

But he wasn't even there! they retorted.

Maybe they were right, but I thought otherwise. There were just too many coincidences. I couldn't dismiss the striking similarities of the Murrah Building explosion to the World Trade Center bombing and to another bombing that had taken place that summer in Saudi Arabia to the same type of building, with the same result. (I'm talking about the Al Khobar Towers explosion in Dhahran, in which nineteen American airmen were killed.) There were other Saudi connections, beginning with Osama bin Laden, the Saudi multimillionaire and arch-enemy of the Saudi royal family. Many Americans hadn't heard of bin Laden until August 1998, when two bombs went off outside the American embassies in Kenya and Tanzania. The bombings, which killed hundreds, were within days linked to bin Laden and his international terrorist network. During the Afghanistan War between the former Soviet Union and CIA-backed Afghan rebels that started in 1979, bin Laden's activities were based in Peshawar in northern Pakistan. Peshawar was the home of the International Islamic Academy, where young Muslims were recruited to join the mujahideen. The International Islamic Academy and Osama bin Laden were specifically mentioned by Angeles in his tape as the seat of all Muslim terrorist training. According to a Saudi intelligence official interviewed by *The New York Times*, bin Laden learned many of his tricks from the CIA during the war. He spent millions of dollars helping the Afghan rebels and was himself the leader of more than 10,000 Arabs who went to Afghanistan to fight alongside their fellow Muslims. After traveling around the Middle East and North Africa, bin Laden returned to Afghanistan, where he now lives, protected by Taliban forces in the southern city of Kandahar. Bin Laden has said that "to kill the Americans and their allies is an individual duty for every Muslim who can do it in any country in which it is possible to do it." He is suspected as the man behind the Al Khobar bombing and another bombing in Riyadh, Saudi Arabia, which killed seven, including five Americans. And he and his worldwide network of terrorists (he spends tens of millions of dollars a year funding terrorist cells in places like Algeria, Egypt, Lebanon, Sudan, Yemen, and, perhaps most relevant with regard to Oklahoma City, the Philippines) are suspected in a number of other attacks.

Bin Laden, with his brother-in-law, Mohammed Jamal Khalifa, had been named by U.S. authorities in February 1995 as among the 172 unindicted co-conspirators in the World Trade Center bombing (indeed, the architect of the bombing was captured in a bin Laden–financed guesthouse, and bin Laden's address was found in his wallet). Both bin Laden and Khalifa were known to have close ties to Sheikh Omar Abdul Rahman, the blind Muslim cleric convicted in the World Trade Center case, so it is not beyond comprehension to imagine bin Laden being involved with an attack against

Americans on American soil. Indeed, as *The New York Times* noted when writing about the East African bombings, bin Laden "has publicly threatened to strike at Americans throughout the world."

And bin Laden visited the Philippines in the early 1990s, around the same time as a man from America whose name was Terry Nichols. (It is probably worth mentioning that CNN, in reporting on bin Laden and the Kenya bombing, noted, "The discovery of the suspected traces of ammonium nitrate and fuel oil suggests that the bomb, which killed 247 people, may have used the same ingredients as the bomb that destroyed Oklahoma City's Alfred P. Murrah Federal Building in 1995.")

The connections kept coming. Bin Laden was known to Ramzi Yousef. Terry Nichols had met Yousef, Angeles said. Ramzi Yousef's brother had been a member of Abu Sayyaf with Angeles. If the government found it reasonable that Tim McVeigh had been willing to travel all the way from Arizona to Harrisonburg, Virginia, just to get a length of detonation cord (this is what one prosecution witness attested to), then was it unreasonable to think Terry Nichols had gone to the Philippines to find somebody to teach him how to make a bomb? In all likelihood, the experiments Terry and James had conducted in Michigan (exploding pop bottles) had been an effort to come up with the right mixture for a "big bang" but—*The Turner Diaries* notwithstanding—every expert I ever talked to confirmed that it was easier said than done. Although I didn't doubt that a man might marry a woman pregnant by another man, I doubted it happened very often with a man who had supposedly been interested, in the beginning, in a mail-order bride from a culture halfway around the world. From all appearances, there was nothing to indicate affection between the couple. At Terry's trial in 1997, Marife couldn't even spell her husband's last name properly, and she was unable to recall the date of their marriage. Meanwhile, aside from the Angeles tape, aside even from the letter Lana Padilla had opened and the batteries of long-distance phone calls to and from the Philippines that couldn't be explained, our own investigations had elicited these statements from various witnesses: (1) Nichols had carried a book with him on how to build explosives; (2) he had specifically asked a Philippines tour guide (by her own statement) if she had any friends in the military or someone who made bombs; (3) his wife had attended school at an institution where there were substantial numbers of radical Muslim students and which Vincent Cannistraro had specifically mentioned as a place we should look into. How, given all this, could I not think that Terry had gone in and out of the Philippines at will, using Marife Torres Nichols as a beard, in order to meet there with conspirators who had taught him to develop and assemble the ANFO bomb?

And there was something else. If this was true—if, that is, Terry Nichols had gone to the Philippines to be instructed by Ramzi and his band in the art and techniques of blowing up a nine-story building—then mightn't he have learned another part of Ramzi Yousef's modus operandi? That it's always most prudent to leave someone else holding the bag?

Bin Laden—Yousef—Nichols. Now a lot of things made sense. Nichols and his brother had been "anti-government" with a vengeance for a long time, since Tim McVeigh was in high school. According to FBI records, in 1988 James had shown the seed salesman a picture of the Murrah Building and talked to him about blowing it up. (The salesman remembered a younger man present who he thought might have been McVeigh, but of course it couldn't have been Tim because he didn't go to Michigan until much much later. That refrain—"he looked like Tim McVeigh, but it wasn't him"—would be repeated throughout the case.)

Whether Terry Nichols had a direct link to bin Laden was not as important to me as the fact that I now had three witnesses who said Terry was in the Philippines asking about explosives and how to make a bomb and carrying with him a book on how to make explosives. I had a witness who claimed, after passing polygraphs, that James Nichols was familiar with the Murrah Building, had a picture of it, and long before he ever met Tim McVeigh, that he and his brother harbored a deep anti-government animus. The Nichols brothers had experimented with pop bottle explosions, but they could never make them work, and that, I suspected, was why Terry Nichols went to the Philippines, and possibly why he returned there. I had learned enough about Terry Nichols that I suspected he was greedy, so for him to part with nearly $20,000 in cash and leave it in care of his ex-wife for his son Josh was proof enough that he was worried about the state of his health in the Philippines. Later, after he was arrested, the word was put out that what he was really afraid of was being killed by the father of Jason, the two-year-old boy Marife had conceived after she promised to marry Terry. But, the government had no evidence whatsoever the putative father even knew about the boy, his birth or his death, or that he had ever threatened Terry or Marife or even contacted her. Besides, if that threat was real Terry simply would not have gone abroad. No, something made him go to the Philippines and I suspect that something was the very thing he feared might result in his death. His supposed farewell message to Tim—"Go for it, you're on your own" was another gratuitous piece of incrimination put in place to serve Terry Nichols's interest at the expense of my client. He knew his ex-wife well enough to know he would hardly be seated in the plane before she would be tearing open the envelope and reading it.

Could have, would have, might have. The truth—the whole truth—stayed tantalizingly beyond my grasp, but only just beyond it. But the most galling part of all, to me, was that the people who *ought* to have been listening, who *ought* to have been probing, who had the power to intimidate and interrogate witnesses, some of whom were within their grasp and custody—I'm talking about our own Federal Bureau of Investigation, not to mention the so-called intelligence gathering agencies of our national government—just weren't interested. Instead of browbeating the minister in Manila to shut down our investigation, why weren't *they* grilling Edwin Angeles?

Presumably, they would say that they'd been there, done that, which was true enough, for we'd run across their footprints during our Philippines investigations, if only superficially. But another bitter truth became clear to me once again: At some point after they'd caught McVeigh and Nichols, and certainly by the time of the grand jury indictment in August 1995, someone high up in the government had ordered that they were simply going to drop all the rest. And by 1996, the last words anyone on the prosecution side wanted to hear were *others unknown*.

8

THE GOOD NEIGHBORS FROM THE CITY OF GOD

There are, as mentioned earlier, more than four hundred active "hate" groups in America, and they can be found in virtually every state of the union. Although they like to maintain, at least for public consumption, that they hate no one—Richard Butler of Aryan Nation proudly called himself a racist but defined the word as "one who loves his race"—what holds them together in a loose confederation is hatred: hatred of the other, the alien, the minority, of anyone, particularly the federal government, who would protect that minority.

No sooner had the bombing taken place than the FBI began to investigate, or reinvestigate, these groups, searching for ties to McVeigh and Nichols, searching for "others unknown." They looked in Michigan, where the Michigan Militia angrily denied any connection to McVeigh and Nichols, and they were in Kingman, Arizona, in force. But it was in Oklahoma itself where the most intriguing and important overlap between the bombing and the extreme right could be found.

Due east from Oklahoma City on Interstate 40, about 180 miles through increasingly hilly terrain, lies the Arkansas border. Aside from the interstate itself and the town of Ft. Smith, Arkansas, this is relatively wild and underpopulated country, the Ouachita Mountains, foothills of the Ozarks, where dirt roads far outnumber paved ones and where people, for whatever reason, who choose to live removed from civilization have long been drawn.

In 1973, a onetime Mennonite from Canada named Robert G. Millar, who had "heeded a call" some twenty years earlier, came to the Ozarks with seventeen followers, including his four sons. There, on a wild, 400-acre tract near the town of Muldrow, Oklahoma, he established "Elohim City"—the City of God. The Reverend Millar preached a mixture of Christian Identity and Odinism and soon came to attract a strange and motley crew of white supremacists, among them one James Ellison and his survivalist Christian Identity group, the Covenant, the Sword, and the Arm of the Lord. In the early 1980s, Ellison had a vision in which he discovered that he was directly descended from King David. Shortly thereafter, Ellison proclaimed himself "King James of the Ozarks" in a ceremony presided over by the Reverend Millar.

CSA grew increasingly violent during the early eighties. Spurred on by King James, they committed acts of vandalism against Jews and homosexuals throughout the Midwest and tried to sabotage a major natural gas pipeline near Fulton, Arkansas. Seeking other targets, they made a list of buildings they earmarked for attack. On that list was the Alfred P. Murrah Building in Oklahoma City. Their plan, according to a federal prosecutor who investigated them in connection with the sedition trial of 1988, called for parking a van or panel truck in front of the building and blowing it up with rockets in launchers detonated by a timer.

In November 1983, Richard Snell, one of King James's lieutenants, held up a pawnshop in Texarkana, Arkansas, with two other CSA members. Believing the owner to be Jewish, Snell shot him in the head, killing him.

Some six months later, pulled over for a routine check, Snell burst out of his car and shot and killed a black Arkansas state trooper. Later that same day, cornered in Broken Bow, Oklahoma, he was wounded in a shootout and captured. The state of Arkansas tried him for murder of the pawnbroker. He was convicted and sentenced to death.

In April 1985, the FBI raided CSA's encampment. King James promptly "abdicated." He was convicted later that year under the federal RICO law for racketeering and given a twenty-year sentence. In 1987, however, after a year in prison, he made a deal with the enemy and became a star prosecution witness in the Fort Smith sedition trial of 1988, the one in which Richard Butler, Louis Beam, and twelve others (Snell among them) were accused. All fourteen, however, were acquitted.

The date of the FBI's initial raid against CSA was April 19, 1985.

In a further bizarre turn to Ellison's story, after he was released from prison and living on parole in Florida, and tarnished though his reputation was in white-supremacist circles, he nonetheless made several extended visits to Elohim City and even managed to live there for a time. He was still there in 1995. Perhaps this was a sign of Robert Millar's magnanimity. As the reverend told *Time* of another person (who will make her appearance later in these pages), "It was not unusual for unstable people to seek us out. The Church of Jesus Christ exists for such people." But it may also have helped that later in 1995 Ellison married the Reverend Millar's granddaughter, Angie, a girl almost forty years younger than he.

As for Richard Snell, he was executed in his Arkansas prison. His last words to the governor of the state were, "Governor, look over your shoulder. Justice is coming."

The Reverend Millar was a witness to the execution, brought Snell's body home, and presided over its burial. A single cross now marks Snell's grave on a slope in Elohim City.

The date of Snell's execution?

April 19, 1995.

Ten years after the FBI raid on the CSA compound. Two years after Waco. Snell executed the evening after the bombing.

April 19, 1985.

April 19, 1993.

April 19, 1995.

Elohim City, it must be assumed, had never stopped being a subject of interest to various federal law enforcement agencies. In 1988, according to later documents produced by the government, the FBI had planned a raid on the settlement. The reason for the raid and the reason why it was called off are unknown, at least to those without access to the files of the Justice Department. Then, as we discovered later, during the winter of 1994–1995 federal officials were actively planning a joint raid on the settlement and requested that

other law enforcement officials put investigations of their own on
hold. This raid was also called off—also for reasons never explained—but it gave substance, after the fact, to the fears the Reverend Millar expressed to two local sheriffs that a raid was imminent
and to the widespread anxiety among people at Elohim, who numbered less than a hundred, that their home was about to become the
next Waco. This also partially explained why the Reverend Millar,
not long after the bombing, felt obliged to call a press conference
denying any involvement by his flock.

Elohim City would continue to fall under suspicion to anyone
who investigated at all seriously. A band of bank robbers who sometimes called themselves the Aryan Republican Army had been holding up small Midwestern banks ever since 1992, sharing the proceeds
with a variety of neo-Nazi groups. In January 1996, the FBI would
break the case, arresting two of the gang, one of whom, Richard
Guthrie, plea-bargained and named names. Guthrie later committed
suicide in his jail cell, but among the people he identified was one
Kevin McCarthy, a nineteen-year-old Philadelphian and a protégé of
Mark Thomas, a Posse Comitatus and Aryan Nation leader in eastern Pennsylvania. McCarthy would confess to having participated in
the crimes. More to the point, McCarthy and Scott Stedeford,
another of the accused, had lived at Elohim City in the period prior
to the bombing, and so had one Michael Brescia, another friend of
Mark Thomas, who in 1995 became, for a time, the John Doe #2
suspect-of-the-month. Both Thomas and Brescia were eventually
indicted on the bank robbery charges.

After the bombing, in other words, the FBI had ample reason to
investigate Elohim City, inch by inch. We knew they'd interviewed
Robert Millar, because they asked him not to discuss the interview,
or let anyone else discuss it, with people who might come see him
on Tim McVeigh's behalf. But otherwise?

Otherwise it was as though they'd drawn an imaginary circle
around the compound, as though they had declared everything
inside the circle off-limits. It was amazing. Amazing, for one thing,
that one of Elohim City's most prominent militants, Andreas Strassmeir, a/k/a "Andy the German," chief of security for the community
and one of its most outspoken exhorters to revolutionary activity,
was only worth one telephone interview to the FBI—at least until

January 1996, that is, *after* he'd left not only Elohim City but the United States too.

And what was plainly flabbergasting—for an organization that had interviewed thousands of people, including Timothy McVeigh's fifth-grade school teacher—was that one Dennis Mahon, a former grand dragon of the Ku Klux Klan, a leader of the White Aryan Resistance (WAR), and a violently antigovernment Tulsa resident who kept a trailer at Elohim City and admitted to having experimented with truck bombs, didn't seem to have interested them at all.

Yet in a letter dated February 6, 1997, Beth Wilkinson, who had by that time become one of the heavy hitters on the prosecution team and whom I considered the Justice Department's mouthpiece, wrote me as follows: "At no time did the FBI consider Andreas Strassmeir or Dennis Mahon a subject of the Oklahoma City bombing investigation."

But I am getting ahead in my story.

For the radical right, the Oklahoma City bombing presented obvious problems. Whatever their private feelings—and many of them had been calling for just such actions for years—white supremacists couldn't afford to applaud the bombing publicly, and for obvious reasons they had to disavow any connection with Tim, Terry, or the Fortiers and, to the extent they could, any of the John Doe #2 eligibles. Yet for them to condemn the bombing vigorously and totally would suggest that all their antigovernment preaching and exhortation, going back over many years, had been just so much bluster. Their positions, as a result, were ambiguous, cautiously taken and expressed.

There was, however, some evidence linking Nichols and McVeigh to the radical right. Among the Daryl Bridges phone calls during early April 1995 were a number to the National Alliance, the organization founded by William Pierce (author of *The Turner Diaries* and onetime aide to the former head of the American Nazi Party, George Lincoln Rockwell). And there was one tantalizing call to Elohim City, at 4:46 P.M. on April 5, 1995. It had been taken by Robert Millar's daughter-in-law. The caller—the government said it was Tim McVeigh—had left a message for "Andy."

During the early summer in 1995 I had received a phone call from a woman I did not know. She had a very distinctive voice, quiet, almost seductive. She said her name was Jo Thomas, adding, almost apologetically, that she was assistant national editor of *The New York Times* and that her job was to supervise their investigation and coverage of the bombing. She wanted to come in and see me, with an eye to establishing a relationship.

I'd already met several reporters from *The New York Times* but not Jo Thomas, so I called David Johnston, the one I knew best. "Who's this Jo Thomas?" I asked, and he chuckled, explaining facetiously, "Well, Stephen, you could say that if I have the power to stop the presses, Jo Thomas has the authority to stop the trucks."

You wouldn't have known it to meet her, but among other skills, she managed to get people to talk to her—all kinds of people. The only trouble we thought she had in the Oklahoma City bombing case, and she must have been greatly vexed by it, was that *The New York Times* simply wouldn't print much of what she must have filed.

The Oklahoma City bombing, Jo Thomas believed, was a conspiracy much larger than McVeigh and Nichols, and it was Jo Thomas who through her tenacity discovered the strange truth about the FBI's handling, or nonhandling, of Andreas Strassmeir. According to the files of the Immigration and Naturalization Service (itself a branch of the Justice Department), Strassmeir, who was technically an illegal alien for having overstayed the last of three visas issued to him by the State Department, had been, in the period before the bombing, the subject of a "sensitive" investigation by ATF. ("Sensitive" was the word used by Special Agent Angela Finley of the ATF office in Tulsa, who will appear again in these pages and who, as will become clear, had a particular reason for being interested in Strassmeir.) But only in January 1996, nine months *after* the bombing and *after* Strassmeir had left the country, did the INS issue the following "BOLO" (be on the lookout for): "Subject is wanted for questioning in Oklahoma City. DETAIN AND NOTIFY FBI SPECIAL AGENT, JOHN R. HIPPARD, OR SUPERVISORY SPECIAL AGENT, RICH BAKER.... SUBJECT IS PARTIALLY ARMED AND MAY BE DANGEROUS."

It had taken the government some nine months to decide that Strassmeir might be relevant after all. Luckily for us, we hadn't been sitting around waiting.

Andreas Carl Strassmeir, born in 1959, came from a politically illustrious German family. His grandfather had been a ranking member of the Nazi party. His father, Günter, had been parliamentary secretary of state in the cabinet of Chancellor Helmut Kohl, and an uncle held a seat in the Bundestag, the German parliament. Although Andreas would later be characterized in the media as a black sheep in his family and as a rogue or loose cannon in the milieus of the American right wing, he was nonetheless well educated and had served as a lieutenant in an elite German Panzer division, with formal intelligence and antiterrorist training.

Strassmeir had apparently come to the United States in the late 1980s. As we discovered later, there was a State Department file on him showing that he entered the country on a tourist visit. But there was the curious code designation "A.O.," which, quite typically, Beth Wilkinson said meant nothing but which Roger Charles, who became a valued investigator for the defense late in the case, proved specially coded Strassmeir's file. According to what Strassmeir later told interviewers, he came to America expecting to work on a special assignment for the operations section of the Drug Enforcement Agency but (mysteriously) the job hadn't panned out. Instead, he had migrated to Texas, where, while working as a computer analyst, he fellow-traveled with members of the Ku Klux Klan and the Texas Light Infantry, then to Elohim City, where he took charge of security and weapons training for the settlement.

His paramilitary activities at Elohim City had scarcely gone unnoticed by law enforcement agencies. For one thing, there was a record of an Oklahoma state trooper having arrested him in 1992 (after his visa had expired) for driving without a license and using false identity papers (in the name of Peter Ward, a buddy at Elohim City). Interestingly, Strassmeir had books on bombmaking in his car when he was arrested, but he was let go, mysteriously enough, without charges being filed. The Oklahoma Bureau of Investigation was aware that small groups of trainees came periodically to Elohim City for arms training with Strassmeir, and Angela Finley, the ATF agent from Tulsa, had aerial photos of concrete bunkers at the settlement and other pictures of Strassmeir working with assault weapons.

Only later did I learn that the FBI had long been aware of Andy the German. In late 1993, Ron Ostrow of the *Los Angeles Times* had covered a visit to Germany by Louis Freeh, head of FBI, during which German security officials asked Freeh about Strassmeir. According to Ostrow, the Germans reported to Freeh that Strassmeir was engaged in neo-Nazi activities in the United States. Freeh replied rather prudishly—presumably he only did so after checking—that the FBI was aware of Strassmeir, was "monitoring" his activities, but observed that "because of our First Amendment, there isn't anything we can do."

Was Strassmeir an agent provocateur? If not, was he on the payroll of one or another federal agency? There were rumors galore, before and after the bombing, and he would certainly appear to have led a charmed and protected life, vis-à-vis American law enforcement. Strassmeir himself would deny vehemently that he'd been on anybody's payroll, at the same time making coy-sounding observations about how easy it was to "penetrate" the American right wing once you learned to speak the language. In May 1996, "living quietly with his parents in a well-to-do area of West Berlin," he was the subject of five interviews and a series of articles for *The Daily Telegraph* (London). "I met the guy [McVeigh] once at a gun show," Strassmeir told the *Telegraph*. "We spoke for five minutes, that's all." He also offered the *Telegraph* his own theory on the informer question—"The ATF had an informant inside this operation. They had advance warning and they bungled it"—while insisting that whoever the informer was he wasn't it.

Whatever he was, Strassmeir's whereabouts during 1995, after he left Elohim City, were shrouded in mystery. Depending on whom you talked to, he had been in Texas or North Carolina or simply traveling around. When we interviewed him in Black Mountain, North Carolina, in November 1995 our interest was largely whether he'd ever met Tim McVeigh and, if so, what they'd talked about. Apparently, though, this sufficed to set off alarm bells. Kirk Lyons, Strassmeir's lawyer, admitted in a subsequent letter to his supporters that he had "spirited" Strassmeir out of the country, via Texas, to Mexico, France, and then Germany. He went on to say that it would be easier to defend Strassmeir and represent his interests when he was in Germany than from a federal prison in the United States—quite a strange statement from a lawyer, who felt compelled to proclaim his client's innocence before anyone had

accused him of a crime. In any case, it was only later, after Strassmeir had definitively returned to Germany, that the aforementioned
BOLO was issued and the American government became "interested" in Strassmeir again, only to have it affirmed by Beth Wilkinson, in 1997, that he'd never been a "subject" of the Oklahoma City
bombing investigation.

Andy the German was not the only lead that had brought
Kirk Lyons and his CAUSE Foundation to our attention.
Lyons, thirty-eight, was a self-styled one-man ACLU of white
supremacy (or, as Morris Dees of the Southern Poverty Law Center
had dubbed him, "the William Kunstler of the right wing");
CAUSE is an acronym for Canada, Australia, United States, South
Africa, and Europe—areas where, in Lyons's judgment, the civil lib-
erties of the white right were endangered. He represented Louis
Beam and Richard Butler of Aryan Nation, among others, and But-
ler had officiated at his wedding. He also represented survivors of
Waco in a civil suit against the federal government. Once located in
Houston, Texas, Lyons moved his operations to Black Mountain,
North Carolina, in 1992, and that was where our investigator
Richard Reyna tracked him down in November 1995.

The first thing Lyons said to Reyna, at their meeting, was that he
knew why he'd come. It was the phone call, wasn't it? The one that
had come into his (Lyons's) office the day before the bombing?

Reyna had no idea what Lyons was talking about, but, trying to
string him along, he said yes, there was that phone call, but he also
wanted to talk to Andy Strassmeir.

Well, so did a lot of people, Lyons countered. He mentioned
"that female reporter" from *The New York Times* and some people
from Interpol. He allowed as how the FBI was probably looking for
Strassmeir too.

Reyna said he only had a few questions to put to Strassmeir—about
Tim McVeigh, of course, and particularly about the April 5 phone call
McVeigh allegedly had made to Strassmeir at Elohim City.

Lyons said he had his doubts such a phone call had ever taken
place.

Reyna said the FBI had documentation that proved otherwise.

Then, much to Reyna's surprise, Lyons agreed to arrange a meeting for him with Strassmeir. Furthermore, it could take place that very day.

Within an hour, Reyna found himself driven by Lyons and Neil Payne, Lyons's brother-in-law and codirector of CAUSE, to a small room off the lobby of a Black Mountain motel. And there was Andreas Carl Strassmeir—and a TV set with the volume turned up so that no one could overhear.

Not surprisingly, Strassmeir was less forthcoming on McVeigh than on his departure from Elohim City. Apparently the latter had been abrupt and involuntary. Strassmeir, it seems, had openly criticized James Ellison's presence at Elohim City, claiming to Robert Millar that Ellison could not be trusted because of his history of getting people into trouble. Ellison, in response, had called Strassmeir a government plant. It was one against the other, and the relative— Ellison had married Millar's granddaughter—had won out. When Strassmeir came back from an errand one day, he found that his belongings had been packed, and Millar, who had already enlisted Kirk Lyons's help, had given him two hours to quit the premises.

During his interview, Reyna had to press Strassmeir and jiggle his memory with a photo of McVeigh in order for him to recall that well, yes, he might once have met someone who resembled Tim. It could have been at a gun show in Tulsa, he said, not long after Waco. Prodded by Reyna, he remembered having traded McVeigh, or the McVeigh look-alike, an old U.S. navy combat knife for a pair of gloves. But when asked how come McVeigh had had a business card of Strassmeir's, which had been found in his possession at the time of his arrest, he said that he'd given out business cards routinely to all sorts of people, at gun shows and elsewhere, and so did other Elohim City inhabitants.

Similarly, on the subject of the April 5 phone call, Strassmeir had little to offer. He told Reyna he'd never gotten a message from Tim. Normally, he said, when calls came into Elohim City for someone who wasn't there or was unavailable, whoever answered the phones left messages in people's mailboxes. Strassmeir claimed he'd never gotten one that McVeigh had called.

In other words, Strassmeir, talking to Richard Reyna, knew nothing. He said he didn't know Nichols or Fortier or James Rosencrans, Fortier's Kingman buddy. And he didn't really know Tim McVeigh, either. In this sense, Reyna's interview, like so many other leads we followed, led to a dead end. (Interestingly, when Reyna interviewed Robert Millar the following month, he reported Millar as having thought it possible that McVeigh had visited Elohim City some time back and that he, Millar, might have met him once or twice. Millar later told the media the same thing. Millar may have been hedging his bets, not confirming a McVeigh visit in case none was discovered, but not wholeheartedly denying one if such a visit was eventually revealed. In fact, on the date the government's theory claimed the conspiracy began, McVeigh was staying in a motel in Vian, Oklahoma, a short twenty- or thirty-minute drive from Elohim City. But the government never gave an explanation for the date. On another occasion, McVeigh was given a ticket by an Arkansas state trooper less than ten miles from Elohim City. And, of course, the April 5 phone call to Millar's residence could hint at some familiarity with Elohim City.)

After the meeting, Lyons offered to take Reyna to meet another of his associates, David Holloway, who was just about to be released from a local hospital. It was Holloway who had taken this other phone call—the long one to CAUSE—that Lyons had initially thought occasioned Reyna's visit. That call had come a day or two before the bombing. According to Holloway, the caller never identified himself, except as "a patriot," but made comments to the effect that the government was out of control, that the lawsuits on behalf of the Waco survivors, even if they won, would do no good, and that it was time for less talk and more action. The caller had also suggested that it was time to "get" some congressmen.

Holloway said he had contacted the FBI on April 24 to report the phone call, but apparently there was never any follow-up as to where the call had come from or who had placed it. Lyons had also reported it to the FBI. Both Holloway and Lyons believed the caller had been McVeigh. I had my doubts, but whether it had been or hadn't been Tim, the FBI's lack of interest was—again—rather surprising.

But the FBI's lack of interest in a lot of things continued to be surprising. Strassmeir was allowed to leave the country, even though there were at least three additional reasons the government should have been dramatically interested in him. One we wouldn't learn about for another year. But the two that became clear much earlier, having to do with Strassmeir's friends, were:

1. Strassmeir had roomed, at Elohim City, with Michael Brescia. Brescia, it will be remembered, was a strong John Doe #2 candidate. He was also a fugitive. And he would later be arrested and charged with the bank robbery gang.

2. Strassmeir was a great buddy of Dennis Mahon, a resident of Tulsa and Elohim City, Oklahoma.

I n a court document, the defense later described this friend of Strassmeir as follows:

> Dennis Mahon is a virulent racist and avowed enemy of the U.S. government. He is the Number 3 person in authority in the White Aryan Resistance movement led by Tom Metzger. There are videotapes featuring Mahon, in full Ku Klux Klan uniform, lighting a cross at a Klan recruiting trip in Germany, and yet another videotape of Mahon firing a semiautomatic rifle during paramilitary training for Klan members. . . . The Iraqi government has given Dennis Mahon thousands of dollars over the past six years. Mahon has admitted to receiving money from Iraq approximately once a month. . . . The money started arriving in 1991 after Mahon started holding rallies protesting the Persian Gulf War. . . . Mahon has been banned from the United Kingdom and from Canada.

A 45-year-old Tulsan who in the past had worked off and on in the aircraft industry, Mahon ran a "dial a Racist" hotline, lived in a rather modest, middle-class house filled with books and videos on Nazi-related subjects, and parked a trailer on the grounds of Elohim City. A physically intimidating man, Mahon was given to outbursts of anger that careened into rages, and he liked to boast that he was a master of disguises.

The British and the Canadians were well aware of him. As *The Sunday Times* (London) reported in January 1994,

Two American extremists, refused entry to Britain last year, have been organizing elsewhere in Europe. Tom Metzger, a former grand wizard in California who now runs White Aryan Resistance (WAR), went to Russia to meet neo-Nazis. Dennis Mahon, of Oklahoma's White Knights of the Ku Klux Klan, has set up Klan cells in Germany, where thirty people have been killed in racist attacks in three years. Mahon was introduced to German fascists by Ian Stuart Donaldson, the late lead singer with the racist rock group Skrewdriver, who was sworn in as a founder member of the British Klan at a secret ceremony in Derbyshire.

The Canadians, meanwhile, had thrown him out a year earlier. At the Canadian immigration department inquiry of January 26, 1993, which resulted in Mahon's eviction, a video was played, the last twenty minutes of which depicted a speech Mahon had made to the Canadian "Heritage Front" the previous February. In it, according to *The Toronto Star*, Mahon was greeted with *Sieg heil!* salutes and told his cheering audience, "You've got some serious Oriental problems." Then, admonishing them to get rid of government leaders who had allowed so many nonwhites in, he said, "Once you take care of that problem, your Pakistanis, Bangladeshis and Orientals will be a weekend operation."

Nice man. And he lived down the turnpike, barely ninety miles from Oklahoma City.

As we would discover later (but the FBI already knew), Mahon knew his way around large ammonium nitrate bombs. According to what he told Rob Nigh in early 1995 during a surprisingly candid interview, the Canadians and British had banned him from their countries because Interpol had him classified as an international terrorist, a fact he repeated to me in a telephone conversation on February 13, 1996. Yet the FBI, amid this mammoth investigation, couldn't be bothered to interview this man.

It made no sense. After all, on April 19, how many Oklahomans had been classified "international terrorists" by Interpol?

In January, 1996—that is, after Strassmeir had returned to Germany—J. D. Cash, the journalist, visited Mahon at his Tulsa home, and their five-hour conversation became the subject of a sworn statement Cash gave the defense team two months later. In addition to his work for the McCurtain County *Gazette*, Cash also wrote for the right-wing magazine *Jubilee*—a connection he used to establish his bona fides with people like Mahon. That January day, he got Mahon to talk quite freely until the subject turned to Strassmeir, and Cash gave voice to his own theory that Strassmeir might well be an agent for the German government. According to Cash, Mahon then became extremely agitated. He wanted Cash to tell this to Mark Thomas and Michael Brescia, who was then staying with Thomas on Thomas's Pennsylvania farm, and went so far as to get Mark Thomas on the phone. Cash managed to talk briefly to Thomas and claimed later that Thomas admitted he was at Elohim City in the days before the bombing but that he had left before Snell's funeral. Thomas then cut the conversation short, and although Mahon tried to persuade Thomas to let Cash visit him in Pennsylvania, Thomas flatly refused. (Later I would send Neil Hartley and Ann Bradley to interview Thomas. Ann persuaded him to talk to her for three hours as they played pool late into the night. Thomas lost the game; he didn't know of Ann's pool prowess, but it broke the ice.)

Then, according to Cash, they got into a detailed discussion of Strassmeir's family connections in Berlin and the further connections between the German and U.S. governments, including the operation the FBI was carrying on, mandated by Louis Freeh and Larry Potts, a top FBI executive, to provide intelligence to the Germans on neo-Nazi activities in the United States.

According to Cash, Mahon said he could think of situations where Strassmeir might have done a great deal of harm to people in the movement and proceeded to work himself up until he placed a call to Germany. Mahon's nonidentical twin brother, Daniel, who spoke much better German than Dennis, joined them at this point. He took over the call when Dennis stumbled and had trouble making himself understood, and in the translation back and forth, what they were saying became very clear to Cash. Whoever it was they were talking to, Dennis wanted him to find out if Strassmeir could be an agent for the German government. Strassmeir had once been his friend, a very good friend, but if it turned out Strassmeir had double-crossed him, then he (Mahon) wanted them to shoot Andreas in both kneecaps, wring a confession out of him, then try to execute him.

One of the reasons Dennis was anxious about Strassmeir was what had happened to Gary Lauck. Lauck was the leader of the American National Socialist Worker's Party, which was affiliated with neo-Nazi groups across Germany. Its publications were highly influential in these circles, because German law forbids the publication and dissemination of Nazi propaganda. According to Mahon, Lauck had told him, a few weeks before the Oklahoma City bombing, that he was planning a trip to Germany. Mahon had tried to talk him out of it. Lauck had gone anyway, was arrested in Copenhagen, and extradited to Germany.

The question Mahon had to ask himself was: Had he, or hadn't he, mentioned Lauck's forthcoming trip to Strassmeir?

By the time I talked to Mahon on the telephone, however, on February 13, he had totally disavowed the kneecaps story. Possibly he found himself being sucked into suspicion himself, caught between the media on the one hand—"that bitch" from *The New York Times* as he characterized Jo Thomas—and higher-ups in the white-supremacist movement. The mention of Louis Beam, Cash had noticed, and the possible linking of Beam to the bombing (a Jo Thomas notion), had upset Mahon a great deal.

In any case, he wanted me to find out who was "spreading this horseshit" about him putting out an assassination attempt on Strassmeir. If I could find that source, he said in his ranting style, then I'd find out "who is behind, or at least financed and masterminded, this whole thing in Oklahoma City."

Needless to say, I was taping our conversation. I asked Dennis if he thought Strassmeir was an informant.

"No, no," he said, calming down. "Andy? I've gotten drunk with him. I've partied down with him. We've screwed the same women." At this he laughed.

You learn a lot about a guy. Andy never had any money. Christ, he'd come here to visit me, and I'd have to pay his gas, give him money for gas money to go back to Elohim City. I'd buy the beer. Andy never had any money, never had a car. His car was always broken down. He always had to borrow somebody else's vehicle to come here to visit. Andy never had a phone. In my experience with these . . . uh . . . informant-type people, they've always got pretty good transportation, they've always got a phone for communications, and they've always got at least enough money to pay their way.

And he concluded that he didn't think Andy had had anything to do with it.

Mahon and Strassmeir.

Michael Brescia and Mark Thomas.

The Reverend Millar.

We kept trying to crack Elohim City, and we were failing. We made charts and timelines, but they didn't quite connect. Reyna, interviewing Millar, found him protective of Brescia—in part, it turned out, because Brescia had been in love with another of Millar's granddaughters. And so, it turned out, had Strassmeir. It was like a joke—all the militant youths of the radical right, some of them (like James Ellison) not so young, falling in love with the granddaughters of the patriarch.

But had they participated in the bombing? And/or: Were one or more of them informers or agents?

As already mentioned, we petitioned the court numerous times to force the prosecution to turn over all information gathered by the CIA and other national security agencies about the bombing. Judge Matsch refused our petitions as such, although he noted—repeatedly—that the prosecution was legally obliged to turn over to us anything that might benefit our client's case. And the prosecution—surprise, surprise—continued to deny that there was anything at all. And the band played on.

But I knew all along that we were missing something. I knew there was something there, in Andy the German and Dennis and the so-called City of God of Robert Millar tucked into the eastern hills of Oklahoma. I knew it by the time of my own first trip to Europe that January. I just didn't know what it was yet, and we wouldn't find out for another year.

Meanwhile, the FBI just wasn't interested.

One of the first things Judge Matsch did after he was appointed presiding judge was to call a meeting of the principals on both sides. (This was while the case was still in Oklahoma

City.) He came down to the federal courthouse and stood at the door, shaking hands with each of us as we entered, and once we were all present, he made two memorable statements.

One was that he hadn't consulted with Judge Alley about the case and wouldn't. Chief Judge Russell, yes, but not Alley. In other words, he wanted to convey to us that as far as he was concerned we were starting on a blank page.

And then he said that he was vacating the trial setting of May 1996, which Alley had already announced would be the beginning of the trial.

"I don't set a case for trial," Matsch announced that day, "until I understand it myself. Only then is it ready to be set, and this case isn't."

The moment he said that, one key element in the government's strategy collapsed. From the beginning, they'd clearly planned on delaying sharing any evidence with us until the last possible minute. This is an old prosecutor's trick in our adversarial system. Hartzler had engaged in "negotiations" with us before, but he kept changing the rules. In October, we'd filed the first of a number of court documents, laying out in great detail how the government had stonewalled us, and in November we had filed our first motion for exculpatory evidence. Exculpatory evidence is that which either shows the accused didn't do it or mitigates punishment, and under *Brady v. Maryland* the government is obliged to share it with us. That first motion, frankly, looked like a telephone book. What we'd done—it was very largely Bob Wyatt's work—was to list every witness mentioned by the media who'd reported having seen this person or that person along the trail of the crime. To cite but one example, someone claimed to have seen four Middle Eastern–looking men leaving the Murrah Building site—and we said in the motion, okay, we want all your information about these. The motion was like a vacuum cleaner, sucking up everything out of the public domain and turning it back on the government. In other words, we knew there were limits to the amount of time Hartzler could or would spend reviewing 30,000 statements, deciding which he would and which he wouldn't give us, and we wanted to flood him into giving us everything.

In the long run, with Judge Matsch's help, the strategy worked. No trial would be set until all the *i*'s were dotted and the *t*'s crossed, which obviously included the sharing of discovery material.

For the moment, I wrote Joe Hartzler a letter, requesting, as a show of good faith, that he give us the 302s on an enclosed list of people. There were eight names on my list: Eldon Elliott, Vicki Beemer, Tom Kessinger (the three from Elliott's Body Shop), Lea McGown (manager of the Dreamland Motel), Daina Bradley, one of the surviving victims, Michael and Lori Fortier, and a young man named Jeff Davis. Jeff Davis made deliveries in Junction City for a local Chinese restaurant. On the night of April 15, 1995, he made one to the Dreamland Motel where—according to the government's theory—McVeigh stayed alone while he completed preparations for the bombing. When Davis arrived at the door of room 25, however, the man who answered and paid was tall, with "unkempt" hair and a strange accent. It certainly wasn't McVeigh, Davis said, and it wasn't Nichols either. Obviously we were interested in speaking with Davis, but as was the case with the others on the list, we had had no luck. In any case, Hartzler wrote me back, saying he had personally reviewed the 302s in question and that he'd found nothing exculpatory in them toward our client.

I was suspicious as all get-out.

I called Pat Ryan—probably this could be classified as a "dirty trick" on my part, for it was thoroughly obvious by then that there was bad blood between Ryan and Hartzler—and I said, in substance, "Patrick, I've been trying to get hold of some 302s pertaining to the case, and Hartzler's told me they're not exculpatory."

I ran off the list of names for him.

"Oh no," he said, "you're entitled to all that stuff. Joe wouldn't tell you it wasn't exculpatory. Some of it is."

"Patrick," I said, "Joe told me that in writing."

"He did?"

"Yes."

"What exactly did he say?"

I had Hartzler's letter in front of me, and I read it aloud.

"Would you send me a copy of that?"

This I did.

Either Ryan talked to Hartzler or Judge Matsch acted (by then he'd made it clear he wouldn't tolerate obfuscations on either side). In any event I got the 302s in question. In fact, they arrived just as I was leaving for England, on January 5, 1996. I read them on the first leg of that flight, and when I got to St. Louis there was a four-hour delay in the flight to London, so I read them again. And reread them. And the more I read and reread, the madder I got.

Not exculpatory? I wanted to shout at the world. Before I boarded the plane, I did the next best thing. I called Rob Nigh and Bob Wyatt at the office.

"You're not going to believe it," I shouted at them, "what these guys have been doing to us! They've misled the media up one street and down the other. They've got a damn weak case!"

They must have thought I was nuts. I'm not usually given to outbursts. But there were Daina Bradley's statements, for starters. She was the woman who'd seen the Ryder truck just before the explosion and, later, had to have her leg amputated on the spot in order to be extricated from the rubble. According to two of her 302s, she had told the feds on two different occasions that the person she saw at the Ryder truck matched the description of John Doe #2. No mention of John Doe #1.

And then there were the Elliott, Beemer, and Kessinger 302s. They were the trio of witnesses at Elliott's Body Shop in Junction City, where the Ryder truck had been rented. All three testified that two men rented the truck together. Not one, but *two*. They were adamant on the point. And the description they gave was not consistent either with McVeigh or the clothes he was wearing at the time.

Not exculpatory, Mr. Hartzler?

According to Tom Kessinger, who was questioned by Special Agent Scott Crabtree of the FBI on April 19, UnSub #1 was wearing "a multicolored uniform" and had short brown hair, close-set eyes, and a medium nose. "His chin was pushed up and out with a wrinkle across it."

Eldon Elliott told Crabtree on April 19 that Robert Kling was a white male, five-foot ten, and wearing an army fatigue or similar military-type clothing.

Vicki Beemer, interviewed by Crabtree the next day, described a white male, approximately five-foot ten, and wearing a drab green T-shirt.

Tim McVeigh was six-foot three. He had a straight chin. A video image taken of him, about twenty minutes before the Ryder truck was rented, at the local McDonald's near Elliott's proved he was wearing jeans and a T-shirt that afternoon.

UnSub #2 (was he John Doe #2?) was described by all three as shorter than UnSub #1, and he was wearing a baseball cap with blue zigzag stripes on it. According to Kessinger, he had a tattoo on his upper left arm.

No, according to Hartzler, none of this was exculpatory.

And then there were the witnesses at the Dreamland Motel. They placed the Ryder truck there on Sunday, which, according to the government, it wasn't. Plus they'd seen someone they'd identified as John Doe #2, and they also had heard other male voices coming from the room McVeigh was supposed to be alone in. And, of course, there was delivery-man Jeff Davis and what he'd seen.

Reading those 302s, it became clear to me that my earlier suspicions that the government had made a deal with the Fortiers because it had a weak case had been right on point. Had I known then about the FBI Lab I would have understood how absolutely crucial it was for the government to get Mike and Lori Fortier to "correct" their statements.

Finally, at the end of that January, under pressure from Matsch, the government gave us the first major batch of 302s. I believe there were some 7,500 in all. But these were arranged in serial chronological order, which meant that if Witness A had given five separate statements they would be scattered throughout. Furthermore, the FBI parceled out the dates. In January, say, they gave us all the 302s for April 30, but it wasn't for another couple of months that we got those for April 29 or May 1. (All of this added, of course, to the ultimate cost of the defense.) Then, as Bob Wyatt began to pick up, for he was in charge of discovery and did a marvelous job of policing what we did get, there were significant 302s "unaccountably" missing. Although the government's data processing systems were highly sophisticated, allowing printouts in a variety of sequences, it took Judge Matsch's intervention to get the government to give us documents in alphabetical order and by coherent categories.

All along, from Joe Hartzler's letter on these 302s to Beth Wilkinson's missive on Strassmeir and Mahon, the government took the same grudging stance: *We will delay as long as we can. We will dodge when we have to.*

It took me a long time to understand that this wasn't just competitiveness on their part or even a desperate need to win—to win at all costs.

There was something else too.

Some thing, or things, that they were hiding.

9

"THIS LEG DOESN'T BELONG TO A VICTIM"

I had already contacted a very distinguished firm of London solicitors, Kingsley Napley, whom Judge Matsch had authorized us to retain as our representatives in the United Kingdom. The firm had been founded, or cofounded, by Sir David Napley, a legend in British criminal law. He had prepared the defense of Jeremy Thorpe, the Liberal leader charged with conspiracy to commit murder in the late 1970s, as well as that of the man accused of the attempted assassination of Princess Anne. Although Sir David had since died, his right-hand associates, John Clitheroe and Christopher Murray, were still with the firm and received me in their London offices at 14 St. John's Lane in Knight's Quarter, along with Ray Tilburey, a retired British army officer who would assist in our investigations.

Kingsley Napley's principal function was to put me in touch with experts on terrorism and explosives, partly so that I could bounce the government's theories off them and get their fix on such evidence, mainly photographic, that I could bring with me. Among those I met were John Bates, recently retired from Scotland Yard's Special Branch and one of Britain's top investigators; representatives of Control Group, Inc., one of the world's largest and best private security and corporate intelligence firms; and Tom Nelson, a trace analysis expert whose father was a prominent Northern Ireland politician, now in the House of Lords, and who had been a key forensic scientist in Northern Ireland against both the Irish Republican Army (IRA) and the Protestant paramilitary militia. Under Margaret Thatcher's regime, police laboratories had been privatized (a reform very worth considering in the United States) and today function completely independently of the police themselves; Tom Nelson now worked for one of these labs. He recommended that I go see a senior forensic pathologist, Bernard Knight, who was also a barrister at law and who lived in Cardiff, Wales. Dr. Knight performed about a thousand autopsies each year. He agreed to see me, and one day I caught the morning train from London's Paddington Station and traveled across England to Cardiff.

Before I go on, though, I need to bring up the story of the extra leg.

In summer 1995, while the grand jury was still sitting, I'd had a quiet tip, originating with an Oklahoma state trooper, that an extra left leg had been found in the rubble of the Murrah Building and that it couldn't be matched to any of the victims. There was nothing I could do with the story myself—true or not, it would almost certainly be denied—but persistent questions from the media were something else. I first gave the story to *The Dallas Morning News*, which quit after it got the first denial, then to *Time*. *Time*, apparently, had more persistence and a lot more clout. I happened to be in Kansas City the next weekend, with other members of the defense team, when the hotel switchboard lit up like a Christmas tree. All the incoming calls, it turned out, were from media people in Oklahoma City who'd tracked me down. They wanted to know what the defense thought about the extra leg. The state medical examiner's office, it turned out, had just put out a press release confirming that the leg did exist and further that it probably belonged to a white male (75 percent probability) and that it had a combat boot on it with some type of military blousing strap attached to the shoe.

Several weeks later, I had a visit in my office from Rick Serrano, a first-rate reporter for the *Los Angeles Times*, who in addition to being an excellent source of information had strong contacts at the Department of Justice. Rick told me, one, that according to what he'd heard they were going to have to announce soon that the leg belonged to a black male, not a white one, and, two, that the existence of the leg was driving the government crazy.

A few days after that, we learned, an all-day meeting was held at the state medical examiner's office in Oklahoma City—attended by the FBI and other government officials—to decide how to deal with the leg, and some forty-eight hours later, a second press release was issued by the same office, accompanied by a press conference, now stating that the leg belonged to a black female. Dr. Clyde Snow, from Norman, Oklahoma, and one of the world's most famous anthropologists, stepped forward at the press conference to accept responsibility for the "mistaken identity" and promptly left on a three-week vacation.

I decided, at this point, that it was time for me to go see State Medical Examiner Fred Jordan.

Jordan had been understudy for some years to A. J. Chapman, a forensic pathologist of unimpeachable integrity who, in my experience, always called it as it was, without regard to which side of the bar it favored. I liked Fred Jordan personally, and he made a good witness in court, but he always carried a hidden harpoon for the defense lawyer. No matter how many times you'd asked him the same question before, once you got him in the witness chair, you would hear him say, "Well, Mr. Jones, I know I may have said that, but I've rethought it and now I believe such-and-such." He was, in other words, distinctly proprosecution and a dangerous adversary.

But this wasn't the courtroom, and in his office he was affable and forthcoming.

"Here's what we know about the leg," he said in substance. "We have eight people with traumatically amputated left legs, and we have nine left legs."

I asked him what the possibilities were that they had buried two right legs with one of the victims. Zero, he said. There was a clear anatomical distinction, and even a first-year pathology student knew it and could spot it. Then he said there was some sentiment in his shop that the leg might belong to Lakesha Levy, who'd been in the social security office when the bomb exploded. The federal government, he said, had given them a young forensic anthropologist named Emily Craig, who'd done a report on the subject.

Jordan gave me a copy of Dr. Craig's statement. It said the leg bone in question was either that of a very small man or a good-sized woman, and there was some indication, from the color, that it was non-Caucasian. Lakesha Levy was a twenty-one-year-old Airman First Class, a black woman of slightly above average build who'd been stationed out at Tinker Air Force base. Jordan showed me her file. It maintained that Levy had both her legs but that the left one was barely attached. Dr. Choy had been the pathologist on the case. I knew her, and, thorough though she was, I doubted she'd have made a mistake like that. If she'd said the left leg was still attached, if barely, then I'd have bet the farm that it was still attached.

(As it turned out, I'd have lost the farm.)

I met Dr. Bernard Knight in his office at the Royal Infirmary, a marvelous old relic from Queen Victoria's reign, in Cardiff, the capital of Wales. I had Dr. Craig's report with me. I showed it to him and outlined for him the government's theory of the bomb, how it had been carried in a truck from Junction City, Kansas, down to Oklahoma City.

Dr. Knight voiced skepticism about the report, but he was much more skeptical still that such a bomb could safely be carried almost three hundred miles. To illustrate, he scooted back his chair, which was on rollers, to a metal filing cabinet and produced a gruesome photograph. It was of a man's body, literally half of it blown away.

The man in the photo, Dr. Knight said, had been an IRA "mule," that is, someone recruited to deliver a bomb. He had been holding an ammonium nitrate bomb in his lap when the car he was riding in hit a bump in the road. The car blew up.

Dr. Knight looked at me over the top of the photograph, saying, "I know your roads in the States are much better than they are in Northern Ireland. But are they that much better?"

More than a hundred members of the IRA and their allies had been blown up, he told me, while carrying explosive devices, and furthermore, some sixty of these had been ammonium nitrate bombs. Until they were able to obtain *plastique* from Czechoslovakia, the ANFO bomb—or "Co-op mix," as Knight called it—had been the IRA's preferred method of terrorism. In Dr. Knight's experience, in almost all cases of ANFO bombings, the intended victims had not had their bodies "disrupted" (that is, blown to pieces), but had died as a result of traumatic injuries caused by the force of collapsing buildings. This, in fact, had been true of the Oklahoma City bombing too.

Furthermore, according to Knight, for a body to be "disrupted" to the extent demonstrated by the unidentified leg, the victim had to have been standing almost directly next to the bomb, and in his experience and observation, that meant the victim was the bomber himself. He referred to it as "scoring his own goal"—the term used in soccer when a defender inadvertently puts the ball into his own net. In his judgment, the leg was just such a case.

Needless to say, I wanted Knight to help us. Instead, he recommended two people he thought better than he. One was T. K. Marshall, who had been chief state pathologist for Northern Ireland and had performed some 2,500 autopsies on bombing victims, many of them victims of ANFO explosions. He also put me on to Dr. Yasar Iscan of Florida Atlantic University. I contacted Dr. Iscan as soon as I got back to the United States, and I would see Dr. Marshall six weeks later, on my second trip to the United Kingdom.

The most mysterious yet fruitful meeting in London came about because of John Clitheroe's contacts in the London Jewish establishment. I didn't expect that any Jewish organization anywhere would go out of its way to help Tim McVeigh, but I, and John, thought there might be some community of interest, and there turned out to be.

We met late one evening—let me call him Mr. Z—and the first thing he said to me was, "Well, I guess you're here to talk about Dennis, Kirk Lyons, and the German." I was dumbfounded. Clitheroe, I was certain, had given no details of why I was there.

All three individuals, it turned out—Mahon, Lyons, and Strassmeir—had strong ties to the U.K. neo-Nazi movement, which served, in turn, as a two-way conduit to the continent. In fact, Mr. Z went on to say, much of the neo-Nazi literature published in the United States was actually printed in Brighton, England, and a recent series of train robberies in France by French neo-Nazis had been engineered and financed from England.

Dennis Mahon, as I knew, had already been barred from the United Kingdom. I was also told that most neo-Nazi groups in Germany, and some in Britain, received financing from the most radical regimes of the Middle East, including terrorist organizations protected by those regimes. The money trail ran from the Middle East to Germany and, through England, to the United States. There was mutual support, fund-raising, and the planning of terrorist actions. Mr. Z described both Mahon and Strassmeir as "dangerous" and "fanatical." After two and a half hours of dialogue, Mr. Z left me with an observation that was as troubling as it was comforting: "If it's any consolation to you, Mr. Jones, I think you're on the right track."

Before I left London, Kingsley Napley set me up with a retired army officer who, I had been told, was connected with British Internal Security or MI5 and had apparently done some chasing of the Provos (the Provisional IRAs, who were the terrorist vanguard of the movement in Northern Ireland). After an impressive lunch at the Athenaeum Club, during which I told him the story of the Oklahoma City bombing in detail, we sat upstairs in the library overlooking the Mall. This stately room was like a posh set in some old movie—complete with drowsing members—and there, over coffee, having heard me out, my host gave me his considered opinion on the bombing.

"I'm not saying your chaps didn't do it," he said.

I'm just telling you that no one else has ever been able to do it that way. Since we've been keeping records, and that goes way back before 1968, there's been no major incident of terrorism anywhere in the world, where anything like this number of people were killed and injured, that was the work of only two men. If it was that easy, we would have bombs going off in London all the time. Terrorism requires infrastructure, supplies, financing, safehouses, a getaway plan, lookouts, engineers, and leadership.

So if your clients are guilty, they and no others, one has to ask oneself: What did Terry Nichols and Tim McVeigh know that the PLO, the General Command for the Liberation of Palestine, Black September, and the Provos of the IRA, and every other terrorist organization in the world that uses ammonium nitrate bombs, didn't know?

"If your clients are guilty, Mr. Jones," he concluded, "I hope, before your government executes them, that you will make them available to the rest of us, so we can find out how they did it."

Two days later, back in Enid, I called Jim Manspeaker. Manspeaker was clerk of the U.S. District Court for the District of Colorado, as competent a clerk of any court as I've run across. I asked him for an 848 meeting with Judge Matsch.

An 848 is a meeting held ex parte with the Court, usually with only the judge and a court reporter present, or, as in this case, Judge Matsch and Manspeaker with a tape recorder. The change of venue motion was still pending at that time, but the judge was in Denver, as I knew, and later that week I drove up, spent the night, and was in his chambers the next morning.

I went armed with an affidavit fifty-six pages long, outlining virtually everything we'd learned so far, including a summary of the trip to London and my first interview with Cannistraro, when he'd recommended I look into Nichols's Philippines connection—all in support of a request for further funding. I was charged up, I must say. I believed that the case was opening up in front of us but that we were going to have to go still further afield—including to the Middle East and the Philippines.

I put the affidavit on the table between us.

The judge asked me what it was.

I explained. I said I'd come to Denver because, quite frankly, for security reasons I was reluctant to file the affidavit at the federal courthouse in Oklahoma City. But I would be happy to leave it with him in Denver.

He asked me to brief him on it instead.

This was the first time I'd ever spent more than a few minutes one-on-one with Matsch, and I seized the opportunity. A great deal rode on it. I must have talked for a good hour, developing the theory that the bombing had to have been an operation far beyond the capacities of my client and Terry Nichols.

I talked for an hour uninterrupted. I outlined for him everything we knew in detail. As he was also the trial judge I had to be especially careful not to prejudice him, not to cross over the line. But I was very specific as to what we had learned, where we thought it might take us, and what we needed: bomb trace analysts, experienced pathologists, anthropologists, terrorism experts, authorization for travel, secure communication, photography, and the like, and other items too sensitive to detail. When I was done, Judge Matsch carefully pushed the affidavit back toward me with his finger. He didn't want me to file it. He said he wanted it locked up in my safe in Enid. But he wanted me to keep going. And he, in turn, would authorize all the expenditures I needed to pursue our investigation.

He told me I had met my burden for the authorization, and he told me something else: "In the future, Mr. Jones, when you seek additional authorization along these lines, just refer to our meeting of this date. I'll understand." After the trial as I occasionally encountered criticism of the defense costs, I had to ask myself how many of these critics would have changed their minds had they been sitting in the room that day, and heard what Judge Matsch heard. Certainly I told myself any judge or lawyer who knew what Judge Matsch knew would have reached the same result, and I suspected any fair member of Congress or the media would have done likewise.

We talked a while longer. He was very concerned about the media and my contacts with them. As I explained to him, citing several examples, we'd used members of the media from the very outset to assist us in pursuing investigative leads. We could never have competed otherwise with all the troops the FBI put into the field or with a prosecution team that had obstructed us every which way. But getting help from the media, even off the record, was a two-way street. As I said, quite candidly, the media, in the quid pro quo of things, had to be "fed."

Judge Matsch understood this, then and later. At one point during the trial, he elaborated on the theme: "Counsel for the accused do not have an institutional structure for investigation comparable to that of law enforcement agencies serving the prosecution. . . . Defense lawyers have a legitimate need to communicate with the news media in preparing for trial. It is not uncommon for lawyers on both sides of a criminal case to do a bit of bartering in the information market."

I couldn't have said it better myself. But at the same time, and he made this very clear, he didn't want me trying the case in the media or prejudicing the government's case unfairly.

It was a fine line.

Still, I came away from that meeting exhilarated. The playing field might never be quite level in the Oklahoma City bombing case—there was just no way it could be—but Judge Matsch was doing everything in his power, given the limitations of his power, to support our efforts for an adequate defense.

O n February 23, we filed a motion with the court requesting authorization to be present at the exhumation of Lakesha Levy's body. The court agreed. Airman First Class Levy had been buried in Louisiana, and Dr. Iscan from Florida and Robert Warren, a recent addition to our legal staff, went as our representatives. When the casket was opened, it was found that the body's left leg was not in fact attached. Dr. Choy had made a mistake, and the government's theory, as DNA tests confirmed, proved correct: The ninth left leg was indeed Lakesha Levy's.

But what about the left leg that had been buried with her body? If it wasn't hers, then whose was it?

The state medical examiner had no match. He and his people still believed that this leg, like its predecessor, belonged to a young black female, but no one could say with certainty. Sex was determined by bone measurement, at least in part, and this newly unidentified leg fell into the gray zone.

The state medical examiner and the government were content to leave it there—an unexplained loose end to the case. And so, outwardly, was I. I never again mentioned the leg publicly or suggested the defense might one day use it. As they say in intelligence circles, I let it "go dark."

At the same time, I got authority from the court to hire T. K. Marshall. Marshall was the expert pathologist Bernard Knight had recommended during our visit in Cardiff. I also obtained a judicial order permitting me to take photographs of the victims out of the country.

The photographic evidence, I should say, had already been a bone of contention between me and Joe Hartzler. That is, I had asked for copies of the pictures without telling him why I wanted them, and he, in turn, had typically refused.

What did I want them for anyway? he wanted to know. Did I really need them? Didn't I realize how god-awful they were, and how terrible it would be if they were ever leaked, and what that would do to the families of the victims?

To which I replied, yes, I understood all that, but this was still a murder case and I wanted the pictures.

It took a court order. More delay, more costs to the taxpayers.

I flew over again to the United Kingdom in mid-March to see T. K. Marshall. This time I showed up at the United Airlines gate with a briefcase handcuffed to my wrist, containing the photographs of the 168 deceased victims. In so doing, I caused no end of consternation to airlines personnel, not to say to any passengers who noticed what was going on, but I had a sealed letter from the judge to the pilot of the plane, explaining who I was and that the briefcase, by court order, wasn't to leave my hands during the flight. The pilot, on reading it, escorted me back to my seat personally, and, at least as far as I know, none of my fellow passengers debarked in New York during the layover.

In addition to the photos, I brought along for Dr. Marshall copies of all the documentation the defense had received till that point concerning the victims and the bomb, including the medical examiner's autopsies. I had four questions to put to him:

- Could he evaluate for us, from these photographs and documents, the degree of professionalism and thoroughness of the work done by the medical examiner?

- From examining the photographs and the various reports, did he have an opinion on whether more than one bomb might have been used?

- What was his opinion on the matter of the leg?

- Was there anything else in the materials before him that we should be aware of?

Dr. Jordan, in Marshall's estimate, had done a tremendous job.

"You know," he told me, "we live with this every day, and we've lived with it for thirty years, but in the States, well, acts of terrorism of this magnitude are virtually unknown, aren't they? This being the case, I can't say anything other than the highest praise for Dr. Jordan and his staff. I tell you, their work was absolutely first-rate."

On the second question—about the bomb—he saw no evidence for anything other than the truck bomb. At first glance, he said, looking at the pictures, there were a couple of victims that might suggest a different type of bomb, but he had excluded it. He personally didn't think a case could be made for more than one bomb.

Then we came to the leg. He readily understood how the mistake had been made. Undoubtedly, he said, two legs that had been severed had been found very close to each other, and the rescue people had put the one with Lakesha Levy probably because it was closest to her body. It would then have been an easy, and common, mistake to think it was attached.

But then Dr. Marshall paused. He eyed me in that way the British have of signaling that they are about to say something important.

"You know," he said quietly, "this leg doesn't belong to a victim."

"What are you telling me?" I said.

"I'm telling you the leg belongs to the bomber. Or at least *a* bomber."

"How do you know that?"

"I have several reasons. You see, in the Western world, there is no such thing as an unclaimed innocent victim. Everyone gets claimed, sooner or later, unless there's a particular reason not to. Now in very large cities, where sometimes a pauper will die, say, of overexposure to the cold or a cause of that type, well, yes, he may not have been identified before his burial. But eventually, even in a case like that, someone will come forward, looking for him.

"But putting a situation like that aside, in a case involving an airplane crash, a bomb, a mass killing, there are *never* unrecovered, unidentified, innocent victims. In all the years in Ireland, we identified every innocent person that was killed. There is never an unknown *victim*."

Marshall pointed out that, in our culture, everyone has somebody, somewhere. A relative, a friend, a neighbor. We care for our dead. Then, too, medical science has progressed to a point of great sophistication in the identification of bodies. DNA testing has made a tremendous difference.

Finally, he said, the very fact that just the leg had been found suggested strongly that it was at, or very near, the seat of the explosion.

Dr. Knight had made the same point, but Marshall had had personal experience. He told me the case of the unaccounted-for penis.

In the aftermath of an IRA bombing, rescuers had recovered the bodies of all the victims. All male victims had their own penises. But there was an additional detached penis that could be connected to no one. Marshall and his fellow investigators had come, inevitably, to the conclusion that the penis could only have belonged to the "mule," the terrorist who had carried the bomb. In addition, there had been some evidence suggesting that the bomb had exploded prematurely, and Marshall said that if he had to guess the bomb must have been resting on something in the bomber's lap—a board or a plank?—that had protected just the area of his penis at the moment of the blast.

Over a year later in the Denver courtroom, Pat Ryan called Dr. Fred Jordan to the witness stand. Pat's was a relatively perfunctory direct examination, but I was able, when it became the defense's turn, to recall Jordan, and I then led him laboriously through the details of how his office had handled the recovered bodies. The bodies had been kept in three refrigerated semis across from the medical examiner's building, with an honor guard from the Oklahoma National Guard watching over them before and after the body bags were carried, one by one, into the morgue. I led Jordan into describing—again, meticulously—the procedures they'd used for classifying the remains, identifying them, naming them, and in particular how carefully and sensitively they'd handled the body parts.

It certainly must have seemed as though I was enhancing the government's case for them, that is, that here was an exceptional pathologist who had done everything right. The jury, the prosecutors, Judge Matsch too, could only have been wondering what on earth I was doing it for.

Then I asked Jordan if they'd been able to match all the body parts to the victims.

No, he replied. But most of the parts they hadn't been able to match up were very small.

But wasn't there a leg among them, I asked? From the government's table, I could hear papers rustling. Maybe they'd guessed what was coming.

Yes, Fred Jordan replied.

And isn't it so that you haven't, to this day, been able to match that leg?

It was suddenly very quiet in the courtroom, and I could have kissed Fred Jordan for his reply.

"You're absolutely right, Mr. Jones," he said. "The truth of the matter is we had eight victims with traumatically amputated left legs missing, and we have nine left legs. We have one leg too many."

I was aware of the jury sitting up straight in their seats, and I caught a smile on Judge Matsch's face. I pushed on:

"Do you mean to tell me that with all your efforts, and with the FBI Laboratory, and Walter Reed Hospital, and the national this and that, and DNA testing, you still cannot match up this leg?"

"That's right," Jordan said.

Pat Ryan joined the fray then, trying to cross-examine his own witness, unable to get very far. The facts, after all, were the facts. And once he was done, while the drama of the leg was still hot in the minds of the jury, I called Dr. T. K. Marshall to the witness stand.

The good doctor's credentials were impeccable. (Fred Jordan— off the witness stand—called him "a living legend" in their field.) And when I asked him the big question, he answered:

"The working assumption has to be, until it is excluded, that the leg in question belonged to a bomber."

It was one of our best moments, and the following morning, *The New York Times* confirmed it on the front page. A picture of Dr. Marshall and me sat atop the headline: "McVeigh Defense Suggest Real Bomber Died in the Blast."

In preparation for what I knew would be an emotionally and physically challenging trial, I took a few days off in mid-December and drove down to Houston, Texas, stopping along the way in Tyler to revisit some of my old haunts, including the elementary school and my high school in Bellaire, Texas, where I had been invited to speak to the debate class. The invitation held special meaning for me, since my early interest in the law had been stimulated by my high school debate coaches, Mollie Martin and Jeanne Wootters. I was surprised to find that there were still faculty members present who were at Bellaire when I was a student more than forty years before.

From Bellaire I retraced my steps to Enid in order to be home by Christmas. A few nights before Christmas Eve, Sherrel told me that I would receive my Christmas present from her that evening. The Enid Phillips Symphony was performing Handel's *Messiah*. Sherrel was to have a role in the performance, but I did not know what it was. I went and, at her request, sat in the balcony. Then, toward the end, as the house lights were dimmed, Sherrel stepped forward to sing, solo, "I Know My Redeemer Liveth." This selection is my very favorite in the entire work, and as I sat there in the darkness and watched her, I knew she was singing it for me. On that evening, with a light snow falling outside, surrounded by friends, listening to my wife sing, I knew it was a special moment that would be with me forever—and that it was her way of telling me how much she loved me and how proud she was of me. In a larger sense, of course, it was also a reaffirmation of the resurrection of the dead in the life to come.

On the last day of 1996, a small convoy headed north out of Enid, Oklahoma, on U.S. 81, in the direction of Kansas. One security car with two armed men led the way, and another brought up the rear. In-between were two large trucks loaded with the office furniture, files, equipment, and documents of the McVeigh defense team. To all intents and purposes, Jones, Wyatt & Roberts was closing up shop in Oklahoma and moving to Denver, at least for the next six months, and the cost of moving all the furniture was but a fraction of what it would have cost to rent or buy it. Furthermore, when the prosecution had moved north from Oklahoma City to Denver with an escort of U.S. marshals and FBI agents, it'd made quite a production out of all the "evidence" it was bringing—evidence that required three trucks to transport. I wanted the defense's case to be just as "big," and so it was, the next morning, New Year's Day, when we unpacked in Denver under the eyes of television cameras.

The security arrangements, though, were not for show. Although I haven't dwelled on it, we'd had our share of threats and incidents, particularly around my home. Early on, Sherrel and I had electronic gates and large arc lights installed at our own expense, to which the court added electronic monitors, motion detectors, and armed guards. In addition to the threatening phone calls—and a few people who'd managed to get close to the house through the woods at the rear, where you had to jump two fences, ford a creek, and cross a briar patch—we'd had drive-by shootings from the highway. Maybe they were all college kids, maybe they weren't. I guess people can get used to almost anything, but it was a little like living in a fishbowl. Denver, we expected, would be the same.

In any case, our little caravan moved steadily north and west across Kansas. Sherrel and I were riding behind the lead car, and it was after dark when we pulled off the highway for a pit stop. We didn't know exactly where we were, only that we'd been on the road a long time and that, tired though we might have been, we still had a long way to go.

I came back out first, just ahead of Sherrel, and I noticed two young dudes wearing cowboy hats who were hanging out nearby. They were giving us the eye. I was just getting into the car when I realized the young men had stepped into Sherrel's path.

"Is that who we think it is?" one of them asked her.

I'm not sure she answered anything.

"And is all that Tim's stuff?" with a wave at the trucks.

Sherrel nodded.

It all happened so fast, I scarcely had time to move. But at that, the two young men took off their hats, stepped out of her way, and with a gallant bow said, "Well then, welcome to Colorado, ma'am."

Without realizing, we had crossed the state line.

PART

III

10

PRIOR KNOWLEDGE

One night in January 1997, shortly after we'd moved to Denver, I had dinner at the Brown Palace with Mike Boettcher of NBC News. The Brown Palace was built by one of Mike's great uncles and he always got special treatment because of the family tie. I knew Boettcher and his brother, Fred, who was a very successful lawyer in Ponca City, Oklahoma, and I always thought NBC really blew it by not letting Mike work full-time on the Oklahoma City bombing. As it was, he came and went, but, even part-time, he was still able to develop more newsworthy material than most other reporters, giving NBC an edge.

In the course of conversation, Mike said, very casually, "Hey, have you heard about this gal that got herself arrested in Tulsa?"

"What gal?" I said.

"That's right. They're saying she was an ATF informant and that she was at Elohim City, knew Strassmeir, and so forth."

There'd been rumors from the beginning about an informant at Elohim City. I'd been told about a *Newsweek* story that had been pulled at the last minute. Strassmeir, himself, in the *The Sunday Telegraph* (London) coverage, had said so, insisting, at the same time, that he hadn't been it. But I'd always thought that could just have been Andy the German's way of covering his own backside.

"*Who's* saying it?" I asked Boettcher.

"She's saying it."

"But who's she? You're not kidding me, are you?"

"No, I'm not. This gal—her name is Carol Howe—she and her boyfriend were questioned by the FBI. Apparently he'd been making public threats about blowing up some more federal buildings. The FBI arrested the boyfriend. He's been charged; she hasn't. It turns out she was at Elohim City before the bombing."

"What's the boyfriend's name?" I asked.

"Viefhaus." He spelled it for me.

"And the girl?"

"Carol Howe."

I found Rob Nigh in the office, after dinner. Neither of us had ever heard of a Carol Howe. I told Rob what Boettcher had said and asked him to get on to Tulsa, first thing in the morning. Mr. Rob, it will be remembered, had gone off to be assistant public defender in Tulsa after he left Enid.

"You're not going to believe this," he said in my office, the next morning, "but guess who's representing James Dodson Viefhaus Jr. as a public defender?"

I had no idea.

"Craig Bryant," he said.

Like Rob, Craig Bryant had once worked for me.

"Craig Bryant? Well, let's get him on the phone!"

This we did, and Craig told us the story. Initially both Viefhaus and Howe had been taken into custody. Howe's daddy, though, was a former president of MAPCO, which is a company listed on the New York Stock Exchange and a very big deal in Tulsa. Apparently Howe had been dating Viefhaus, who had some kind of tape recording on his answering machine in which he threatened to blow up federal buildings. Carol Howe's voice was allegedly heard on the tape too, and the prosecutors had said at the arraignment that they were going to charge both of them. According to the indictment, Viefhaus and Howe were cofounders of the Nationalist Socialist Alliance of Oklahoma and had used the telephone line at the house they shared in Tulsa as an information line for the Aryan Intelligence Network. Armed with a search warrant, the FBI had raided the house and discovered not only the tape but also materials that could be used in bombmaking and a virtual library of how-to manuals.

But when the indictment had come down, only Viefhaus had been named.

"I wanted him to stay away from this woman," Craig said. "Obviously, she was a snitch and she'd set him up," he continued. "I didn't want him to have anything to do with her. Well, two or three days after that, the phone rings and it's Carol Howe, and she's mad as hell. 'You got it all wrong,' she tells me. 'The reason they didn't indict me was because I know about Oklahoma City and Mahon and Strassmeir. I love him, and I didn't set him up, and I'm not a snitch, and all that stuff they found in the house was stuff I got for the ATF from Elohim City.'"

As soon as we got off the phone with Craig Bryant, I called Allen Smallwood in Tulsa. Smallwood was Carol Howe's lawyer, a very good lawyer too. Carol's daddy had hired him, I supposed, but Carol's daddy had no interest in helping Timothy McVeigh, and Smallwood had little enough to share with us. Still, once we got the court papers from Tulsa, it became pretty clear what had happened: A small-scale FBI operation mounted against Viefhaus had accidentally bumped into something it never should have bumped into, namely, Carol Howe.

I requested an immediate meeting with Judge Matsch. I told him what we'd found out—that the government had had an informant at Elohim City.

Needless to say, Beth Wilkinson had been expecting this. When Judge Matsch asked her if it was true, she said, yes, that it was, but only up to March 1995.

"But why," I wanted to know, "weren't we told about this before?"

Wilkinson had been waiting for this too.

Why, Mr. Jones, of course you were told about this. It was in Batch Number So-and-So, Insert Number Thus-and-Such. You received it in January 1996.

I knew there had to be a "but-for" in that, somewhere.

I wasn't wrong either.

"Of course," Wilkinson said, "I can understand how you couldn't find it right away. There were some misspellings in it."

"Do you have a copy with you?" I asked.

Of course, she didn't.

She'd succeeded, at least, in breaking the momentum. I went back to the office and, sure enough, there it was, an insert describing an interview, conducted on April 21, 1995, by Special Agent James

R. Blanchard of the FBI and Special Agent Angie Finley of the ATF with "FINLEY's confidential source 'CAROL.'"

In earlier filings with the court, answering to specific court orders that all 302s and related inserts pertaining to Mahon and Strassmeir be furnished to the court and us, the government admitted it had "neglected" to include this insert. Because of the misspellings, Beth Wilkinson told Judge Matsch, their system's search mechanisms failed to turn it up. Her carefully crafted denial may have been correct, but I simply did not believe Beth Wilkinson's statement. Arguably, because of the misspellings and incompleteness a defense computer scan or even attorney review, in isolation, might not have picked up its significance, but it strains credulity that Beth Wilkinson's attention hadn't been called to the whole incident. She and the government had to have known what it was. Perhaps they were hoping it would slide past us because of the misspellings, and it did. But for the arrest of Viefhaus, we would not likely ever have caught it or forced the government specifically to call it to our attention.

The worst of the misspellings was "B-o-b L-a-m-a-r." Ask a computer to search for Robert Millar and not even the most sophisticated of programs known to man would come up with Bob Lamar. Elohim City was spelled "Elohim" once and referred to afterward as simply "EC", Strassmeir was spelled as "Strasmeyer," and Mahon as "Mehaun." Carol Howe was referred to only as "Carol." (These "misspellings," I must say, made me as suspicious as I could be, in that Angela Finley had participated in the interview, on which the insert was based, with FBI Special Agent Blanchard. Every other report Finley filed herself—and there were many—had these names spelled correctly.)

As for the defense, since scanning is an expensive element in a computer system, we'd waited until we made the move to Denver, at which point we'd had the software we wanted custom-designed and installed. We were just going online about the time we first heard of Carol Howe. Although I'm sure every last piece of the thousands of pieces of paper we'd been given by the other side had been handled by one or more of our attorneys, we'd missed it. Without a last name for "CAROL" and with the misspellings, it had simply slipped between the cracks. We'd had it for a year.

According to the insert, "Carol" had started going to "EC" in June 1994, introduced there because she'd called a racist hotline owned and operated by one "Dennis Mehaun," who did paramilitary training at Elohim City. She said Strassmeir, in September and October 1994, had "discussed assassinations, bombings, and mass shootings." He "frequently talks about direct action against the U.S. Federal Government."

She described Elohim City residents as being "ultra-militant white separatists" and said that Odinism was popular among the younger members. She named *Mein Kampf*, *The Silent Brotherhood*, and *The Turner Diaries* as required reading. She said a Branch Davidian flag hung in the Elohim City church and that there was, on the one hand, a lot of hatred toward the government for the Waco raid and, on the other, the fear that Elohim City could be next.

And then, there was this paragraph:

MEHAUN has talked with CAROL about targeting federal installations for destruction through bombings, such as the IRS Building, the Tulsa Federal Building and the Oklahoma City Federal Building. Mehaun has also discussed a plan for destroying power lines from Oklahoma City to Catousa, Oklahoma, during the hottest time of the summer. MEHAUN reasons this will create a panic, and without air conditioning, mass race riots would begin.

And this revelation:

"Carol" told her interviewers (on April 21, 1995, two days after the bombing) that she thought she had seen the two men identified in the composite drawings as UnSub #1 and UnSub #2 at Elohim City. She thought they were two brothers, whom she knew as "Pete" and "Tony." When she saw television pictures of Tim McVeigh, she said they didn't look like Pete.

And all of it right in our own files the whole time. And ending with this paragraph:

CAROL attempted to use ATF equipment to make a consensually recorded telephone call to MEHAN [sic] on April 21, 1995, but was unsuccessful in reaching him. SA FINLEY supervised CAROL in these attempts.

We were amazed. But this, as it turned out, was only the beginning.

In Tulsa, Carol Howe replaced Smallwood as her lawyer with Clark Brewster. During an in camera hearing in Tulsa relating to the Viefhaus case, Angela Finley, Howe's old handler at ATF, admitted that Howe had been her paid informant. Howe, meanwhile, had already given the first of several interviews to J. D. Cash of the McCurtain County *Gazette*, and there was a sudden jolt of media attention to this otherwise obscure case. In this fevered climate and possibly in an effort to muzzle her, the federal prosecutors decided to indict Howe too.

After the indictment, Clark Brewster demanded to see Howe's ATF file, and the court so ordered. Brewster took one look at it and told Judge Michael Burrage, who was presiding over the case, that it was exculpatory to Timothy McVeigh. With the judge's permission, he wanted to send it to Judge Matsch. Burrage told him to go ahead, and he did.

And there it was. Judge Matsch called us over on a Sunday morning. Beth Wilkinson read it first, and then I did.

I must confess that some, but not much, of what Judge Matsch gave to us that Sunday I had already seen. And this is how.

One morning, just after the news of Carol Howe had come out—this was before her indictment, when Alan Smallwood was still representing her—the phone in my Denver apartment rang at about 7 A.M. It was Larry Mackey, the number-two prosecutor on the government's team. He was calling to tell me that Carol Howe was going to give a press conference that very afternoon, at which she would claim that the government, thanks to her, had prior knowledge of the bombing, and he wanted to know if I would join with them . . . in denouncing it!

I was dumbfounded. I respected Mackey and rather liked him. One reporter said of him that he was the type who could cut your throat and you'd never know it because he'd be smiling the whole while. She meant that as a compliment! As for me, I'd found him straight and highly competent. Why, though, was he calling me? How on earth could he be asking me to join the prosecution in affirming that there'd been no prior knowledge?

Was this some kind of trap, I wondered? Or a sign that they actually *had* had prior knowledge? Were they trying to do what H. R. Halderman, Nixon's chief of staff, once said *couldn't* be done, that is, "putting the toothpaste back in the tube?"

Although I kept it to myself, I was skeptical about there being any press conference. As far as I knew right then, Carol Howe had disappeared. There were rumors that she was hiding out on the family ranch, somewhere in central Texas. I'd had our own bloodhounds looking for her too, and we suspected she was holed up in the family condo at Vail, Colorado. Knowing Smallwood and imagining her father, I thought the last thing in the world she would do was hold a press conference. Besides, I'd heard nothing about one from the media people.

"Larry," I said, "how could I possibly agree with your side when I don't know what information Carol Howe gave the government in the first place?"

It was a very logical answer. And so, I guess, was his response.

"The FBI will be in your office in two hours," he said. "They'll have all her statements. You can see for yourself."

They probably figured I was going to get to see it all anyway. I'd been pressing the discovery issue through the court, and the government's stalling had begun to antagonize Judge Matsch. Getting me to help them was undoubtedly a long shot, but they may have been scared enough to try it, because a Carol Howe press conference, if there'd ever been one, would have been a blockbuster media event. In fact if she'd actually held one and said before the media right then what she would say later, I doubt the government would have dared indict her.

The FBI agents didn't show up in my office till 2 P.M. I suspect this was because the file was being sanitized in the meantime. All there was was a slim folder of summaries of Carol Howe's reports and statements, fragmentary to say the least. I couldn't take any notes, make any photocopies, and they sat with me while I read them, but the statements confirmed what Mackey and his cohorts feared. She had been an informant for many months. She had been to Elohim City. She had been polygraphed and passed. She had been paid for what she was doing. Although there was no one direct proof of "prior knowledge," a number of things Howe had said certainly would have suggested to any experienced investigator that there was the real possibility of a revolutionary act of terrorism emanating out of Elohim City.

After all, six months before the bombing, Howe had reported to Finley that Andreas Strassmeir—a known neo-Nazi with access to weapons, serving as director of security in a Christian Identity compound and associating with people clearly linked to prior plans for attacking the Murrah Building—had been tired of the inaction and had talked of murder, assassination, bombings. As her report made clear, the federal government and its employees and facilities were the target. Once again, intelligence—in this instance the ATF and FBI—had refused to accept, or act on, the possibility of what was staring them in the face. What was the point of having a paid informant inside Elohim City? So that Agent Finley in Tulsa could file her reports and nothing be done about it?

Meanwhile, 168 people were dead.

After I finished reading the summaries, I handed the folder back to the agents. I asked them to tell Mr. Mackey I couldn't assist him. As it was, Carol Howe never held her press conference.

There is a highly unpleasant sequel to this episode. A few days later, in a letter to Beth Wilkinson about Carol Howe, I made an oblique reference to the phone call I'd received from Mackey. Two or three days after that, he himself called me. He denied that we'd had any such conversation. I had the distinct impression he was speaking "for the record" and that another person or persons might have been listening in. I therefore made some noncommittal response, but sometime later I had occasion to catch Larry alone, and, looking him straight in the eye, I asked why in hell he'd denied that he'd called me when we both knew he had?

He returned my stare.

"You're right," he said. "I did call you."

"Then why call me to tell me you didn't?"

"Look," he replied. "I'd gone out on a limb. I was the only one who wanted to call you in the first place. The others said you would use it against us. I went ahead and did it anyway, and so they made me call you back and deny it had ever happened."

I'd figured as much. He didn't say who "they" were, and I didn't ask him. I simply told him to consider the matter closed. And so it was.

But the matter of Carol Howe was far from closed, and it was incumbent upon us to learn quickly all we could about her.

She was born into an affluent Oklahoma family. Petite, blonde, and very attractive, she had been an accomplished equestrian, a Miss Teenage America contestant, and a Tulsa debutante. She became a white supremacist, by her own account, in February 1994, after she was accosted by three black men who chased her onto the roof of a building and pushed her off. In the fall, she severely damaged both heels, a condition that continued to plague her several years later.

She met Dennis Mahon, she said, by calling him on his racist hotline, and not long after that she became his lover, although later she started legal proceedings against him when he threatened her. It was Mahon, nevertheless, who introduced her to Elohim City, and it was through Mahon that she met, to quote her ATF file, "Andy LNU, German male, who is head of security for Elohim City."

Howe went undercover for ATF on August 25, 1994, having been recruited by Special Agent Finley. No one outside ATF knows for certain how or why she was recruited, but the overture to her occurred almost immediately after she had filed for a domestic protective order against Mahon in Tulsa County District Court. Mahon's name would certainly have been familiar to the ATF's Tulsa office. Probably, ATF got wind of what had happened and, after a little investigative work on Howe's background, decided she was reliable. She passed a polygraph test, signed an ATF contract that said that she had agreed to assist in an official investigation for the bureau, and was given the code designation CI–57230–183 (abridged in Finley's reports to CI–183). She was paid $125 per week. During the period she worked for ATF, she forwarded some seventy reports and passed periodic polygraph tests. Finley's own first report was labeled "Sensitive," which in the ATF system means that copies of it automatically went to her Tulsa boss, to Lester Martz, the special agent in charge of the Dallas office, and to ATF headquarters in Washington. Finley's file was labeled "White Aryan Resistance, W.A.R.," and it was assigned to a category entitled "Terrorist/Extremist."

Finley, after identifying Mahon as the local leader of WAR, relayed the following from CI–183:

> Mahon has made numerous statements regarding the conversion of firearms into fully automatic weapons, the manufacture and use of silencers and the manufacture and use of explosive devices. . . . Mahon and his organization are preparing for a race war and war with the government in the near future, and it is believed that they are rapidly stockpiling weapons.

None of this in and of itself would have startled anyone accustomed to white-supremacist rhetoric, but, according to a later report from CI–183, Mahon had bragged that some five years before, in Michigan, he had made a five-hundred-pound ammonium nitrate bomb and blown it up under a truck.

After a November 1994 visit to Elohim City, CI–183 reported him to Finley, who in turn reported that "Andy LNU" (who of course turned out to be Andreas Carl Strassmeir) was out to "destroy the United States Government with direct action and operations such as assassinations, bombings and mass shootings." It was time, Andy was saying to anyone who happened to be listening, to stop talking and start blowing things up.

In the ensuing months, CI–183 spent a great deal of time at Elohim City, sometimes weeks at a stretch and almost all weekends. Reverend Millar, according to her reports, was preaching preparation for the holy war to come. CI–183 also reported that Mahon and Strassmeir made three trips to Oklahoma City, one in the company of Millar—in November and December 1994 and again in February 1995. Although Howe accompanied them only on one of these trips, she believed they were casing targets, and there was discussion of the federal buildings in both Tulsa and Oklahoma City. She claimed she reported this to "Angie." The government, of course, later denied this, as they sought to discredit everything Howe did and said. And by pure coincidence—of course—Agent Finley's monthly report for December 1994, at roughly the time Howe would have been passing on this information, had somehow disappeared from the ATF archives and was never found.

With the cat out of the bag, thanks to the ATF file and the media rush to seize on this new twist to the story, the government, true to form, fought to limit the damage. They made much of how Carol Howe had been terminated as an informant some three weeks before the bombing because of an alleged suicide attempt, her instability, her unreliability. They quoted Special Agent Finley's deactivation note, saying that "CI–183 was no longer loyal nor competent to operate as an informant for ATF." Oh yes, they admitted, she had been reactivated after the bombing and outfitted with a wire, but just to make a quick run back into Elohim City. But then there was the following, which they couldn't erase—a report from Special Agent Finley dated May 22, 1995, and signed off on by her boss, David E. Roberts, resident agent in charge (RAC) of the Tulsa Office, on its way up the chain of command.

I quote it in its entirety:

This is a 30 day status report in the investigation of the White Aryan Resistance and the violations of federal firearm, explosive and conspiracy laws in both the Northern and Eastern Judicial Districts of Oklahoma.

On April 20, 1996, this agent was contacted by CI–53270–183 in regard to the bombing in Oklahoma City, Oklahoma. CI–183 stated that he/she believed suspect #2 resembled one of the residents of Elohim City, Tony Ward.

On April 21, 1995, this agent, along with Special Agent John Eisenhoover, traveled to Tulsa to pick up CI–183 and transport him/her to Oklahoma City. CI–183 was debriefed by Special Agents from ATF and FBI. A lead sheet was then completed. It was determined that CI–183 would be sent to Elohim City to obtain any intelligence relating to the bombing.

On April 29, 1995, CI–183 met with area W.A.R. leader, Dennis Mahon, and obtained several video tapes regarding the movement. CI–183 stated that they discussed alibis for April 19, 1995 and the components of the explosive. CI–183 stated that Mahon mentioned the name of a man familiar in explosives who lives in Illinois. Mahon used the name Pierson, however, he was not sure. CI–183 stated that Mahon could have been referring to Paulson because he cannot remember people's names.

On May 2, 1995, CI–183 traveled to Elohim City and stayed for three days.

On May 3, 1995, this agent met with CI–183 and debriefed him/her. This agent then took CI–183 to Oklahoma City to meet with ATF and FBI agents for further debriefing. CI–183 stated that while he/she was inside, a news crew was also there doing a story and that he/she was asked to stay out of sight. CI–183 was excluded from the daily worship meetings due to the media attention. CI–183 did speak to an individual who stated, 'There is a big secret out here.' CI–183 was also informed by Zara Patterson IV that James Ellison was now residing at Elohim City, however, CI–183 did not see him. Ellison was the former leader of the Covenant, Sword and Arm of the Lord in Arkansas. CI–183 stated that he/she had viewed the freshly dug grave of Snell, the man executed in Arkansas on April 19, 1995 for the slaying of an Arkansas trooper. CI–183 was informed that Robert Millar had attended the execution and transported the body to his compound for burial. CI–183 stated that individuals spoken with were supportive of the bombing of the building in Oklahoma City.

On May 18, 1995, this agent met with CI–183 to discuss returning to Elohim City in order to determine what the 'big secret' is and to attempt to identify suspect #2.

On May 22, 1995, this agent was contacted by CI–183 who stated that he/she had been contacted the previous day and informed that he/she had better not go to Elohim City. CI–183 stated that the person called again on this day and gave him/her the same warning. CI–183 did not reveal the source at this time. CI–183 then stated that he/she had seen the numerous television broadcasts about Elohim City and was too frightened to go.

On May 24, 1995, this agent was informed by RAC, David Roberts, that Robert Millar suspected CI–183 of being a confidential informant. It was determined that CI–183 would not be sent to Elohim City at this time or in the future.

This investigation to remain open.

The two names that may be unfamiliar in the above are Paulson and Patterson. Paulson, spelled that way, means nothing to me. Paulsen, with an *e*, could have referred to Paulsen's Military Supply, a store near Madison, Wisconsin. A business card from the store was found in the Mercury Marquis at the time of Tim McVeigh's arrest, and David Paulsen, the son of the owner, was someone McVeigh had met at gun shows. But how Carol Howe might have known of David Paulsen I cannot say.

Zara Patterson was another Elohim City resident, already known to the defense. (Richard Reyna had interviewed him in January 1996.) Patterson apparently believed, in hindsight, that Strassmeir had been an agent provocateur, and interestingly, in marked contrast to what Mahon had told me in our phone conversation around the same time, Patterson observed to Reyna that whenever Strassmeir wanted to buy something, he just pulled out his credit card.

However, I've quoted Finley's end-of-May status report in full not for Paulson or Patterson or even to commend its spelling but because it undermines the prosecution's "case" against Carol Howe. If "he/she" was so "unreliable" that she had to be dismissed, then why was "he/she" sent back into Elohim City after the bombing? Finley is quite explicit on the subject. At her debriefing of April 21, which we already know from the 302 insert with the garbled spellings was conducted by FBI Agents Blanchard and Finley, *it was determined* that Howe be sent back in.

Moreover, as will become clear, Howe did this at considerable personal risk and—as we learned still later—at a premium in pay. And some three weeks later, Special Agent Finley is talking to her about going back in yet another time. Are we to assume Finley took this initiative on her own? Of course not. The investigation of the bombing was in full stride, and the FBI was by then fully in charge. Elohim City, as the status report attests, was a focal point of attention (for everyone except, according to Beth Wilkinson, the government), as well as a potentially dangerous place to be. Certainly, Finley had to have been acting with the knowledge and approval of her superiors and, one would have to think, with the knowledge and approval of the FBI.

Finally, the mission was called off by Finley's boss. It was RAC Roberts who learned that Reverend Millar was suspicious of Howe. How he learned that, we don't know. Perhaps it was the FBI that told him. Or some other informant? (It would be worthy of a Mel Brooks comedy were it not also part of the awful tragedy of the bombing, but at various times virtually every one of the principals at or around Elohim City—Strassmeir, Mahon, James Ellison, Robert Millar himself—was suspected of informing.)

CI–183, "unreliable" though she may have been in the eyes of the prosecution, nonetheless stayed on ATF's books, after she was reactivated, until late 1996. She considered herself to be in danger, at one point even asking the FBI for protection (she was turned down), and in April 1996 Special Agent Finley wrote a "threat assessment" report, approved by Roberts, that contained the following:

> This informant is involved with the Oklahoma City bomb case which is pending prosecution in Denver and was the key in identifying individuals at Elohim City, which is tied to the Oklahoma City Bombing Case.... The FBI is the lead agency on this case, however many other federal state and local agencies are involved. Individuals who pose immediate danger to CI–53270–183 are: (1) Dennis Mahon, (2) Members of Elohim City, and (3) any sympathizer to McVeigh, i.e., militias.... This agent has known CI–53270–183 for approximately two years and can assert that this informant has not been overly paranoid or fearful during undercover operations. This agent believes that he/she could be in serious danger when associates discover his/her identity.

Clearly ATF viewed Carol Howe as an asset of some value. Certainly Agent Finley did, as did her boss, David Roberts, and presumably Lester Martz in Dallas. What individual FBI agents may have thought, we do not know, although it was enough, presumably, to have sent her back into Elohim City with a wire in the days immediately following the bombing.

As for the prosecution, by early 1997 they viewed Carol Howe as an ever-present danger to their case, and they were ready to go to any lengths to squelch and/or discredit her. They had some success too. Don Thrasher, a dogged and resourceful producer for ABC's *20/20*, and Roger Charles, a retired Marine Corps officer who'd been a freelance journalist and who worked with Thrasher as an assistant producer (and later joined the defense team as a highly valued investigator), had been following the story, thanks in part to my leads and with some help from J. D. Cash. Barbara Walters had done a *20/20* piece in January implying, without coming right out and saying it, that the government had had prior warning of the bombing. Then Thrasher and Charles succeeded in getting an off-camera interview with Carol Howe and, in mid-February, were about to take the conversation onto Peter Jennings's primetime Evening News when at the eleventh hour the piece was killed. Thrasher was told that all of a sudden ABC News didn't find Howe "credible"—this despite the polygraph tests and the fact that everything she had told Thrasher and Charles was born out in the historical documentation. I was told by ABC News employees that the Justice Department had called repeatedly, importuning the network not to run the piece, and while ABC News would certainly deny they were pressured, I believe they were. The piece never aired.

Fortunately, NBC and Tom Brokaw saw it differently. Mike Boettcher did the reportage—balanced, fair, and not at all inflammatory. He simply told the truth, according to the record, as I've done here. None of this, of course, deterred Beth Wilkinson from writing to me, in the extraordinary last paragraph I've already mentioned of her letter to me dated February 6, 1997:

> As you know, in the days following the bombing the FBI and ATF pursued thousands of leads based on information obtained from a variety of sources. At no time did the FBI consider Andreas Strassmeir or Dennis Mahon a subject of the Oklahoma City bombing investigation. Nevertheless, agents collected information regarding these individuals and many others in hope of identifying any of the perpetrators.

Rereading this statement today, I can only say what I thought at the time: *Either Wilkinson was lying, or the Federal Bureau of Investigation, on whose findings the prosecution was based, was extraordinarily incompetent and unbelievably obtuse.*
There is no other possible explanation.

11
PHONE CALLS

From the very beginning, two things drove the prosecution absolutely to distraction. One was the prior knowledge issue, the idea that someone, somewhere would produce irrefutable proof that this or that branch of the federal government—be it the FBI, ATF, or U.S. Marshal's Office or the State Department, CIA, or some other agency you and I never even heard of—had known ahead of time that the Murrah Building was going to explode. The second was the merest suggestion of foreign sponsorship.

Every time one or the other came up, the government either denied it or struck back or both. Vehemently, venomously. Sometimes it was left to the people onstage, such as the time Joe Hartzler referred publicly to me and my "screwball theories." (Joe subsequently called me to apologize but then, in open court, denied that the reference was to me! This was quite a surprise to Nolan Clay of the *Daily Oklahoman* and Terri Watkins of KOCO-TV in Oklahoma City, who had video and audio recordings of his original statement.) But there were also subtler instances, where you could feel movement and manipulation behind the wings even though it was unclear who was pulling whose strings.

I'm thinking of Beth Wilkinson, who in April 1996 stated flatly to Judge Matsch in open court that the prosecution had no evidence of foreign involvement in the bombing. Not that the prosecution had no hard evidence, no credible evidence, no persuasive evidence, no qualified evidence. But that they had *no* evidence.

I'm thinking in the same context, if I may backtrack, of the strange case of Vincent Cannistraro.

As I've mentioned, the government, having long ducked and delayed and stonewalled on the production of evidence we were entitled to, took, under pressure from Judge Matsch, the very opposite tack. They drowned us with material. All at once they would cascade 302s on us in a great dumping—some ten thousand 302s arriving virtually at the same time—in totally helter-skelter form. There could be, for instance, four or five or six 302s pertaining to one person, but you'd never know it until you went through the whole batch, one by one. And this is what we were obliged to do, a slow and painstaking and arduous task that all of us on the defense team shared in but that sometimes produced nuggets of information. And sometimes, as is clear from the following 302 insert, these nuggets were pure gold.

Three-oh-twos, as noted, were interviews carried out by FBI agents. Witness statements, in other words. "Inserts" were more like internal memoranda, written by FBI agents, of so-called non-relevant material. This one, if I'm not mistaken—Number 174A–OC–56120–SubE–6998, dated April 19, 1995—had slipped through in a batch of some seven hundred separate items. It was written up by Special Agent Kevin Foust in the Washington Metropolitan Field Office (WMFO), undoubtedly just after the telephone call it described, and it read as follows:

A telephone call was received 4/19/95 at WMFO from VINCENT CANNISTRARO. The call was received by SA KEVIN L. FOUST.

CANNISTRARO is identified as a retired high-ranking CIA official who has worked closely with WMFO in the past, specifically on the Pam Am 103 case. CANNISTRARO currently works as a consultant to ABC News in Washington, D.C. CANNISTRARO reported the following information:

CANNISTRARO received a telephone call at his residence earlier in the afternoon of 4.19.95. He described the caller as a Saudi Arabian citizen who works as a counterterrorist official for the

Saudi royal family. This person is basically responsible for developing intelligence to help prevent the royal family from becoming victims of a terrorist attack. The Saudi official said he was calling from Jeddah, Saudi Arabia.

The Saudi official told CANNISTRARO that he (the source) had information that there was a "squad" of people currently in the United States, very possibly Iraqis, who have been tasked with carrying out terrorist attacks against the United States. The Saudi claimed that he had seen a list of "targets", and that the first on the list was the federal building in Oklahoma City, Oklahoma. The second target was identified as the INS office in Houston, Texas, and the third target was the FBI office in Los Angeles, California.

CANNISTRARO could not comment on the reliability of the information, nor could he corroborate it. CANNISTRARO stated that he had known this Saudi individual for the past 15 to 20 years. CANNISTRARO promised to share any additional information that he might learn about this report, or any others.

Obviously the call, if Cannistraro had received it when he said he had, that is, during the afternoon of April 19, had nothing to do with prior knowledge or prior warning. The call would have been placed in the evening, Saudi Arabia time, some twelve hours *after* the bombing. What was surprising, assuming Cannistraro's account was accurate, was the impression that a high-level official in any intelligence service anywhere, calling twelve hours after the event and claiming to have seen the Murrah Building on a list of targets, would have had no knowledge that the target had already been hit. This in the era of the internet and CNN.

When I first read the insert, I had no idea who Special Agent Kevin L. Foust was. Probably, if I noticed his name at all, I'd have thought it was just the person who picked up the phone when Cannistraro called, because that was the tone in which it was written. But I learned, in the course of things, that Special Agent Foust was no Johnny-come-lately. He was a senior specialist in counterterrorism, with at least one very major investigation under his belt. He and Cannistraro, I learned further, had worked together before.

Needless to say, Vince Cannistraro had made no mention of the call from Saudi Arabia during our January meeting.

In March—March 1996, that is—I had occasion to see Laurie Mylroie in Washington. Mylroie, who was now working for us as an expert on Middle East terrorism (Cannistraro himself had recommended her to us) joined Ann Bradley and me for lunch at the Occidental restaurant. I braced her with the story of Cannistraro's Saudi connection.

At first, Mylroie feigned ignorance, but when I pushed, asking why Vince wouldn't have told me about that, and she being a good friend of his, she said, "No, no, it just didn't happen. He never got any telephone call like that. If that's what the FBI is saying, they must have made it up."

Probably, I raised both eyebrows, one after the other.

"Look, I know Vince," Laurie said. "I love Vince. What he told the FBI was that an attempt would be made on President Bush's life when he went to Kuwait. But that was in '93, maybe '94. After Bush had been defeated in the election in any case. So that's what they must be mixing up."

"Laurie," I said, "I don't believe that for a minute. You're telling me that, in the midst of the single greatest act of terrorism in the history of the United States, a rogue FBI agent, down in the bowels of the Washington office with nothing but time on his hands, decided to commit a federal crime?"

"I don't understand what you're saying."

"I'm saying that under Title 18 of the United States Code paragraph 1001 it would have been a false statement for an agent to say he'd received such a phone call from the former chief of operations for the CIA counterterrorism division when he hadn't."

"Ohhh," Laurie said. "Well. You know, I think maybe you ought to talk to Vince about this."

I said, "Great. Where is he? I've left messages at both numbers I have for him."

"Well, why don't I call him and see if he'll be somewhere where you can call him in an hour or so?"

This she did. About an hour later I had Cannistraro on the phone.

"Steve, how are you?" he asked after I'd introduced myself.

"Fine," I replied. "I'm pursuing this matter of the telephone call you received from a source in Saudi Arabia."

"Steve, I just. . . . Well, I just don't remember that. I remember calling them about a threat on Bush if he went to Kuwait, but—"

"Vince," I interrupted, "I've got a copy of the FBI insert sitting right in front of me. Is what you're saying that the conversation never took place? That you never called Foust? Vince, I have a lot of trouble believing that in the aftermath of the bombing of the Alfred P. Murrah Building, an FBI agent had nothing better to do than invent a conversation between you and Saudi intelligence."

There was a pause. I was about to say that I had corroboration of sorts, but I didn't have to.

"Maybe I did receive such a call," Cannistraro said. "Now that I think about it, it sounds familiar. Strange, but I'd altogether forgotten about it."

Strange indeed. Had it happened? Well, yes, he thought it actually might have happened. But it didn't add up to anything, et cetera, et cetera.

"Well," I said finally, "what did happen?"

"Steve, I just don't know. I did get the call, yes, and I reported it. But I just don't know if it was credible or not."

This was a curious statement too. Cannistraro, according to the 302, had known, or claimed to have known, his Saudi caller for fifteen or twenty years. I learned later that "credible or not" Cannistraro had also reported it to the CIA and that the Saudi official held the rank of general.

I had all this in mind when Beth Wilkinson, ingenuous as ever, announced to the court that the government had no evidence of foreign involvement, and I pounced with the Cannistraro 302.

Wilkinson's retort was that there was nothing to it. "Oh, that?" she seemed to say. Mr. Cannistraro himself had said that the source was not credible. Besides, the government had no corroborating information.

Wrong.

I stood up in court.

"What do you mean, the source is not credible?" I asked. "He is clearly credible to the king of Saudi Arabia. According to this information, he's a senior official in the intelligence service, the mission of which is to protect the royal family. So at least in his own country he's credible. And Mr. Cannistraro has known him for fifteen to twenty years. Furthermore," I said, "you do have corroboration, at least in part."

I was referring to a call that had come in, the day of the bombing, to the FBI's Los Angeles Crisis Center. We knew of it, but it wasn't until the following September, in a formal letter addressed to Mike Tigar and myself and begun in characteristic bureaucratese—"In compliance with our ongoing *Brady* obligations"—that Beth Wilkinson acknowledged the call as follows:

> *Unknown Caller From An Islamic Group.* The crisis center in Los Angeles had received information that an unknown caller from an Islamic group (NFI) had claimed responsibility for the April 19, 1995 bombing of the federal building in Oklahoma City. In addition, the caller supposedly stated that the FBI and INS offices in Houston and Los Angeles were also targeted. No other details were provided. Additional information regarding this claim of responsibility has been requested from the field office. We will provide additional information if appropriate.

What makes this corroborative, of course, is the identification of the offices in Houston and Los Angeles as targets, both mentioned in the call Cannistraro had received. That Cannistraro did get such a call seems to me irrefutable, although none other than Joe Hartzler took a stab at it. One night in Denver, Joe, Larry Mackey, Rob Nigh, and I had dinner together. When the conversation came around to the Cannistraro call, Joe put his fork down and said, in all seriousness, "Did you ever stop to consider that he just made that up? Just made it up out of thin air?" And I thought to myself, *Sure, a man with one of the highest security clearances in the country, who served on the National Security Council staff and ran the counterterrorism division of the Central Intelligence Agency, has nothing better to do on the afternoon after the worst act of terrorism in our nation's history than call the FBI and invent this story, thereby committing a crime.*

Of course, it is conceivable that Cannistraro embellished it—the Saudi source's message—in reporting it to Foust, although I can't imagine why he would have done that. It is also possible that both Cannistraro's Saudi source and the unknown caller in Los Angeles were engaged in a disinformation campaign, seizing the occasion of the bombing to point a finger at their enemies in the Middle East. But there is another reason—a second FBI document, as I will shortly relate—to believe that the warning was genuine.

Almost immediately after our exchange before Judge Matsch, however, I had occasion to realize the lengths Wilkinson and the government would go to protect what they saw as their own interests. Just before Tim McVeigh moved up to Denver in early April, Pat Cole of *Time* had done a strong interview with him. Pat, it seemed to me, wasn't averse to helping us, or at least to being even-handed in his treatment of the case. He'd also worked at the CIA. In order to keep our relationship going, I shared a copy of the Cannistraro 302 insert with him. We were both taping our conversation, and I still have my tapes to prove that I was showing him the 302 insert off the record and for background only. (On that basis, no judicial order was violated.)

The following week, however, I picked up *Time* and there it was—not only was there the story of the Saudi phone call but also a statement from Vincent Cannistraro that Stephen Jones had mis-quoted him! According to Cannistraro, at no time had he ever told Stephen Jones that he had received any information from a Saudi official about a bombing *prior to April 19*.

The italics are mine. So was the unprintable vituperation that burst forth when I read it.

I called Pat Cole.

Before I even had a chance to blow off a particle of steam, he said, "I know why you're calling, Stephen, but I didn't do it. It was Elaine."

Elaine Shannon covered the Justice Department for *Time*. She was also a close pal of Beth Wilkinson, according to Cole. One didn't have to be a rocket scientist to connect the dots.

"You've just showed me how this game works," I said to Cole. "I tell you something and you tell New York. New York tells Elaine and Elaine tells Beth. But if Justice tells Elaine something, does New York tell you? So you can tell me? No. What we've got here is a one-way street. If you ever decide to open it up to two-way traffic, then you call me."

After unloading on Pat, I wrote a formal letter of complaint to Joëlle Attinger, *Time*'s chief of correspondents, pointing out that not only had they burned me as a confidential source (I had it on tape that Pat Cole and I were talking off the record) but also—far worse—they had let Cannistraro off the hook by allowing him to turn his denial into a "prior warning" story, when that had never been in question. According to Pat Cole, I stirred up a hornet's nest inside *Time*, but as they like to say in New York, that and a buck-fifty would have gotten me on the subway.

(Some three weeks later, Beth Wilkinson had the audacity to stand up in court, holding the relevant issue of *Time*, and complain that Stephen Jones was leaking information to the media! This was, of course, not true. I'd made it crystal clear to Cole that our conversation was off the record. And I'd learned from Beth: I was able to reply that I'd never told *Time* that Vincent Cannistraro had had a warning phone call before April 19, 1995.)

Trafficking with the government, particularly when it involves such sensitive issues as prior knowledge, requires the patience and persistence of a bloodhound. The Cannistraro story, for instance, didn't end with *Time*. Sometime later, a second FBI document on the subject came into our hands. Another 302, numbered 173A–OC–56230–D. It was written by a "Supervisory Special Agent" of the FBI, but his name had been blacked out on the copy we were furnished.

Although it referred to an investigation that had taken place on April 19, 1995, the 302 itself was dated June 18, 1996.

That was one curious thing about it. But not the only one.

Supervisor BLANK wrote as follows:

I, Supervisory Special Agent [BLACKED OUT] contacted a confidential source the evening of April 19, 1995, regarding the bombing of the Federal Building in Oklahoma City.

This source, who has provided accurate and reliable information in the past, advised that a source of his, within the Saudi Arabian Intelligence Service, reported that the Oklahoma City bombing was sponsored by the Iraqi Special Services, who contacted seven (7) Afghani Freedom Fighters currently living in Pakistan. His source further advised that the sponsor was concealed from the Afghanis and that the mercenary contractors may not be aware of the real sponsor.

This source advised that, in addition to the Oklahoma City operation, two other bombing attacks were planned. The second operation was to occur at the Houston Field Office of the Immigration and Naturalization Service; the third was to occur at the Los Angeles Field Office of the FBI. His source was further advised that the time frame would be "soon."

I alerted the proper authorities and attempted to verify this information through contact with other "sources."

I was advised by my confidential source that only one other individual possessed this information within the United States. I was advised that this person would be passing this same information to his U.S. Government contacts in Washington, D.C. My confidential source further advised that I should not view this similar information as independent corroboration of the information I had been given by him.

I confirmed that the New York case agent forwarded my information via teletype to FBIHQ and other concerned Government agencies.

If Foust's original 302 insert and Supervisor BLANK's 302 are considered together, contradictions as well as corroborations quickly arise, and so do questions galore:

- What prompted Supervisor BLANK to write this second report over a year after the fact? Presumably he'd made some sort of notes when he initiated the contact on April 19, 1995, but why did he wait till June 18, 1996, to put them into a formal report?

- Someone must have ordered him to do this. Why? Who could this have been? Who was he protecting, other than himself?

- Was the "accurate and reliable" source of BLANK's 302 Cannistraro himself? At first, it certainly sounds like it. But if so, how does one explain the discrepancies in details between Cannistraro's call to Special Agent Foust and BLANK's version?

- Among the discrepancies were these. The Cannistraro source said the hit squad was very possibly Iraqi. The BLANK source is unequivocal: They were Iraqi-sponsored Afghani freedom fighters. The Cannistraro source talks of the Oklahoma City bombing as though it has yet to happen. BLANK's source knows that it has already happened. BLANK adds the further detail that the Afghanis may not know who is paying them to do the bombing. He also talks about a New York case agent, whereas Cannistraro deals entirely with Washington. Finally, he is told that one other individual in the U.S. has this information. Would that be Cannistraro?

◆ If, however, BLANK's source wasn't Cannistraro—and on closer examination, it doesn't appear to have been—was the source (once removed from BLANK) "within the Saudi Arabian Intelligence Service" of the second report the same as the "counterterrorism official for the Saudi royal family" of the first report? In other words, were the two Saudi informers who gave the information in the two reports really one and the same person? And if so, why, in the Cannistraro report, was the informer apparently unaware that the bombing had already taken place?

◆ Finally, why did Beth Wilkinson feel compelled to tell the court, "We have no knowledge of any foreign involvement"? And why, according to Cole, had she tried—successfully—to manipulate *Time*? And why (if it was she) did she see to it that Supervisor BLANK wrote his retrospective report in June?

We have entered the Kingdom of Murk.

Later in 1996, I explored as far as I could at the other end—the Saudi end—but I succeeded in clarifying nothing. If I've dwelled so long on the Cannistraro incident, it is less to give vent to the immense frustration I felt at the time than to show what we were up against, over and over again, in probing for what had really happened.

And we had no one to help us. Not the federal government certainly. And not even, as I will show, Judge Matsch.

The prior knowledge issue was hardly the sole province of the defense teams. From the very beginning there were people who had known or heard or seen something, or thought they had, and wanted to come forward, and tried to, only to be dismissed or ignored or even, in some cases, ridiculed by a law-enforcement establishment that wanted no part of what they had to say. Into this category would go not so much the warnings received in March and April, already cited, from the U.S. Marshal's Office and the Israeli government. These could be dismissed as too general in nature to have application to the Murrah Building or even Oklahoma City, and so, strangely, could the rumors that percolated through right-wing and militia circles at the same time to the effect that "something big" was in the offing. Besides, the right-wingers were always talking big.

Harder to handle, though, was the reported bomb scare, one week prior to the bombing, that had people briefly evacuated from the Murrah Building. Or the reports like those from the assistant chief dispatcher at the Oklahoma City Fire Department who, in the face of denials from his superior, maintained that the FBI had phoned in a warning on April 14. Or the eyewitness reports of hard-to-explain sightings on the day itself.

For instance, there was the sheriff's bomb squad truck, with trailer, parked in the vicinity of the federal buildings. Several eye-witnesses saw it—too many to be explained away—around 7:45 A.M. that day, although it was definitely gone by the time of the bombing. At various times in the investigation, its presence was (a) denied, (b) part of a training mission that had been scheduled for noon, or (c) the result of someone from the sheriff's office running an errand. As for (b), if there was a training mission scheduled for noon, why was the truck there at 7:45 A.M.? As for (c), why was the errand-truck towing a trailer?

And what of the dog patrols spotted at dawn in the vicinity of the old federal building two blocks away? A licensed private eye, Claude Criss, reported having seen sniffer dogs—three dogs, he thought, and six to seven handlers—near the intersection of Harvey and McGee as late as 8:15 A.M. That intersection is one block from the federal courthouse, two from the Murrah Building.

The sniffer patrols were forever denied by law enforcement.

There were also the rumored morning absences of ATF personnel from their Murrah offices. In order to counter the implication that they had had prior warning, which they vehemently denied,

ATF devised various stratagems. It had pictures distributed of an agent with his right arm in a sling who claimed to have been injured in the blast. It also floated the story of two intrepid agents who had survived the five-story free fall in a Murrah Building elevator.

The only trouble was that in a sheriff's video the agent with the sling was seen outside the building, shortly after the arrival of the rescue teams, unharmed and shaking hands with one of the law-enforcement people. The sling, it seems, came later. Also, as mentioned earlier, when experienced elevator inspectors studied the wreckage, they determined that none of the building elevators had gone into free fall with people inside.

Probably it was ATF's own fault, therefore, that a good year after the trials people were still saying there had been no ATF personnel in the building when the bomb went off. In fact there were several ATF agents on the ninth floor, including the head of the Oklahoma City Field Office. But none was injured.

Some of the other rumors of prior warning certainly seemed outlandish, but they have persisted, and the clumsy, often abusive efforts on the part of law enforcement to quash them have only lended them staying power. To this day, there are people who are convinced the bombing was an ATF sting operation gone sour. There are others who say the building was under close surveillance because of an anticipated attack all during the night of April 18–19 but that the surveillance was called off at 6:00 A.M. Still others remain convinced there were other bombs inside the building and that a single Ryder truck bomb could never have wreaked the damage alone.

One of the reasons these stories persist is, to be sure, the government's track record at Ruby Ridge and Waco, to which, in terms of prior warning, the World Trade Center bombing must be added. In that case, the FBI had actually had its own informant inside the conspiracy, one Emad Eli Salem, until, mistrustful of what he was telling them, they pulled him off the case shortly before the explosion, thereby losing control of their own operation. No matter how the Justice Department tried to explain away its own actions, the World Trade Towers disaster—six dead, a thousand injured—was also an FBI disaster. Unfortunately, that misadventure only made the FBI more defensive, more secretive, more arrogant, and more abusive and dismissive in the way it treated people whose stories conflicted, one way or another, with its own theory of the case.

Among those who felt most disenfranchised, in this way, were the surviving victims of the Oklahoma City bombing and members of surviving families. Although officials at all levels of government paid obeisance to their grief and their suffering, and although the prosecution knew that victims' testimony, sprinkled throughout the presentation of their case in court, could have an overwhelming effect on the jury, the prosecutors and FBI systematically tried to silence or discredit anyone who challenged their version of what had happened. It was because of this that Glenn and Cathy Wilburn, grandparents of two young boys who had died in the explosion, started their own investigation, aided by and sharing information with several media journalists, also joining forces (before Glenn Wilburn died and Cathy carried on alone) with State Representative Charles Key.

Charles Key, whether by conviction or political motive or both, became—outside the defense teams themselves—the focal point for criticism of the government's investigation. Among other things, he made the accusation to J. D. Cash "that the Federal Grand Jury was purposely shielded from witnesses who saw Timothy McVeigh with other suspects both prior to and immediately after the bombing." He was highly outspoken in his demands for investigations distinct from that of the federal government, be it in the form of state legislative committee or a local grand jury. As a result, he became the object of a negative campaign spearheaded by the two largest papers in Oklahoma, the *Daily Oklahoman* and the *Tulsa World*, and inspired by the state's two leading politicians, Attorney General Drew Edmondson and Governor Keating himself, who asserted that Key and others like him were "howling at the moon." Tim McVeigh and Terry Nichols were seen by most survivors as arch-villains who fully deserved the death penalty. As a result, the victims' groups and the defense teams had little direct contact. But we kept close tabs on their activities. For the prosecution, meanwhile, the victims remained a constant irritant. It fell to Pat Ryan, on the government side, to try and placate fellow Oklahomans and reassure them periodically that there was nothing "sinister" about the prosecution's investigations and no attempt to conceal and cover up. But that was a tough sell in our state, where distrust of the federal government takes many forms and where the very actions and omissions of the prosecutors themselves too often belied their protestations of good faith.

It is no accident, therefore, that Charles Key prevailed. In summer 1997, an Oklahoma County grand jury began hearing evidence independently of the federal government, although the latter has done its best to thwart and obstruct the process. As of this moment, the grand jury continues to sift evidence and listen to the testimony of witnesses.

L et us come back, now, to the phone call that came into the Executive Secretariat at the Department of Justice in Washington, the morning of April 19, 1995.

It will be remembered that when the phone rang that morning at extension 2171 James Howard Miller, one of three receptionists in the department, picked up. A call, he learned, was being transferred to him—a crank-type call, he later said. There were two witnesses to Miller's talking on the telephone: Kimberley Tolson, who worked in the Executive Secretariat, and Russell Stuart Green, a courier from the criminal division of the department.

Both, by their own accounts as well as that of Miller, were standing near him as he talked.

On April 27, 1995—eight days, that is, after the bombing—Miller was interviewed by Special Agent Basil Doyle of the FBI, and another telltale 302 entered the FBI archives. According to what Miller told Special Agent Doyle, the anonymous caller said: "I'm nobody special. The Federal Building in Oklahoma City has just been bombed. I'm standing across the street from it. I can see it from where I'm standing."

The caller then hung up.

In Miller's account, Stuart Green, the courier, was standing there while he took the call, and, because he was talking, Kimberley Tolson came to the front desk to sign Green's log sheet for the delivery. After he hung up, Miller told Tolson and Green what the caller had said, then time-stamped the log sheet. As he told the FBI, he didn't take the call seriously because such calls often came his way, but when about one hour later someone came into the office and said the federal building in Oklahoma City had been blown up, Miller said he reported the call to his supervisors. By then, they and others in the office were watching the TV news coverage.

The following day, according to what Miller told the FBI, Stuart Green brought the log book back, and they discovered that the time stamp on the previous day's document was 9:38 A.M. Or, to put it in Special Agent Doyle's precise words, the time stamp "was 9:38, eastern standard time (est), which is at least 24 minutes prior to the bombing in Oklahoma In Oklahoma City."

Miller, according to what he told Doyle, then checked the time stamp and discovered that its clock was approximately six minutes fast. This would have made the time of the call 9:32 A.M.—eastern standard time, according to Doyle—or thirty minutes prior to the bombing.

Kimberley Tolson and Stuart Green were also the subjects of Doyle-generated 302s. Both corroborated Miller's story. Tolson said she was preparing for the 10:00 A.M. mail pickup for the Drug Enforcement Administration when she went to Miller's desk to sign Green's log for the document. Once Miller hung up, Tolson said, he "stated that a Federal Building just blew up in Oklahoma City." Green remembered this as, "There has been a bombing in Oklahoma," and remembered saying, "You're like the president, everyone calls you to tell you what's going on." Then, according to his 302, Green asked Miller to time-stamp his log book "real quick" so that he could "get back to work."

There was only one problem with Doyle's 302 pertaining to the Miller interview.

On April 19, 1995, both Washington, D.C., and Oklahoma City were on daylight saving time—and had been for seventeen days. Therefore, if what Doyle wrote down was right and the call did come in at 9:38 A.M. *eastern standard time*, then that would have put it thirty-six minutes *after* the bombing, not twenty-four minutes *before*. Clearly Doyle had made a mistake, and there was a simple explanation why. The first Miller 302, although it covered an investigation that had taken place on April 27, 1995, carried a "date of transcription" of February 28, 1996. In other words, Doyle only got around to typing up the interview, or having it typed up, ten months after it had taken place. By then it was winter, that is, standard time, and an agent accustomed to referencing time and time zones in his reports would easily have incorporated an erroneous "eastern standard time." The time stamp could only have referred to daylight saving time and the call, whatever its message, had preceded the bombing by a half-hour—but such was the atmosphere of paranoia we all lived in, such that when the defense team started challenging the government on this subject in late 1996 we convinced ourselves prosecutors were going to claim the time stamp was still set according to eastern standard time—seventeen days after the changeover—and therefore that Doyle's 302 for Miller "proved" the call had come in after the bombing, not before.

But the prosecution never claimed that. Instead, it set about "adjusting" the story in a different way. In October and November 1996, a year and a half later, the FBI simply "reinterviewed" Miller, Tolson, and Green. They did it this time in the presence of a member of the prosecution. His name was Aitan Goelman, a special attorney to the attorney general (SAAG).

O n August 20, 1996, when the first three 302s emerged from the stack of more than twenty-five thousand we had received from the FBI, I wrote Joe Hartzler requesting that the three people—Miller, Tolson, and Green—be made available for interviews. I also asked for any information that might have bearing on the subject, including anything concerning the time-stamp clock, plus a copy of the document Ms. Tolson had stamped, the time that was stamped in, and whether the clock was correctly set.

We received no answer to this letter. The prosecutors must have realized they had a major problem, for two things were fairly certain. First, it strained credulity that a person standing across the street from a Murrah Building that was smoking and in ruins would call the Department of Justice in Washington, D.C., as opposed to 911. Secondly, anyone standing across the street from the building when it blew up wouldn't have been in any condition to make such a phone call, and it is highly unlikely that any of the phones in the neighborhood would have been working.

On October 14, I made the same request to Hartzler, again in writing. Again, no answer. We were simply ignored.

On October 16, Special Agent Doyle was sent to reinterview Miller. According to his new 302, when we finally saw it, Miller had nothing of significance to add to the first interview, other than to say he couldn't recall if the caller spoke with an accent or who in Justice had referred the call to him.

Then, on November 15, a different FBI agent, David R. Brundage, interviewed Miller for a third time. This interview, as I mentioned, was in the presence of SAAG Aitan Goelman, and this time it was held in Denver. (Interestingly, in contrast to the tardy Doyle, Brundage transcribed his 302 on the same day as the interview.) And Miller, more than a year and a half after the event, now changed his story—but in what at first blush seemed to be insignificant ways. This time, Miller said that the anonymous caller named the building in Oklahoma City, although he, Miller, didn't recognize the name, and this time Miller recalled hearing traffic noise behind the caller's voice.

Miller also recalled Stuart Green arriving at the reception counter. Miller was still on the phone. Green was delivering a package of internal communications. Kim Tolson was also near the reception counter when he ended the phone call. Miller remembered telling them both about the call, also that neither of them seemed concerned. He then "*took the transmittal log sheet, which accompanies Green's deliveries, signed and date stamped it.*"

The italics, above and to come, are mine. (The reader will not immediately understand why these "revisions" were important. I didn't when I first read them. But bear with me.)

"*Approximately ten minutes, but no more than twenty minutes after receiving the anonymous call,*" Miller and others in his office heard the news. The building had in fact been bombed. Miller then told others the story of the phone call. And then, to quote from Brundage's 302, "Later that day, attempts were made to determine the exact time he had received the call by examining Green's transmittal logs. Miller had no independent recollection of the time of the call but stated that the most accurate means of establishing the time of the call would be to review Green's transmittal logs and locate the one that he had signed and date stamped the morning of April 19, 1995."

Then, on November 19, also in Denver and also in the presence of SAAG Goelman, Brundage reinterviewed Stuart Green:

Green stated that with regard to this particular delivery, he stood at the receptionist's counter while waiting for Miller to complete his telephone call. Green cannot recall if anyone else was behind the counter. After completing the telephone conversation, Miller stated that the caller had said something about a bombing in Oklahoma. Green told Miller that the call was important and that he, Miller, "should get on it."

As Green and Miller were discussing the telephone call, Green's supervisor, Penny Chiarzia, entered the Executive Secretariat's Office and joined the conversation. Green advised that Chiarzia shared his concern about the seriousness of the bombing. Green recalled Miller handing him a single transmittal log, but he does not recall if Miller had been the one to sign it. After leaving the Executive Secretariat's Office, Green, carrying the single transmittal log, walked with Chiarzia back to their office, arriving less than five minutes later.

Then, on November 25, back in Washington, D.C., this time, and with Special Agent Basil Doyle investigating once again, but also in the presence of the ubiquitous Goelman, Kimberley Tolson was reinterviewed. This time, Tolson was more meticulous in describing her daily routines. She made at least four trips each day to the front of the office, she said, to distribute mail, sometimes as many as ten trips or more. Sometimes too, in the first mail distribution of the day, she has mail left over from the previous evening as well as what might have come in during the morning.

On the morning of April 19, she was already on her way back to her cubicle, toward the rear of the office, when Miller was hanging up the telephone. Stuart Green was at the front desk, making a delivery. After Miller relayed what the caller had said—"A building has just been blown up in Oklahoma City"—Tolson, disbelieving, said, "Yeah, right," and went back to her cubicle.

She believed it was Miller who signed for the delivery. She had no recollection of signing herself, and when she was confronted with her previous statement, she didn't deny having said she'd signed, but she had no recollection of it now.

At the end of Tolson's 302 is a telltale statement that makes clear the overriding reason for all this flurry of reinterviewing, as well as the presumably vigilant presence of Aitan Goelman: "Tolson was told that counsel for Timothy McVeigh had requested to speak with her. She was told that the decision to speak with counsel for the defense was hers to make. She was encouraged to have a government representative with her during any interview."

O n December 10, 1996, two months after my second request, I finally received a letter from Aitan Goelman, apologizing for the delays. It referred to the reinterviews—copies of the 302s would be forwarded to me shortly—and offered James Miller alone for us to interview, provided a representative of the government was present. Goelman also said he was enclosing a copy of "the complete delivery log."

The "complete delivery log" consisted of two sheets of paper. One sheet was a transmittal form from the criminal division to the Executive Secretariat. It described a document, presumably the document or package to be delivered, with two long identification numbers and the name "Troland." At the bottom of the page was a "Received by—Date" line, and the signature above the line was Kimberley G. Tolson, the date, 4/19/95. The date, however, was written, not stamped. And there was no time stamp.

The second sheet of this "complete delivery log" was a blank page with large type across the middle of it: "1B3895."

If Goelman and his bosses were simply trying to antagonize us, they deserve a presidential commendation.

I wrote back three days later, ignoring the question of the delivery log and simply stating that since Goelman had interviewed all three witnesses working at the Justice Department I wanted to do likewise.

Goelman replied on January 6, sending me the 302s of the reinterviews. Green and Tolson, according to his letter, had refused to be interviewed. Furthermore, it wasn't Department of Justice policy to force employees to submit to "undesired interviews." Four months after our initial request, Goelman now informed us that Green had a mental handicap (apparently not severe enough to keep him from working for the Justice Department) and that Tolson was three months into a complicated pregnancy.

Our next stop—as it so often was—was Judge Matsch.

We wanted to interview those witnesses. We wanted the time-stamped documents. We so moved, formally.

Through Goelman's formal response to our motion, the purpose of all the reinterviewing became clear. The government, it turned out, now had a new position on the matter. To wit:

> Miller, who does not independently recall the time of the call, remembers that Stuart Green . . . had been delivering a document to the Office of the Executive Secretariat when the call came in. Miller remembers that he personally signed for his delivery. Mr. Green's delivery log reveals that Miller signed for only one of the several deliveries that Mr. Green made to the Executive Secretariat on the morning of April 19, 1995. The log sheet for this delivery was time-stamped at 10:26 A.M. Eastern Time, which (correcting for a time-stamp that apparently ran six minutes fast) was 18 minutes after the bombing. Miller also remembers telling co-workers Kimberley Tolson and Green about the content of the call. All of the log sheets and reports of interview have been provided to the defendants.
>
> In the immediate aftermath of the bombing, Miller was shown a single log sheet. It was for a delivery that Green made at 9:38 that morning. Miller was then under the mistaken impression that Green had made only one delivery to the Executive Secretariat that morning. The FBI interviewed Miller, Green and Tolson, and the 302s of these interviews were produced to the defense in the normal course of discovery. In the initial FBI interview, Miller tied the phone to Green's 9:38 A.M. delivery. He later corrected himself after seeing a complete set of delivery log sheets from the morning of April 19, 1995.

In other words, one and a half years after the bombing and their first FBI interviews, Miller, Tolson, and Green had changed their stories—seemingly innocuous changes but designed to fit a shifted set of facts. The 9:38 delivery, signed for by Tolson, was *not*, after all, the one that had interrupted the phone call Miller was taking from the streets of Oklahoma City. That call only came in at 10:20 A.M. eastern daylight time, that is, *after* the bombing. The bombing had taken place eighteen minutes before. The caller was simply telling what he was seeing—that part of it now made sense—and Miller relayed the news to his coworkers.

It was clever and it fit, more or less. It also made Judge Matsch suspicious as all get-out.

He ordered all three witnesses flown out to Denver to his courtroom. Mentally handicapped or not, pregnant or not, the three witnesses appeared in due course, and on a Saturday morning, during a closed proceeding, we were given the opportunity to examine them under oath.

"This is a proceeding," Judge Matsch explained to each of them at the outset, "to learn whether you have any pertinent information with respect to the case that's being tried here [in *United States v. McVeigh*]. So I directed you be brought here so that counsel can question you."

And so I did—a kind of minitrial before the trial—with Aitan Goelman in attendance to object, on occasion, and to conduct brief cross-examinations.

In fact, the three witnesses no longer needed Goelman, except possibly as a reminder. They knew what they were supposed to say. They stuck with the stories of their November 1996 302s. Nothing I asked or brought up succeeded in shaking them. Yes, they realized there were contradictions, discrepancies between what they'd said in November 1996 and what they'd said in April 1995. But when I brought these to their attention, well, as Kimberley Tolson said, "It was such a long period of time ago."

They just couldn't remember. Over and over again, they couldn't remember. They could remember everything they'd said in November 1996, but April 1995?

No.

Of course they couldn't.

It was such a long period of time ago.

As Judge Matsch put it, once we were done with Stuart Green, who was the last to be interrogated, "Well, I don't know where you intend to go from here, Mr. Jones. Perhaps you don't either, at this particular moment."

Judge Matsch was right.

I'd lost. I didn't know where I was going with it either.

But nobody had won.

This is why I've devoted space to a story that went nowhere. This is why I chose to start this book with the anonymous phone call from the streets of Oklahoma City, a phone call that never made it to the trial.

Because nobody *won*.

Timothy McVeigh didn't win, but neither did the people of the United States of America. Neither, for that matter, did Aitan Goelman, although he ought to have gotten a raise for his efforts (for all I know, maybe he did).

Of course, the call came in at 9:32 A.M. eastern daylight time, that is, before the bombing occurred. That was Miller's, Tolson's, and Green's memory at the time, memories corroborated by a time-stamped document, by Kimberley Tolson remembering that she was getting ready for the 10:00 A.M. mail. It was only a year and a half later, when we tried to introduce the evidence of the phone call, that their stories changed, "supported" by a new document that somehow hadn't been found before. For five months the prosecutors stalled, ignoring our request to interview these three Department of Justice employees. And when they finally arrived for direct examination, the three witnesses simply shifted their stories to accommodate Aitan Goelman's new theory.

I don't mean to pick on Goelman. He was making a career for himself in the Department of Justice, and I'm sure he'd only done what he was told to do. By delay, by obfuscation, by withholding, and finally by the careful coaching of three witnesses, he had neutralized what the government obviously saw as a big problem.

And by a highly clever feat of legerdemain too. I mean to say it took imagination to take a troubling set of facts and make it right. Assuming Miller was telling the truth as to what the caller had said, no one had ever been able to explain how someone could claim a building had exploded a half-hour *before* it happened. It didn't make sense. But with Goelman's time switch, everything worked just as the government needed it to.

Well, didn't it? Doesn't it?

Well, more or less.

Trouble is, it fails to answer the big question: Why on earth would a person standing on the street in Oklahoma City, amid debris and death and smoke and flames and sirens, call the Justice Department—in Washington, D.C.—to report the disaster eighteen minutes after it had occurred? If you were such a person—a "nobody special"—would it ever have occurred to you to do this? After, presumably, having first needing to call Washington directory assistance to get the phone number? (Unless, of course, you're one of those rare Americans who carries the telephone numbers of the federal cabinet in your head.)

Somewhere inside me—I realize how naive this sounds for a county-seat lawyer in his fifties, naive too for a lawyer who had been arm wrestling with Justice Department appointees for a good year and a half—but somewhere inside me I still believed. Still believed, that is, in the truth. Still believed that the role of an investigative and law enforcement branch of government, even more than winning cases in court, is to get at the truth and expose it.

But this was all eroding now. I knew in my heart that what had happened with Miller, Tolson, and Green—and Aitan Goelman—had nothing to do with truth.

A man's life was at stake—Tim McVeigh's life, my client—but this was about something else. This was about spin. This was damage control. This was being able to say, once the defense started asking questions, that the phone call didn't happen when the clerk who took it, and his witnesses, once said it had.

It was Vince Cannistraro trying to deny he'd ever gotten a phone call, and Beth Wilkinson's brazen assurance that there was no evidence of foreign involvement.

But why? Why were these things so important to the government?

Because they wouldn't tolerate even the faintest whiff of prior warning. Strange as it may sound, any whiff mobilized the government like a ten-alarm fire.

It was almost enough to make one a believer in prior knowledge, wasn't it?

But there was another consideration too.

If there had been a phone call from the streets of Oklahoma City announcing the event half an hour before it happened, who could have placed such a call?

Only someone who had known what was going to happen.

But how could he have known what was going to happen unless he was one of them?

Same thing for Cannistraro's Saudi connection. Within hours of the event, a Saudi intelligence source called his old CIA buddy to tell him what he knew about it.

But how could he know anything if the crime was perpetrated, purely and exclusively, by a pair of drifters nobody ever heard of?

Two phone calls, from opposite parts of the globe, both calling Washington, D.C. Two phone calls that, in the government's eyes, had to be disavowed.

Why?

Because both, in totally different ways, turned the government's theory of the case into toast.

12

LOOKING GOOD

At 4:00 P.M. on the afternoon of February 26, 1997—a Wednesday—the entire McVeigh defense team met behind closed doors on the twenty-fourth floor of Denver's Total Building South. The purpose of the meeting was to hear reports from our team leaders and to analyze the strengths and weaknesses of the government's case and to see where we stood.

The atmosphere was very serious, as though this was a kind of dress rehearsal in a theater—very up. We were highly energized.

The trial was six weeks away.

We had long since organized into six teams, each with its leader, each leader reporting to me. Rob Nigh was deputy principal defense counsel and leader of Team 1, whose task was to prepare us for the first stage of the trial—that is, the guilt/innocence stage. As one organizing principle, we had broken all the FBI 302s into seventy-two categories, ranging from Tim's elementary school experiences to the rental of the Ryder truck at Elliott's, the Dreamland Motel, the arrest on Interstate 35. Then the members of Team 1, all lawyers, had written prosecutorial memoranda. They took the 302 witness statements and the lab reports and wrote detailed presentations proving Tim's guilt beyond a reasonable doubt. Once they'd done this, they turned around and, as defendants, engaged in deconstruction. They took the government's case apart piece by piece, highlighting where it was vulnerable and rebutting in defense memoranda supported by the same 302s and the physical evidence.

Amber McLaughlin, who'd been with us since 1995, had reviewed with our telephone experts the records of nearly 150 million telephone calls that the government itself had analyzed. She and Cheryl Ramsey, who had just joined us and was a former judge and prosecutor, prepared the cross-examination of the government's experts. Robert Warren, who'd joined us right out of law school, had carefully analyzed the so-called robbery of Roger Moore in rural Arkansas. Although Tim had an alibi, we wanted to prove, if we could, that there'd never been a robbery. Another group had listened to hundreds of hours of taped interviews of Jennifer McVeigh and her mother, and especially the Fortiers, indexing and transcribing passages we might use at trial.

Jeralyn "Jerri" Merritt concentrated on identifications by eyewitnesses, aided by two of the nation's leading experts in the field, Elizabeth Loftus and Gary Wells, and anticipating, from the 302s and their grand jury testimony, what key witnesses such as Tom Kessinger and Vicki Beemer would say on the stand. Jerri also set out to prevent the government from introducing expert opinion on handwriting, who, we were reasonably sure—based on past experience with this unit—would testify that Tim McVeigh had written "Robert Kling" on the truck rental form.

A late arrival to Team 1 was Christopher Tritico, a first-class trial lawyer from Houston who'd been strongly recommended by Richard "Racehorse" Haynes, a legendary criminal defender in Texas and a friend of mine. Chris would take over all the forensic examinations and cross-examinations in the trial, and, taking into account the strictures Judge Matsch put on the defense, he did a fine job building on Bob Wyatt's "gnat's eye" examination of the documents.

Four of our investigators were also part of Team 1. David Fechheimer had the primary task of building up information to impeach and contradict government witnesses. Josiah "Tink" Thompson, who'd written a best-selling book on the Kennedy assassination called *Six Seconds in Dallas*, set out to disprove key elements in the government's case. He became a virtual citizen of Junction City, Kansas, trying to track down people there who'd seen either Tim or the yellow Mercury there on the Sunday afternoon before the bombing when the government was going to try to prove he'd driven to Oklahoma City and been retrieved by Nichols. Roger Charles, meanwhile, who'd just joined us subsequent to the ABC News/Carol Howe debacle, had Elohim City and the issue of prior knowledge in his sights.

Team 2 was headed by Dick Burr. If Tim was convicted of murder, the jury would then decide his punishment in the second stage. Dick Burr had spent his entire professional career opposing the death penalty, and his personal commitment to the cause was very strong. Although his jury experience was limited, he had an encyclopedic knowledge of the death penalty statues and a great deal of experience in postconviction proceedings. So did his (now) wife, Mandy Welch. We also had on board Maurie Levin, a wonderful and well-organized lawyer from Austin, Texas, and Randy Coyne, a University of Oklahoma Law School professor and author of a widely used textbook on capital punishment.

Team 3 was Bob Wyatt's bailiwick. Initially, its function was to gather all the evidence from the government as it came in, examine it, catalog it, index it, and—most of all—make sure we'd gotten everything we were entitled to. This last, as I'm sure I've made abundantly clear, was a colossal task. But as information came out about the FBI Lab and its deficiencies, I needed one person to oversee our effort there, and Bob was ideal. His most effective work in the entire span of defending Tim was behind the scenes, that is, organizing the experts to attack the FBI Lab itself and preparing Chris Tritico for the trial. It was Bob Wyatt, moreover, who conducted the lengthy in camera deposition of Frederic Whitehurst, which Judge Matsch had ordered over vigorous government resistance.

Team 4, headed by Mike Roberts, managed our administrative needs. Mike made sure everyone got paid, including our experts, that our vouchers were honored by the court, and that the myriad motions that had to be filed with respect to housekeeping and administrative details got done. It fell to Mike to deal with all the bread-and-butter elements that made our operation function, like negotiating our rent, our lease, our parking, and so forth.

Team 5 was the academic expert on the death penalty and that was Randy Coyne.

Team 6 was litigation support, in the person of Sam Guiberson. It fell to Sam, for instance, and Chuck Miller, our computer guru, to take in all the government's discovery, some of our own, and material we received from Mike Tigar and screen it, read it, enter it into the computer, and design programs for its retrieval.

Each team reported in that Wednesday afternoon—where we were, what we still had left to do. It took several hours, and darkness had fallen by the time my second-in-command and I retreated for our own postmortem.

Mr. Rob—Rob Nigh—looked at me, I at him.

"Well, Boss," he said, a half-grin on his face, "I think we've got 'em."

It was beginning to look that way.

"Looking good," I replied.

Cautious as experience had taught me to be, my old belief—that whatever it took the government was not going to permit itself to lose this case—was finally eroding. Just recently, the *National Law Journal* had run a brilliant, as well as favorable, piece of reporting by the Denver investigative reporter Ryan Ross, under the headline: "A McVeigh Acquittal?"

Maybe we were about ready, I thought, *to remove that question mark.*

Why did we feel so confident as a group? And I so cautiously optimistic? For the simple reason that the government couldn't prove guilt beyond a reasonable doubt. There was honest doubt embedded in their case. As for me, from an examination of all the evidence, I was convinced Tim McVeigh was not guilty and that the jury should so find.

The government's strategy was like a table with six legs. They could lose one leg and the table would stand, two and the table would still waddle.

Three legs gone, the table would be tilting.

Four? Collapse.

Rob and I reviewed it that evening—for the umpteenth time.

Leg one was McVeigh's political beliefs. Okay, we couldn't dispute these. Yes, he'd read *The Turner Diaries*, had given it away, had sold it. Yes, Tim distrusted the government. Yes, he had made inflammatory statements on occasion. They had quotes from his letters, witnesses to testify. The U.S. marshals, he believed, had committed murder at Ruby Ridge, and the FBI and ATF had been responsible for the deaths of the Branch Davidians at Waco. But even taking into account his extreme language, most of his political views—anti–free trade, protecting our domestic industries, opposing affirmative action, opposing government's intrusions into our personal lives—were no different than those of many blue-collar workers whose families had once supported FDR but who had switched to Ronald Reagan and were now vehement critics of William Jefferson Clinton. Tim's feelings about Waco and Ruby Ridge were probably shared by at least 10 million Americans and would have been by more if they'd followed the stories attentively. The only difference was that Tim had written letters and had engaged in polemics, but nowhere in his writings was there any plan or exhortation to kill federal employees. One message the government claimed he'd left on Jennifer's word processor read, "Die, you spineless bastards, die," referring to the U.S. Marshals Service, but the president, members of Congress, the FBI, and other law enforcement agencies got similar communications all the time. In and of itself, the curse on the marshals meant nothing. Tim's rhetoric could become extreme, but it was scarcely a blueprint for murder or guerrilla warfare.

The second leg rested on the Fortiers. Among the things Michael and Lori would testify to were the following:

- Tim had talked to them about taking direct action against the government and blowing up a building.

- Tim had shown Michael the Murrah Building.

- They knew the date of the attack.

- Lori had made a false ID card for Tim and had wrapped explosive blasting caps in Christmas wrapping for him.

- Tim had told Michael about the Roger Moore robbery and had enlisted his help in finding a storage place for the arms in Arizona and transporting them there.

- Tim had used a small amount of ammonium nitrate to blow up a rock, as a demonstration, in the Arizona desert.

The problem was this: With one exception, the Fortiers' proposed testimony had been available to the government through newspapers and national television. The exception was this: A weak link in the government's theory was the location of the getaway car. According to prosecutors, it was parked and ready for the bomber after he abandoned the Ryder truck. For the government theory to work, however, the car must have been nearby to allow McVeigh time enough to reach the Billings exit on Interstate 35, where Trooper Hanger was waiting. But given the government's timeline, the car sat three days in the alley next to the YMCA building without being moved; the fact no person reported seeing it stretched the imagination. In fact, the government couldn't produce a single witness claiming to see the memorable yellow car, because the one or two witnesses prepared to testify that they'd seen the Mercury in downtown Oklahoma City also reported seeing Tim McVeigh with another, never identified, man sitting inside—and that was no help at all to the government.

The prosecutors tried to "solve" their problem in two ways. One was the key. In a search for debris from the Murrah Building, prosecutors would claim that a key had been found, in pristine condition, in the alley next to the YMCA building and, further, that this key fit the Ryder truck. Obviously, McVeigh had dropped it there on his way to the getaway car. (In one of their classic shell games, trying to hide the existence of the key as long as possible, they sent us a photo of it on the ground, amid literally one hundred thousand other photographs, and simply labeled in their accompanying inventory as "miscellaneous debris." Fortunately, in our laborious review and matching-up of these photos, we'd noticed the key and started asking questions about it. After considerable hemming and hawing, and to Judge Matsch's vast irritation, the government finally admitted in open court that the key in the photo was *the* key.)

But even the key in and of itself was insufficient for the prosecutors' needs. They had to have testimony. Enter Michael Fortier. Not that Michael Fortier had seen the Mercury in the alley; but as part of his cooperating with the government, he would testify that during their trip to Oklahoma City Tim had pointed out the alley as the place he would park the getaway car.

Everything else, as I've said, was old news by the time the Fortiers "corrected" their statements. But all their testimony, including the story of the car, was developed and massaged during many meetings with the FBI and government prosecutors until it emerged in the Fortiers' proffers (offers of proof). What the government wanted was enough testimony to incriminate McVeigh— but not enough to prove the Fortiers themselves were members of the conspiracy. It was a fine line, but over time and with help the Fortiers evolved their stories to meet the government's needs.

Although it remained possible that the Fortiers were telling the truth, they also, as we knew, had ample motives to lie. Their exposure to potential drug charges and other crimes unrelated to the bombing was far greater than the charges to which Michael ultimately pleaded guilty, and Michael also had dreams of fame and fortune through the sale of his story. What we were counting on (and what actually happened) was that they would come across initially to the jury as appealing witnesses, cleaned up by Joe Hartzler and prepped within an inch of their lives, which we would counter with our videotapes of the ragged hippie pair who'd once proclaimed their innocence and their ignorance to any TV camera that turned in their direction.

The third leg was forensic, and I want to come back to it, because the closer we came to trial, the more the government had to rely on it. Suffice it to say that we had our experts lined up. Among them was Brian Caddy from Scotland, a professor of forensic science who taught the only class in the United Kingdom on trace analysis and had been appointed by the British home secretary to investigate allegations of incompetence as to the Ministry of Defense's laboratory and its IRA bombing investigations. Another fine recruit for us was Dr. John Lloyd, a fellow at the Royal Society of Chemistry who had helped reverse the conviction of the Birmingham Six. (The case had been a cause célèbre in England. In it, six men, convicted of blowing up a Birmingham pub, were released, years later, largely because of inadequacies in the forensic evidence.) On the basis of the first FBI Lab reports that we'd been able to send them, both Caddy and Lloyd were scathing in their critiques. Although our motion to suppress all evidence emanating from the FBI Lab on the basis of incompetent and unscientific procedures was about to be denied by Judge Matsch, in another sense, the best was yet to come. I'm talking about the report on the FBI Lab issued by the inspector general (IG) of the Department of Justice. The government, under pressure, had finally investigated its own mess. For a good year, our friends on the prosecution side had, typically, been trying to hide its existence, then delay its publication, but it was now in draft form.

The fourth leg was the telephone records, the allegation that Tim had made calls on the Daryl Bridges debit card. Whether he had or hadn't, the prosecution was obliged to "work backward" in order to try to prove that theory—yet another feat of legerdemain that left it with, as I will outline, the same problem it faced with the FBI Lab. Debit cards are sold in this country by the tens of thousands. One can prepay and then call anywhere in the United States for around twenty-five cents per minute. One can even use them to place international calls. According to the FBI, Terry Nichols, who used many aliases, had filled out the card application, this time using the name Daryl Bridges. The FBI also claimed Tim had signed a money order used to purchase time on the card, but Judge Matsch, as skeptical as I was about "experts" in this field, would rule testimony about the alleged handwriting samples inadmissible.

One problem with debit cards is that they only create a record of whom the call is made to, not where it is made from. The latter is irrelevant, because at twenty-five cents a minute you can call across the country or across the street. Typically a debit card owner gets no billing statement showing where-from and where-to, and in fact there is no electronic chain of billing information. In the Oklahoma City bombing case, one had to be reconstructed. A further obstacle to the government's efforts was the multiple calls made at or around the same time, making it impossible to say if—to invent an example—the call placed at a McDonald's on Interstate 40 outside Albuquerque, New Mexico, is the same one that was received at, say, the M.I.T. admissions office in Cambridge, Massachusetts.

In addition, one important call in the government's chronology—to Elliott's Body Shop in Junction City the morning of April 14 inquiring about the truck rental—didn't, as I've described, even show up on the Daryl Bridges calling card records. This was the unfortunate "computer glitch"—a convenient enough explanation for a significant missing link.

Finally, as we quickly learned, there is massive fraud in the country involving debit cards. People have figured out how to surf and make use of a card that belongs to someone else. Apparently the truly skilled telephone con artist can even make it appear as though a call has originated from an entirely different pay phone than the one he is using. All sorts of such tricks made the telephone record potentially unreliable as evidence, and we were confident we could raise reasonable doubt in reasonable minds.

The government, in other words, had a leg to stand on, but we had ample rebuttal.

The fifth leg was "Robert Kling" and eyewitness identifications. If the government couldn't prove that Tim was Robert Kling, it was in deep trouble. But prosecutors were going to drop their key witness, Tom Kessinger, because, as we'd found out, he had multiple criminal convictions on his record. When David Fechheimer first began to check into Kessinger for us, he'd interviewed his former wife, who'd advised Fechheimer to "ask down at the police station." An excellent tip. Kessinger's record featured a RICO drug conspiracy among other testaments to his reliability, and he'd even once been charged with "terrorist threats" against his girlfriend. Furthermore, Kessinger's landlord had told Fechheimer that Kessinger hired a lawyer and was looking to get his hands on the $2 million reward.

Kessinger, it will be remembered, had given the details of the sketch the FBI had relied on in their search for John Does #1 and #2. He, not Beemer or Elliott, had been considered by the FBI as having the best recall and memory of the facial features of Robert Kling. But now the government didn't dare put him on the stand.

Vicki Beemer, meanwhile, who actually handled the rental transaction at Elliott's and had been exposed to Kling the longest, told the FBI she simply couldn't identify Tim as Robert Kling.

This left Eldon Elliott, a man, we'd discovered, with past financial difficulties—including problems with the Kansas state tax commission—and who, I thought, clearly hungered after the reward. Elliott's testimony was incredible not just because of his willingness to modify and accommodate his story to help the government; when he went to Fort Riley early on April 20 to help with the sketches he asked Vicki Beemer whether Kling had had a beard! This was a man he'd seen, for something between five and twenty minutes, just three days before!

Of course Elliott and Kessinger had since identified McVeigh as Kling. (In Elliott's case, it only took him forty-eight days, by which time even Tibetan monks in the Himalayas knew that Timothy McVeigh had been identified as John Doe #1 and was the FBI's principal suspect.) But what about the government's least favorite subject, the famous, or infamous, John Doe #2? The shop had rented one truck on Saturday and two on Monday, including Kling's, and one or two on Tuesday—we're hardly talking Grand Central Station in terms of business activity—and all three witnesses were categorical: Two men, Kling and another, had picked up the truck on Monday. Vicki Beemer had in fact told the grand jury in 1995, in answer to a question from Hartzler, that she was "absolutely 100% certain" there'd been two of them, and that was also her testimony in Denver.

As previously described, the government, ever resourceful, had found an ingenious way around the John Doe #2 problem. Kessinger, after a meeting with the prosecution's Scott Mendelhoff, realized he'd been confused all along. The man he'd *thought* had been with John Doe #1 (or Kling, or McVeigh)—that is, John Doe #2—was Todd Bunting. Bunting, who resembled John Doe #2, had come in on *Tuesday*, not *Monday*, and he'd been in the company of Sgt. Michael Hertig, who more or less resembled John Doe #1. Hence his confusion.

But Kessinger wasn't going to testify, and Vickie Beemer would be no help. Not only had she refused to identify McVeigh as Kling; she also knew Sergeant Hertig, which made it all the less likely that she would have confused the Tuesday and Monday customers.

Could the government make it fly without them? Wouldn't the jury want to know where they were? And wouldn't they inevitably ask themselves that if the witnesses had been that wrong about John Doe #2, mightn't they also be wrong about John Doe #1? Turning the questions around: Were they really going to condemn a defendant to his death on the basis of this kind of identification?

In addition, there were all those storage sheds that Tim and Terry had allegedly rented, some with witnesses, but that had been cleaned and swept and vacuumed and tested and swabbed, with nothing of an incriminating nature to be found. Nothing at all. The government would try to claim that Tim and Terry had robbed the quarry near Marion, but it had no evidence whatsoever linking Tim to it. And it would try to show that Tim had sought to purchase anhydrous hydrazine at the race track in Topeka, but even if he had—and the eyewitness's identification of Tim was questionable at best—the argument of the government's own forensic experts was that nitromethane had been used—not anhydrous hydrazine. In other words, as Mr. Rob pointed out, prosecutors were going to argue that Tim McVeigh must certainly have purchased strawberries at the store because he'd asked for the price of pears!

The fifth leg was at best wobbly.

The sixth leg was Trooper Hanger. This one we couldn't deny. The time, date, place, and circumstances of McVeigh's arrest in the yellow Mercury Grand Marquis were incontrovertible facts. But between the time McVeigh was in Junction City during the weekend, conflicting as the testimony was, and his arrest on Interstate 35 near Perry an hour and a half after the bombing on Wednesday, there was such a snarl of John Does #2s (and maybe #3s and #4s) and contradictory eyewitness accounts that the prosecutors could find only one solution in the end. When they presented their case at trial before the jury, the period from Monday to Wednesday was going to be "the Great Void." (Curiously, Trooper Hanger, a trained and observant law enforcement officer, had made no connection between the Tim McVeigh he arrested and the sketch of Robert Kling as John Doe #1.)

Furthermore, with regard to the sixth leg, there was an underlying fallacy to the government's theory that we intended to exploit fully. If, for the sake of argument, their theory was correct, then the two conspirators had gone to great lengths, and very considerable expense, to build their deadly bomb. McVeigh had traveled the country looking for parts and components. He had engineered the robbery of a friend in order to raise money. He had used all manner of aliases and disguises and subterfuges in order to pull it off.

Yet this arch-criminal had spent all of $250 on his own getaway car.

Why? Was this really all he could afford?

The Mercury Grand Marquis was nearly twenty years old. It had a gas gauge permanently plunked on empty, a gas cap that literally had to be pried open. And Tom Manning at the Firestone store in Junction City also had to sell McVeigh extra cans of transmission fluid because the transmission "had problems."

97,000 miles?

It could as well have been 197,000 or 297,000 depending on how many times the odometer had turned over.

In addition, there was a huge spot of primer on the driver's side. (For easy identification?) And that master touch of inconspicuousness: no license plate on the rear when he was stopped by Hanger. (Even James Nichols—no great friend of Tim's—offered in an interview that there was no way Tim McVeigh would have driven without a license plate.)

Some getaway car. Such careful planning, for a man who, the government was going to contend, was careful enough to bring along earplugs to keep from being deafened by the blast.

How were they going to square the two McVeighs: The indigent, none-too-bright drifter, or the mastermind who had planned and executed the largest terrorist act in our history?

Or were there—perhaps—two McVeighs?

Or were they going to argue, somehow, that Timothy James McVeigh *wanted* to be caught? And if he had wanted to be caught, why would he bother calling a bail bondsman and lawyer when he was booked in the Noble County Jail?

Six legs.

Not a one was what you would call solid. Although there is no percentage in trying to predict a jury's reactions, there was wobble everywhere we looked—the basis, at least, for reasonable doubt. And that made forensic evidence—the fourth leg of the table—absolutely pivotal.

For those of us who grew up during the early age of television, by far the most resourceful, dedicated, determined, and courageous of our small-screen heroes were FBI agents. Other crime fighters may have made us titter—I'm thinking of Sgt. Friday and the Los Angeles Police Department as depicted in *Dragnet*—but the Federal Bureau of Investigation was serious business. We know now that J. Edgar Hoover was a master manipulator, the orchestrator of a media campaign that presented an organization as infallible as it was indefatigable. The FBI agent of our youth was a kind of Superman-in-training, and he was backed by the most rigorous and ingenious crime lab in the world—the very model, we were told, of forensic science in action. Who would ever have thought to criticize the FBI Lab?

Well, one man did—and indefatigably.

His name was Frederic Whitehurst. A Ph.D. chemist and Vietnam vet, Whitehurst worked at the FBI Crime Lab as a supervisory special agent from 1986 until his suspension a decade later, when he was physically banned from FBI property. He was the classic whistle-blower. For almost a decade he wrote reports, letters, complaints criticizing the shoddy practices of the lab and the irresponsible performances of some of his colleagues. He should have been a national hero—and to many he was. But to the FBI he was a pariah, someone it finally had to get rid of. In 1998, the FBI reached a settlement with Whitehurst's lawyers, whereby he was fired but received a payment of $1.2 million, which, if reasonably invested, would be the equivalent of what his lifetime pension would have been. He was also paid a second, undisclosed sum in lieu of damages.

That Whitehurst's patient efforts to reform the lab internally ever became public knowledge was due to a fortuitous slip in the World Trade Center bombing case, when a sealed transcript inadvertently made its way into the public record and was discovered by ABC-TV investigative reporter Brian Ross. Ross interviewed Whitehurst, and although Whitehurst's personality came across on television as somewhat inflexible, his carefully measured and sincere words must have sent a shudder down the collective spine of official Washington. Much later, after our trial, John F. Kelly and Phillip K. Wearne would publish the whole story in *Tainting Evidence: Inside the Scandals at the FBI Crime Lab* (New York: Free Press, 1998). If it is true, as has been suggested, that Frederic Whitehurst was to the FBI Lab what John Dean was to Richard Nixon's White House, then Kelly and Wearne, as reporters, did to the lab what Carl Bernstein and Bob Woodward did in the Watergate case.

Whitehurst wasn't the first to criticize the lab or understand the contradiction at the heart of its forensic work. In a nutshell: Was a lab researcher a scientist first or a special agent? Was his first allegiance to the truth or to Department of Justice prosecutors? The debate, in the past, had always been resolved in favor of the latter. It is conceivable too that before the age of DNA typing, advanced trace analysis, and sophisticated statistical comparisons by computer a more subjective, seat-of-the-pants approach to crime-solving in the lab might have been tolerable. But that freewheeling, proprosecution approach had infected the lab, deeply corrupting its findings. Take the FBI Lab's Chemistry and Toxicology Unit. One would think that such a unit would be run by expert, diligent scientists. In fact the head of the unit, Roger Martz, doesn't even have a degree in chemistry. When asked to examine the residues found in McVeigh's clothing at the time of his arrest, Martz sloppily handled the clothing without bothering to swab or vacuum the evidence (standard procedure in any normal forensic evaluation) and concluded that the clothes linked McVeigh to the crime. This conclusion was all the more remarkable because in order to conduct such analysis properly one needs to look at the evidence under a microscope, something Martz didn't find necessary. Perhaps Roger Martz has such incredible eyesight that he doesn't need a microscope, and perhaps his body is so sterile and clean that he can freely touch sensitive evidence without any fear of contamination, and perhaps despite not having been academically trained as a chemist he knows something everyone else doesn't. But it was no surprise to the defense that his results, as we shall see, varied considerably from those obtained by a scientifically trained investigator.

Kelly and Wearne, in *Tainting Evidence*, would cover the major cases of the last decade in which forensic examination played a significant role—the Unabomber, Ruby Ridge, O. J. Simpson, the World Trade Center, as well as the Oklahoma City bombing—and the impact the FBI Lab's problems had on those prosecutions. The only one of these cases of direct interest to us was the World Trade Center bombing. Not only had it involved a truck bomb (diagnosed as a urea nitrate bomb by FBI experts); the same forensic investigators who'd worked on the World Trade Center investigation had also been assigned to the Oklahoma City case: David Williams and Steve Burmeister.

(It is worth noting that two days before the Oklahoma City bombing Frederic Whitehurst was evaluated by his superior, whose

evaluation was approved, in turn, by his own superior. Whitehurst
was called the most outstanding forensic chemist in the lab's explosive trace unit. But two days later, when the Murrah Building
exploded and 168 people died, Whitehurst was left at home—presumably because he was considered politically unreliable.)

David Williams was head of the Explosives Unit at the lab. A
zoology major, he had joined the unit in the 1970s, then served five
years in a field office before returning in 1987, when he became
Whitehurst's and Burmeister's boss. As Kelly and Wearne have
pointed out, Williams was the one who boasted, "I knew within two
hours of entering the World Trade Center what type of bomb we
had and how big it was." Such statements, and the backward logic
that led to them, would end up getting Williams in deep trouble—
in 1997, after publication of the inspector general's report, he would
be kicked out of the lab—but in April 1995, when he and Burmeister arrived in Oklahoma City, he was still riding high, and within
hours of the bombing he had been named crime scene manager.

The IG investigation into the lab had in fact already begun. In the
beginning it was low-key, a routine audit, and even after it began to
examine accusations by Whitehurst that reports of his had been
altered by his superiors, the idea was for the IG and the FBI's internal audit people to work hand-in-hand. By mid-1995, though, as
news of the investigation and Whitehurst's charges began to leak
into the media, it became clear—to the FBI as well as the IG office—
that too much was at stake, and the IG took it over entirely, though
its sphere was limited to three units in the Scientific Analysis Section: Explosives, Materials Analysis, and Chemistry-Toxicology.

The McVeigh defense knew some of what was going on. We certainly knew about Fred Whitehurst, and in September 1995 we
moved to get copies of all his reports and complaints and permission
to interview him. There began the endless, and by now familiar, arm
wrestling between us and the prosecution, as expensive and time-
consuming as it was frustrating, with our trying to pry information
free and Beth Wilkinson—who else?—given the task of obfuscating,
delaying, and hiding when necessary.

The skirmishing continued throughout 1996. Bob Wyatt was in
charge of it for the defense—the motions, the requests, the preparation for court hearings, the amassing of such information as we

could get our hands on, the scathing comments of our own experts as lab reports were doled out to us. To cite but one example, we asked repeatedly for manuals and protocols—a protocol being a statement, outline, or guideline of standard operating procedures, step by step, complete with anticontamination measures—that the lab experts would systematically follow. Any laboratory of any kind could reasonably be expected to have protocols and follow them, but it turned out that in the exalted confines of the Scientific Analysis Section no orderly manuals devoted to protocols existed! Finally, in fall 1996 we were given a selection of what were called protocols, which to the eyes of our experts weren't protocols at all. Some of them, embarrassingly enough, were handwritten. As Dr. Lloyd observed, throwing up his hands when confronted with a sudden deluge of lab-generated paperwork that came to us in November, "There was a general pattern—the use of degraded, unchecked equipment, the reporting of positive results when they hadn't done the tests to draw any such conclusions, a whole range of problems."

Meanwhile, there was the missing IG report. The vaguer Beth Wilkinson became about its whereabouts, the more we knew we were onto something radioactive. It was one of those any-month-now deals, beginning in April 1996 and stretching into the next year. However vague Ms. Wilkenson was in her words to us and the court, the message was clear: If there was any way the prosecution could have flushed the report down the toilet, it would have; failing that, it was going to fight to the death to keep us from getting our hands on it.

And with good reason.

By January 1997 we knew there was a completed draft report. It was kept under the tightest security while the FBI reviewed it, but there were enough leaks to make us keep the pressure up, and in March, meanwhile, the National Association of Criminal Lawyers went to court to compel its release, fearing that the FBI might get it sufficiently watered down to blunt the appeals any number of defense advocates were planning to make because of it.

Finally, on April 5, 1997, that is, when jury selection in the trial was well under way, the report was published. It was devastating.

The whole report made for fascinating reading, and citing just its summary will make the points amply:

- that David Williams worked backwards and actually could prove nothing about the makeup of the bomb from forensic evidence;

- that Roger Martz fudged when interviewed by the IG investigators and finally admitted his own negligence;

- that J. Thomas Thurman, overall chief of the Explosives Unit, had simply looked the other way;

- and that, along the line, Steve Burmeister had been encouraged to "alter" his reports.

The following is quoted verbatim from the final IG report:

Williams' September 5, 1995 report contained several serious flaws. Just as he had done in the World Trade Center case, he offered an opinion about the velocity of detonation (VOD) of the main charge that was unjustified. His statement about the VOD of an ammonium nitrate fuel oil (ANFO) explosive—the explosive allegedly used in the bombing—was incomplete. His categorical identification of the main charge as ANFO was inappropriate based on the scientific evidence available to him. Here, Williams did not draw a valid scientific conclusion but rather speculated from the fact that one of the defendants purchased ANFO components. His estimate of the weight of the main charge was too specific, and again was based in part on the improper, non-scientific ground of what a defendant had allegedly purchased. In other respects as well, his work was flawed and lacked a scientific foundation. The errors he made were all tilted in such a way as to incriminate the defendants. We concluded that Williams failed to present an objective, unbiased, and competent report.

Williams' supervisor, J. Thomas Thurman, did not properly review Williams' report. Thurman left too much discretion to Williams to include certain opinions, and Thurman allowed certain conclusions to stand even though he told us that he now does not agree with them and cannot justify them, and the conclusions are unsupported in the body of the report.

All cases handled by the Laboratory deserve professional, diligent treatment. Williams' and Thurman's performance in the

Oklahoma City case—a prosecution of enormous national significance—merit special censure.

Serious flaws. Unjustified. Incomplete. Improper. Nonscientific. Lacked a scientific foundation.

This is the government talking, mind you. This isn't the McVeigh defense, or even Frederic Whitehurst. This isn't the media. This is the inspector general of the United States Department of Justice talking, the federal government's own watchdog.

Is it any wonder Beth Wilkinson tried to hide it?

In its recommendations concerning personnel, the IG report read as follows:

CTU Chief Roger Martz lacks the judgment and credibility to perform in a supervisory role in the laboratory. If Martz continues to work as an examiner, we suggest that he be supervised by a scientist qualified to review his work substantively and that he be counseled on the appropriate manner for testifying about forensic work. We further recommended that another qualified examiner review any analytical work by Martz that is to be used as a basis for future testimony.

EU Chief J. Thomas Thurman deserves special censure for his inadequate supervisory review of Williams' report in the Oklahoma City bombing case. Because we concluded that all examiners in the EU, including the Chief, should have a scientific background, we recommended that he be reassigned outside the Laboratory when that restructuring occurs.

EU examiner David Williams should be reassigned outside the Laboratory. Although we did not find that Williams had perjured himself in the World Trade Center case, his work in that case and in the Oklahoma City investigation demonstrate that he lacks the objectivity, judgment, and scientific knowledge that should be possessed by a Laboratory examiner.

Is it any wonder that David Williams, Roger Martz, and J. Thomas Thurman were nowhere to be found when the prosecution published its list of witnesses for trial? Or that it fell to Steve Burmeister, their subordinate, to carry virtually the entire expert testimony for the prosecution?

The report was devastating to the FBI, the Justice Department, the prosecution. Devastating, finally, to the country.

This third leg on the table, then, the forensic leg, which in such a highly circumstantial case ought to have been one of the prosecution's strongest legs, turned out to be one of its weakest. We had already seen the effect of an attack on a forensic laboratory in another high-profile, highly circumstantial case. I'm referring to the way Barry Scheck and company all but obliterated the Los Angeles Police Department's laboratory in *California v. O. J. Simpson*. The way things looked to Rob and me that February night, we saw no reason why we couldn't hold the FBI Lab to the same scrutiny.

So yes, when it came to the prosecution's six-legged table, we were looking good indeed. We'd come a very long way too. We'd prevented a trial before any Oklahoma judge, and we'd obtained the change of venue. Severance followed. In addition, Judge Matsch had issued a number of favorable evidentiary rulings. For example, he'd overturned an earlier ruling by Judge Russell that McVeigh's refusal to give handwriting samples could be used against him at the trial. Our jury would hear no opinion evidence whatsoever on handwriting; Judge Matsch wouldn't permit it.

And while the thrust of our defense was going to be to attack the government's case (because the burden was on them to produce evidence of guilt beyond a reasonable doubt, not on us to prove innocence), we also had Carol Howe to talk about, and all those nice folks from Elohim City—Andy and Dennis and Robert and the (former) king of the Ozarks plus Ramzi Yousef, Edwin Angeles, and Terry Nichols's other friends in the Philippines.

Looking good.

The media certainly saw it that way. What had been perceived, two years before, as an open-and-shut case and a pro forma trial was now looking like a close contest of uncertain outcome. As Rick Serrano, the *Los Angeles Times* reporter, would say, at this point "the defense held the hot hand." Even ABC's *20/20* aired a fifteen-minute segment suggesting that the government had had prior knowledge of the bombing. As for the trial itself, more than two thousand journalists from all over the world were seeking press credentials to cover it. We were a scant six weeks away.

No wonder there was disarray on the prosecution side! According to some of our friends in the media, the government's lawyers were at each others' throats. The old cracks between the Oklahoma remnant and Joe Hartzler's contingent had split wide open, and Larry Mackey's efforts at making peace between the two factions had apparently failed. Meanwhile, some FBI agents had had enough of being jerked around by the prosecutors—who could blame them?— and were openly showing their disdain, and ATF people were just as openly enraged with the FBI, saying its theory of the case was all wrong. Finally, each of the leading government lawyers had begun leaking stories to favored media sources—stories that pointed the finger at the others.

I'd seen this happen before, although never on this scale. It was a clear sign of panic.

Maybe it really *was* time to take the question mark off that *National Law Journal* headline.

S till.
As long as I was talking to Rob Nigh, I couldn't help but be buoyed by his optimism. We'd worked so hard, so long, and sometimes wanting is believing. I'm not going to say I was convinced we were headed for an acquittal, but we certainly had a hung jury in our sights.

Once I was alone, however, a sense of caution returned. Call it a trial lawyer's sixth sense, if you will, but in my private self I felt a measure of uneasy foreboding. Almost two years had passed since I'd taken the assignment, and during that time I'd come to know, close up, how powerful the forces marshaled against us were and to what lengths the minions of the Justice Department would go in order to win.

The old thoughts came back: Susan Otto's strange and Cassandralike pronouncement that day in John Coyle's office. And my own version of it, which was that the government didn't intend to lose this case. What that really meant, to me, was that everyone at Justice couldn't *afford* to lose it. Certainly Janet Reno's job would be on the line if they did, and Louis Freeh's, for they belonged to an administration in Washington that harbored not the slightest loyalty to perceived losers. Maybe, by now, the prosecutors and the special agents who worked for them had come to hate and distrust each other, maybe they were tripping over their own egos and ambitions, but someone among them—Hartzler? Garland? Gorelick?—had to have a plan.

Someone did. But before we could sniff it out, disaster suddenly and unexpectedly befell the defense.

13

"THE DALLAS MORNING NEWS HAS BEEN THE VICTIM OF A HOAX"

It started with a phone call from Robert Hillman the morning of Thursday, February 27, the day after we had gathered the defense team together and taken stock of our case. Hillman was a reporter for *The Dallas Morning News* Washington bureau, but he'd been in Denver, helping out with the paper's coverage of the trial, and he asked if he could interview me later in the day.

"Sure," I said, "come on over."

To which he replied, "It'll only take a minute. Incidentally, where are you going to be tomorrow afternoon, at four o'clock?"

"Tomorrow afternoon? How come?"

"Well, Pete Slover wants to talk to you then."

Pete Slover and Arnold Hamilton were the two reporters from the paper I usually talked to. I knew them fairly well. Both had been out to the house for lunch in Enid, and Arnold had been the first media person I'd told, back in 1995, about the missing leg.

"Actually," I told Hillman, "tomorrow afternoon I'm going to be on the road to Enid. By four o'clock, I should be somewhere in central Kansas. Car phone connections are pretty poor. I don't know if he'll be able to get through to me. Isn't this something we can talk about now?"

"Not with me," he said. "But you might try Pete at the office."

This I did, and when I found Slover, I explained that I'd be on the road the next day.

"Why can't you tell me what it is?" I asked him. "I'm not going to scoop you, God knows. If it's a reaction you're after, let me give it to you now, provided I can, and I'll keep my mouth shut."

"I don't have it now," he said guardedly. "I won't have it till tomorrow afternoon."

I pushed him to tell me what "it" was, without success.

"Isn't there some place I can be sure to catch you?" he said.

"Well, you can try," I answered, "but I can't promise anything."

What was weird about this was that in all the hundreds, if not thousands, of contacts I'd had with the media, this was the first time someone had tried to pin me down to a specific time of day—other than for a live television broadcast. But Slover wasn't television, he was print.

I didn't get it.

And when Hillman showed up for his interview there was nothing remotely newsworthy about what he asked me. On the contrary, all he basically wanted to know was whether I thought Tim McVeigh could get a fair trial in Denver. If anything, I was irritated by having to answer. Did he really think I was going to say no, that we couldn't? After all, we were the ones who'd petitioned the court for the change of venue, and we'd seen nothing up to this point to suggest choosing Denver had been a mistake.

But the combination of these two inexplicable and rather bizarre events—Hillman's anodyne questions and Slover's insistence that I be available at a specific time, sufficed to put me on my guard. Something funny was going on. I called Sherrel in Enid and told her I'd decided, on a hunch, that I'd better stick around in Denver.

Sure enough, about 3:30 P.M. the next afternoon, Slover called me. I was in my Denver office. I turned on my tape recorder.

STEPHEN JONES: Hello?
PETE SLOVER: Mr. Jones?
JONES: Pete, how are you?
SLOVER: I'm okay. Thanks. How are you?
JONES: Fine, thank you.

SLOVER: The story I'm working on is a story that's based on defense internal documents that recount interviews with your client, in which he said that he did the bombing as well as some of the underlying overt acts, and I need to ask you about what that sort of information—not the information I'm working on the story, but the information that was apparently transmitted to your team by Mr. McVeigh in these interviews—how it affects your defense, and—uh—whether you are aware of it.

Verbatim, from the transcript of our conversation.

My first thought was that this was about the oldest trick in the book. You pretend you have something—some defense material, or something McVeigh allegedly said—and you go fishing. It had happened to me before. I'd never known Slover to do it, but there's always a first time.

"Well, Pete," I said, "I couldn't possibly comment without seeing what you have, because as far as I know, you don't have anything and you're just fishing."

I suggested he send over a copy of whatever it was. Without seeing it, I said, there was no way I was going to give him any kind of comment.

He ducked sending me anything—for good reason, although I didn't understand why right off. Then he launched into a description of what he had—"specific excerpts," he called them. He claimed there were two interviews, one in July 1995, one in December, both between McVeigh and a defense staffer. In one of them, he said, apparently reading, "McVeigh insisted he was the one who drove the Ryder truck." He went on from there. McVeigh allegedly said they'd bombed the Murrah Building by day rather than by night because they'd wanted "the body count." Slover cited other "details" having to do with James Nichols, who, as far as McVeigh knew, had known nothing about the bombing unless Terry had told him, and Marife Nichols, and the Roger Moore robbery, and the Marion quarry burglary, and how he, McVeigh, had once filled out an application to become a member of the Ku Klux Klan.

None of it, to tell the truth, sounded remotely familiar to me.

I gathered myself together.

"I don't presume to know what everybody has said at any given point," I said,

and certainly I haven't been present every time Mr. McVeigh has made statements to people that you call defense staffers. But either one of two things has happened here. I'm not saying that it is because I don't know. Either you have been given some disinformation that has been typed or printed up or given to you in some fashion, or else you have possession of stolen material that *The Dallas Morning News* is not supposed to have. Specifically, stolen documents. I intend to bring this matter immediately to Judge Matsch's attention, and I want to know the name of your editor and the lawyer for *The Dallas Morning News*. And I want to discuss the serious consequences of publishing a story that is either absolutely false on its face, because I don't know whether such documents exist, or you have documents that you are not supposed to have that will seriously impact the date, the time, and the place of this trial, but more importantly lead to an investigation of *The Dallas Morning News*.

The more I talked, the more I worked myself up, the quieter he became.

He gave me the name of the newspaper's lawyer in Dallas, Paul Watler. He started to give me his immediate supervisor, but I told him I wanted to go further up the chain. He then suggested that since I was talking legal action I'd better talk to Watler.

I replied that I would, as soon as I'd talked to Judge Matsch.

We had a fairly elaborate document retrieval and scanning capability in our system, but we must, by then, have processed pieces of paper in the millions, and though I gave instructions to start searching, using certain key words, it could take hours to find the documents Slover had referred to, if indeed they were ours. Meanwhile, some ten minutes later, having already advised Jim Manspeaker, the clerk of the court, of what had happened, I had Paul Watler on the phone.

Watler knew full well why I was calling. Pete Slover was no dummy, and in fact he'd been educated as a lawyer himself. Watler claimed this had been no "ruse" on Slover's part to lure me into commenting, and he denied that the documents in question had been stolen but rather had been obtained through "usual news gathering methods."

We jousted and postured over the phone, as lawyers will. Matsch had put a gag order on the participants in the case, and the documents, if they were real, were clearly protected by attorney-client privilege, as well as Matsch's protective order.

Watler said that they felt themselves under no legal constraint not to publish a news story based on the documents. I warned him that if the newspaper did this it would not only disrupt the trial but also bring the whole judiciary—judges, appellate courts, other lawyers—down on their heads. Legalities aside, it would be the pariah of the media.

In the meantime, though, even as I was haranguing Paul Watler, our phones had started ringing off the hook.

The worst had just happened.

At 4:00 P.M., clearly afraid it was going to be either scooped or enjoined, *The Dallas Morning News* published the story on its internet website. It had "legally obtained" defense documents, it told a global audience, proving that McVeigh had confessed to a defense investigator. Now, if Timothy McVeigh had ever made a genuine admission of guilt, he would not make it, in passing, to an investigator; he would make it to me as his counsel. And I would not write it down. *The Dallas Morning News* either misunderstood or misrepresented the document it had used. But the damage to the defense would turn out to be incalculable.

The media clamored for a statement, and this was simply not something we could ignore. We told them we were going to the courthouse at 5:00 P.M. Meanwhile we worked frantically to prepare documents necessary for filing a lawsuit against *The Dallas Morning News*, and at 5:00 P.M. the defense team marched out en masse to see Judge Matsch.

It had started to snow. I remember walking alongside Dick Burr and saying, "I hope we're doing the right thing. There's something going on that doesn't smell right."

Judge Matsch looked at the lawsuit, then at me through those glasses that magnified his eyes.

"Are you sure you want to file this?" he asked me.

I realized he was trying to tell me something.

"No," I answered.

Then he leaned forward in his chair, and he said, "Don't, then," and I took the papers back. Then he called the government lawyers in. Needless to say, poker faces or not, they had to be jumping for joy inside when I explained briefly what had happened.

I asked Matsch to lift the gag order so that I could respond to *The Dallas Morning News*. He did, and back down the elevator we went, and out the front doors of the courthouse, where now it was snowing, to beat the band.

There must have been a hundred reporters waiting outside, with lights, microphones, and all the paraphernalia they use for "breaking stories." I walked out, bareheaded, into the maelstrom of bright lights and falling snowflakes, and I realized the only possible strategy was to be bold.

"*The Dallas Morning News*," I announced, "has been the victim of a hoax."

(In fact, it would turn out that I was correct, but not in the way I then thought.) Appealing to the basic liberalism of most reporters, I told them I now understood what Pres. John F. Kennedy had meant when he called *The Dallas Morning News* one of the most irresponsible newspapers in the country. (The occasion for this had been when the then-publisher insulted the president in the White House dining room. In fact, the paper, which when I was growing up had been considered Texas's premier newspaper, had in fact gone into decline during the sixties under ultraconservative ownership. More recently, it had made something of a comeback, with new leadership, new reporters, and investments in technology.) A large number of those present thoroughly enjoyed my kicking their rival in the backside, and their questions were friendly for the most part, the worst of them being if we intended to ask for a delay in the trial or a change of venue.

I said no, not at present, and as soon as I could, I ducked away and went back to the office. We still hadn't found the document or documents in question. I was walking down the hall when I ran into Randy Coyne, with whom, I admit, my relations had been sometimes strained. He asked me if I was aware that a member of the defense team, a man I'll call X, had recently had lunch with Slover and Hamilton?

I was furious with Coyne. How could he even suggest such a thing? Didn't he realize that X was an old, dear, and loyal friend of mine?

I went back to my office, brooding on what he'd said. It hadn't so much as occurred to me that X might be a possible culprit—if there even was one. But a crisis of major proportions was upon us, and if anybody thought that by doing nothing it would all blow over— well, it wouldn't. That Friday night I sent out word that I wanted all members of the defense team, at least all those who were in the United States, to fly to Denver that night or early the next day— including X. In the meantime, the staff was still conducting a scanning search to see if they could find a document that remotely resembled what *The Dallas Morning News* had.

I went back to my apartment. Several hours passed, and the document still couldn't be found. I again read *The Dallas Morning News* internet story and noticed the word "waterbed" in it. We had hundreds of thousands of documents in our system that referenced the bombing, or McVeigh, or other key words, but darned few, I would have thought, that used "waterbed." I got onto the office and told them to get the litigation support people to sweep everything for "waterbed."

And there it was, forty-five minutes later.

It was unfamiliar to me, to Rob Nigh, to Ann Bradley, and to Bob Wyatt. But it had been prepared by somebody on the investigative wing of the defense team.

What in the name of God was going on?

We made every effort to find that somebody. It turned out he was overseas, but it took us the better part of twelve hours to find that out.

The next morning, the story was front-paged in the Denver papers. *The New York Times*, however, barely mentioned it, and then only in passing. *Hedging their bets*, I thought.

Now I had to find out how *The Dallas Morning News* had gotten its hands on it—and what else they had.

I called Amber McLaughlin in and asked her to interview, first separately, then together, two people whom I suspected. Neither mentioned anything about a lunch with Slover. Then I saw them separately myself.

The first person incriminated X. Allegedly, X had taken a defense laptop computer out of the secretary's office on the day in question and had told the secretary not to say anything about it.

If true, this was shocking news, for it meant, quite possibly, that the internet story was only the tip of the iceberg.

I interviewed X. It was extremely painful. Loyalty counts in my book, and we'd been friends for so long. I simply couldn't believe what seemed to have happened. But I couldn't not believe it either.

X denied everything. I gave him every opening to speak, and to speak in confidence, but it did no good.

I frankly didn't know what to do, and time was running out. I had never seen the document in question, and I was astounded by what I read. I wasn't even sure how on earth it had gotten into our files. I knew McVeigh hadn't truthfully confessed to anybody, and the "conversation" certainly didn't represent the facts of the case as I understood them. At the same time, the author was a careful and experienced person. There had to be an explanation. Could it be that he was trying to shield interviews he'd held by intermingling comments by the client—real or made up—thereby protecting them under attorney-client communication or attorney-client work product? If that was it, it was convoluted as all get-out.

I called a staff meeting that afternoon. Everyone crowded into the conference room. The atmosphere was tense, and to a large extent, I suppose, that was due to me. They all knew why we were there. I didn't have to elaborate.

"Someone among us has betrayed us," I announced to the group. That word *betrayed* was the euphemism of the year, but I let it stand. "I'm appointing Bob Wyatt to be our 'Inquisitor General,' with Amber to assist him. Their assignment will be to get to the bottom of it, and let the chips fall where they may. I have every confidence they will get there too."

I paused, letting them think about it. Letting X think about it.

"At the same time," I said, "I'd still prefer that the individual responsible for it simply own up to it. I'm going back to my apartment now. I'm going to be there alone. And I'm going to stay there until the person responsible comes to see me."

With that, I abruptly got up and walked out of the room.

I knew I had to be careful, because the media had our building staked out everywhere they could hide. Channel 9 from Oklahoma City had tried to film us through the glass facades of our offices and had to be shooed away by our security people. But there was a connecting, closed-in walkway from our office building to my apartment building, and I used that as a means of avoiding attention.

I waited.

Around 7 P.M., the phone rang. It was X. He wanted to see me. I told him to come on over.

There was something surreal about it, the two of us sitting facing each other, alone, in a Denver apartment, thirty-six floors above the street, with snow on the ground outside. We'd had a professional relationship for many years, one of mutual confidence and marked by X's discretion and loyalty. I'd relied on him many times, in many situations, and his work had always been of the highest caliber. But it went beyond that. He had always been welcome in my home. He knew my family, my children. Only now did I realize that we had already had our last conversation as friends.

He told me the story—up to a point. He'd had a lunch date with Hamilton and Slover at the County Line restaurant in Oklahoma City. This was back in January. He'd driven to the restaurant. He had the defense laptop in his car, and it was loaded with a number of specific databases of ours. In the past Slover had helped X by providing him, on the sly, with some inconsequential documents *The Dallas Morning News* had dug up while investigating the case. Now, in the sort of quid pro quo that goes on frequently behind the scenes of a big case, X planned to return the favor. In this instance, Slover wanted to see some FBI 302s that we'd been given. The laptop presumably had those 302s, but it also had much, much more.

What happened next was hazy. After lunch, X had gone with the two reporters to the Oklahoma City office of *The Dallas Morning News*. He'd had the laptop with him. Hamilton had more or less disappeared after they got to the office. According to X, a telephone call came through for him on his cellular phone. Slover suggested that he might want to take it in his car, and he'd done that. Leaving the office. Leaving the laptop.

When he came back, X said, Slover left almost immediately, not even bothering to say goodbye.

Of course, X had had no business being in Slover's office. He'd had no business going to lunch with him and Hamilton. We had a written policy—it was all in a memorandum that everybody received—that all communications with the media went through me, with the sole exception of the Tulsa people, whom I'd had Rob Nigh take care of, because he'd worked and lived there, and Ann Bradley, who sometimes did liaison work. (In fact I'd been roundly criticized for the policy, from within as well as without, but I had a number of reasons for it, and ego—my own—wasn't one of them.) There was no authority for a defense subcontractor—be they a lawyer or investigator or staff member or secretary—to have lunch with a representative of the media. Much less go to his office with him. Much less carry a loaded defense laptop.

Yet this is precisely what had happened.

As soon as Slover left the office that day, X said, "I knew I'd just been fucked."

But had he called me to tell me?

No.

And later, as he admitted, when Slover had told him he was going to run the story, had he called me to tell me? When I might still have been able to prevent it?

No.

I didn't press him as to why he'd done it. Maybe I knew he'd lie, and I didn't want any more lies. He had known well that the laptop had been fully loaded. There were lots of easy ways that he could have given Slover the 302s (if Slover ever truly asked for any such documents) without giving him a chance to steal everything. Whether X had carelessly left the laptop in the hands of Slover when he went to take his call or whether that was just a story to mask a more overt betrayal didn't concern me much at the moment. I had to deal with the fallout, and it was as serious a crisis as anything I had ever faced as a defense attorney. The story that our client had confessed had already circled the globe. That was bad enough. But there was something else that was potentially worse. I had already asked Maria Ryan, who was much involved in our day-to-day operations, to pinpoint the day X's laptop had been loaded and what it would have been loaded with. Within two hours, she found partial answers, and I then asked Ann Bradley to begin a systematic study of certain classes of documents to see whether it was likely *The Dallas Morning News* had them.

Meanwhile, X tried to tell me he was sorry. But the damage had been done. He had betrayed the defense, he had betrayed our client, and he had betrayed our friendship. There just simply weren't words to express the sad frustration I felt or, I suppose, words that X could use to explain why he'd done what he did.

"This is a dangerous situation," I said grimly. "Very dangerous."

"I know that," he said. "Look, I'm sorry. What do you want me to do?"

"I want you to go home. I want you to stay there. You're not to talk to anybody about this. Nobody, is that clear?"

He nodded.

"You're off this case. I'm never going to be able to use you again, and you'd better hope to hell I can limit the damages this time." In fact, because I needed to control the damage, I promised X that I wouldn't use his name publicly if he would, before leaving, help me piece together exactly what *The Dallas Morning News* now had and cooperate with us if we needed him to.

The disaster, in fact, turned out to be of monumental proportions. *The Dallas Morning News*, we calculated, was now sitting on well more than 100,000 documents, assuming it'd been able to break our security passwords, which I guessed it had, and these documents included all 30,000 FBI 302s and inserts as well as all of our and Mike Tigar's investigative reports shared under reciprocal discovery, not to mention all sorts of internal defense memos and chronologies. *The Dallas Morning News* now had the names and addresses of confidential contacts in foreign countries—such as the Director in the Philippines—and confidential memoranda evaluating sources in the federal government, here and abroad.

The laptop even had included documents that had been filed with the court under seal. There were mountains of these, papers that by court order were not to be released to anyone. Depending on what had been downloaded, there could have been motions, rulings on motions, confidential memoranda. *All* of our expenses, invoices, vouchers, reimbursements were court-sealed documents. They were, in effect, court secrets, and *The Dallas Morning News* had them. It was safe to assume it'd been through all of it by now, backward and forward. There was nothing—at least nothing yet—to keep it from running a story a day, or two or three stories a day. This was clearly the biggest scoop in its history.

How could we go on? How could we possibly hold the trial?

Although we're accustomed to reporters obtaining documents on the sly, it isn't always legal to do so, and in this case it was clear that Pete Slover had committed a crime (not, as I would later discover, for the first time). A lawyer himself, he had to know the meaning of "attorney-client work product" and "attorney-client privilege" and know too that he couldn't have such material legally unless I or Tim McVeigh had authorized it. At the very least, he had knowingly received and used—or misused—stolen property. Paul Watler's statement—that the paper had come by the documents through the "usual news-gathering methods"—was plain wrong, and I wondered how much Slover had told the lawyer about how he'd acquired them.

After X left, I called Slover at his home number. I got his answering machine.

I left a message that went like this:

Pete, I know all about lunch at the County Line restaurant and your meeting afterward at your office in Oklahoma City. You may well have committed a crime. You need to call me immediately, or have your lawyer call me.

Then I left the same message for Arnold Hamilton.

Two minutes later, no more, Slover called back. He was breathless, as though he might be hyperventilating.

"Pete," I said, "on second thought I don't want to talk to you. I'm going to try to save your ass, not for your sake but for the sake of an old friend of mine whom you corrupted. You better have Watler call me."

About half an hour later, having heard from no one, I called the paper's city desk in Dallas and asked to speak to the senior editor. When he came on, I identified myself, and asked if he was aware I was trying to reach their lawyer. He said he was.

"Wherever he is, you'd better get him on the phone to me," I said. "I assure you, once he hears what I've got to say, he's not going to resent your butting in on his Saturday night."

Maybe twenty minutes went by, and then it was Watler, peeved and agitated.

"Paul," I started in, "*The Dallas Morning News*, Pete Slover, and possibly Arnold Hamilton have committed a series of federal crimes."

He interrupted me, wanting to know what sections of the code had been violated. I told him I didn't know the section numbers off-hand but that he could get them from his criminal lawyer Monday morning. Meanwhile, these were the facts: Without authorization from me or my client, a member of the defense team had given a defense laptop computer to Slover at the paper's Oklahoma City office, whereupon Slover downloaded the files to a computer either in his office or in Dallas or both.

The paper therefore had material that belonged to the FBI, or that the FBI would lay claim to, material that was sealed by court order, and confidential defense documents including material protected under attorney-client privilege. Unless the paper had a signed authorization by either my client or me, there was no way they could have it "legally."

Almost immediately, Watler's attitude changed. I deduced from this that Slover had indeed lied to him and the paper.

"What are you going to do, Stephen?" he asked me.

"It's not what I'm going to do, it's what you're going to do."

"What do you want us to do?" he asked.

I said, "I want you to gather up every last shred of these records, all your disks too, and either you send them to me or you take custody of them yourself. I want your pledge that you'll never use them again. Then I want to sit down with you and your editors and tell you why you don't have a confession from Tim McVeigh. And then you're going to print a retraction."

"What will you do if we don't?"

"That's academic," I said. "You're going to. But let's leave it like this. If I don't have your agreement by 2:00 P.M. tomorrow, I'm going to call Judge Matsch and the United States Attorney and tell them I have possible evidence of a criminal violation by *The Dallas Morning News*."

That's where we left it.

The next morning I appeared briefly on David Brinkley's *This Week*. Of course, the "confession" was all the pundits wanted to talk about. I was noncommittal, however, and careful at the same time not to say anything that would antagonize *The Dallas Morning News*, because I realized I was asking them to eat a large amount of crow.

Just before 1 P.M. Denver time, Paul Watler called me. All he wanted to know was whether I'd meant 2 P.M. central standard time or mountain standard time.

It was a good sign. I told him mountain time, that he had another hour.

One minute before the deadline, he called back.

"We have a basic agreement," he said. "The position of *The Dallas Morning News* is that they're going to gather all that stuff up—in fact they already have, and they've given it to me and we've locked it up." He continued: "They're never going to use it again for any news-gathering or editorial purposes, they will have no access to it, they will never even refer to it again. Then, we want to have a conference with the judge over the phone this afternoon, telling him what we've done. But we're not going to sit down with you, and we're not going to print a retraction."

Interestingly, Watler had agreed to two things I hadn't asked for: that they would never refer to the "confession" again in their news coverage and that they would file a statement with the court accordingly. The refusal to print a retraction was a fig leaf, a face-saving response. If they'd obtained the documents "legally," there would have been no reason to talk to the court or commit to never to using the materials again. Whether they feared contempt (not a remote possibility), a grand jury investigation, or the spectacle of two of their employees, Slover and Hamilton, slowly twisting in the wind in the presence of media competitors, I can't say. But they were clearly sounding retreat.

I called Jim Manspeaker to tell him what had happened. He confirmed that the judge wouldn't talk with *The Dallas Morning News*. Later that night I got a copy of the newspaper's statement. It didn't go as far as I'd wanted at first, but it would do. I thought the people of Denver—and elsewhere—were smart enough to realize that if the story had a factual basis, *The Dallas Morning News* wouldn't be marching in the rear, holding a white flag.

Meanwhile, on Sunday afternoon, I'd learned the real story of Tim's so-called confession, when J. D. Cash, the journalist from eastern Oklahoma, issued a press release and faxed a copy to our office. I had no idea what J. D. was doing, and I had no hand in it, nor did anyone else on the defense team, but J. D. stepped up to the plate, and he hit a virtual home run.

According to his statement, a defense investigator had shown him the document and told him it was a hoax, one he'd devised in order to gain an interview with a very dangerous, and very high-ranking, white supremacist. It was a ploy to convince the prospective inter-viewee that McVeigh had "accepted responsibility" for his deed and was being a "good soldier" in protecting others involved. Yet if someone got antsy lest we be looking for someone else to accuse, the document "proved" that McVeigh himself accused no one.

The idea that our man could have done such a thing was less fanciful that one might think. Nobody knew, least of all the media, the extent to which we had cultivated members of the neo-Nazi and Christian Identity movements. It was not something we broad-casted, and I had largely stayed out of it. The extreme right, as I have mentioned, had ambivalent feelings toward the McVeigh defense. On the one hand, McVeigh was accused of having done what the extremists themselves had long since sworn to do. On the other hand, the heat was on. The enemy—ZOG—was knocking on their doors. It was time to lie low and speak softly.

But our investigators had spent hundreds of hours tracking these people down in their territory—that is, in the wilds of western North Carolina, Arkansas, Arizona, Nevada, Utah, Montana, Idaho—and they'd used whatever they could as bona fides to get people to talk to us. Tim's "confession" was one such tool. I admit it had been a risky bluff. Now it had backfired badly.

A few reporters expressed incredulity that we would have con-cocted such an elaborate hoax to win over a prospective witness who, we believed, might have played a role in the bombing. Perhaps the media would have understood it better if we'd been able to tell them of Rob Nigh's experience. Mr. Rob had once interviewed a top "official" in a racist organization who, the minute Rob walked in, pulled a gun on him, which he then put on the coffee table between them; he then pulled out a rifle that he set across his knees during the entire hour-and-a-half conversation. Without my going into details here, a couple of our investigators had visited some highly dangerous folks, some of whom had served time for serious crimes and some of whom, if they hadn't, had yet been accused of them. The skeptical reporters didn't know either—nor did we want them to—of the elaborate system we had in place to screen incoming packages, or of the elevators that didn't come to our floors after quitting time because our floors were locked off, or even of the security measures around my house. And they certainly didn't know that one of our lawyers was authorized to carry a concealed weapon, and I kept a pistol in my desk drawer, and beneath my mattress I kept a loaded shotgun. In dealing with the ultra–right wing, suffice it to say, we were not dealing with ordinary people.

That the hoax statement came from J. D. lended the story credibility too. J. D. was a unique figure among the regulars who'd been covering the case from the beginning. Not only had he frequently scooped other reporters because of his special sources in law enforcement in Oklahoma and among the radical right, but he simply didn't buy the government's accepted line—and never had. His reputation for fierce independence encouraged people to talk to him who never would speak to a Barbara Walters or a Mike Wallace or a Tom Brokaw.

In due course, when a name surfaced as the investigator in J. D.'s statement, he found himself in a difficult position. He was, after all, licensed by the state. His supposed use of a false document put him right on the edge, particularly a document he was said to have created himself. Furthermore, if he'd perpetrated the hoax on them too, the right wing would be on his neck, and there was reason to worry about how some of them would react if they felt they'd been scammed.

The name denied any participation, and since not all defense investigators or sources are publicly known, it was difficult for the media to dig any further. When the media asked me what I thought—between J. D.'s claim and the denial—I simply answered, "I don't have a dog in that fight."

B y Sunday night, then, between *The Dallas Morning News*'s "nonretraction" and the J. D. Cash statement, I thought we were in a position to weather the storm. But then, just before 7 A.M.

Monday morning, Roger Charles, who had recently joined us and was very plugged in to the media, called to tell me Ralph Langin was on the *Today* show.

Langin was *The Dallas Morning News*'s editor. I tuned in NBC on my TV set, and there was Langin, and I couldn't believe my ears. Not only was he defying Watler's self-imposed gag order by talking about the affair, but he was *justifying* what they'd done! And denying any responsibility for having done wrong.

He spoke as if their own statement didn't exist!

This can't be, I said to myself. But there he was.

I called Ann Bradley at her apartment and told her to notify the media that I would hold a press conference at 11 A.M. at the Embassy Suites hotel.

She asked me the subject.

"A character-building experience for *The Dallas Morning News*," I replied. "One hour before high noon."

Before the press conference, and as soon as I could get everybody assembled, I held a quick meeting in my apartment of the defense lawyers. I gave them the blow-by-blow of what had happened, briefed them on what I now knew about the so-called confession, and told them I was about to roll the dice. If I failed, it would be my neck, not theirs. I would have to resign as McVeigh's chief counsel, and I didn't want to take any of them with me. But I was doing what I felt I had to do, given what I perceived as an attack on the integrity of the American judicial process.

So downstairs I went, into another crowded room full of lights, cameras, microphones, and wall-to-wall reporters spilling out into the hallways. Some TV stations carried it live—CNN, Oklahoma City, Denver. I began with a detailed statement of what had happened, the statutes that had been violated by Slover and his paper, how dangerous it was, how unfair. I stressed the illegality of what they'd done and the total lack of professionalism.

When reporters started questioning me about the confession itself, I conceded that it was a document from our files without going into details. It was only a few hours later, after we'd learned that CBS was running a segment to the effect that we had fabricated a statement to get a witness to change his testimony, that I put out the whole story, basically endorsing J. D. Cash's statement—which brought the sharks out again.

When I got back to the office afterward, the whole staff, which had been watching on television, was waiting for me in the conference room, and they all stood up and cheered. (After the trial, McVeigh told the *Buffalo News* that our relations had been strained. But at the time, he thought it was my finest hour.)

There was one more arrow left in the quiver, and I let it fly. *The Dallas Morning News* had called a press conference of its own, following mine. I urged Christy O'Connor of Fort Worth Channel 11 to ask the right questions. Christy, a very talented reporter who gave tenacity new meaning, grilled Paul Watler relentlessly, rattling him to the point where he apparently dropped the microphone and canceled the rest of the conference. To add spice to my chili, Christy then wangled an off-the-record interview with the publisher of *The Dallas Morning News* who admitted to her that they'd been shocked and disappointed that not a single other newspaper in the country had come to their support. That was true. As Jo Thomas of *The New York Times* put it to me, what newspaper would ever want to be the subject of an hour-long press conference, carried live, accusing it of theft, of abusing the system, and of depriving Tim McVeigh of his rights to a fair trial?

In hindsight, there are several points I need make about this affair. One is that Slover had gotten himself into trouble several years before. According to a story in *The Dallas Morning News*, Slover had been criminally prosecuted for staying after hours in a county clerk's office in Ellis County, Texas. He claimed at the time that he'd been inadvertently locked in, but phone records showed that Slover, rather than calling for help, had made a very lengthy call from inside the clerk's office to *The Dallas Morning News*. He was indicted for burglary but allowed to plead guilty to a misdemeanor offense (Slover was fined $1,000 and ordered to perform 150 hours of community service). Slover was also a lawyer by training, and as such he had to have known he'd gotten his hands on our files illegally and that X wasn't remotely authorized to give them to him.

The reason Slover called me that Friday afternoon, presumably with the phone in one hand and his finger on the start button to his printing press, was (1) to cover his ass, and (2) to give me a chance to say something he could use. The reason he wouldn't fax me the document was that he feared I would recognize its origins. He didn't want me to know everything he had.

But there is a distinction, of sorts, that should be made between Slover and his paper. I suspect, as I said earlier, that he may have misled Paul Watler, and probably his editor and publisher too, because from what I saw he no longer covered the story for the duration of the trial. The *Today* show aside, *The Dallas Morning News* did act responsibly once Watler learned the truth, and as far as I know his commitment to impounding the material and never using or mentioning it again was carried out fully.

Some people later asked me why I decided to spare Slover and *The Dallas Morning News* after all they had done. After all, there was plenty of grounds to sue. But I knew that legal action might not be our best move strategically. If we sued, then the stolen files could become part of the public record. As there had been violations of federal statutes, the files could get into the hands of the FBI. So we were stuck. I also had to take into account the slim chance that any jury would feel like awarding someone like Tim McVeigh damages. Finally, what would a lawsuit have done but open up the whole can of worms all over again? We'd been thrown from the horse, but instead of yelling at the animal we simply had to dust ourselves off, get back on, and keep riding.

O ur recovery was short-lived. Once, as I've said, I felt compelled to refute the CBS story and, in so doing, endorsed J. D. Cash's press release, the critics came out in force, reminding me that lawyers can't make false statements, they can't make false statements with potential witnesses, and so on. (As though I didn't know that.) I had violated no code of ethics, but I found myself suddenly having to spend my time on the defensive.

A few days later, Tim called the court clerk's office. He announced that he wanted the court to fire me. He'd decided that he wanted a particular member of the defense team (with whom he was barely on speaking terms) and three others, none of whom was an experienced

trial lawyer, to take over his defense. It was an extraordinary develop-
ment. Some months later, Tim would say publicly, *The Dallas Morning News* affair had strained our relations. Why wouldn't he blame
me for X's blunder? I was, after all, the one who hired the person
who had now betrayed him. But at the time, Judge Matsch would
have none of it. He assured me that I was still in command, that I had
the confidence of the court, and that if, on the contrary, I wanted to
fire anybody, he would support me 100 percent.

Instead, I called a meeting of the defense team, the first of several
on the issue. We were still on the case, I told them, and I further
pointed out that responsibility among us was indivisible. Judge
Matsch had made it clear that if I was discharged, which wasn't
going to happen, then so would everyone else.

And then, at the beginning of the following week, disaster struck
again. Ann Bradley burst into my office with the news that *Playboy*
had published a story on the internet about a defense chronology
for Tim McVeigh. Not long after, Sam Donaldson called from ABC
to tell me they now had the chronology too.

Defense chronologies existed for any number of people connected to the case, either as suspects or witnesses. There were
chronologies for Terry Nichols, Marife Nichols, James Nichols, the
Fortiers, among others, and of course Tim McVeigh. They were
built from a variety of sources: press clippings and the media, FBI
302s, other discovery sources, defense interviews. There were
hearsay items included, and speculations, usually highlighted by
question marks. The chronologies were updated and revised from
time to time. Items were dropped (usually because they were dis-
proved, became irrelevant, or had been replaced by new facts) and
others added. The one for Tim McVeigh ultimately grew to more
than five hundred pages. The chronology in question, the one *Playboy* based its story on and ABC had purchased, was matched to a
chronology Amber McLaughlin had prepared in January 1996.

I don't want to dignify the seller by giving his name, so, charita-
bly, I'll call him "Stringer." A *stringer*, according to my dictionary, is
a part-time or freelance reporter, a wannabe full-time hack.

Stringer had apparently touted the document as one based upon
conversations with McVeigh. An inexperienced reporter who wasn't
a lawyer might well have thought that made sense, for it was

stamped "Attorney-Client Communication, Attorney-Client Work Product, Privileged and Confidential." The defense, however, put the same bold legend on virtually every document it generated. In fact I have my doubts that McVeigh had ever seen his own chronology. This is not to say that routine elements in it couldn't have come from him, but there were egregious errors that couldn't have been true if McVeigh actually was the bomber. For instance, Stringer had McVeigh describing himself driving on an Oklahoma City street leading to Interstate 235 when the street in fact doesn't go there. He had McVeigh claiming that he bumped into a postman at a time when there was no postman on the street. A bigger example—one made from whole cloth—had McVeigh telling his attorneys that the bomb had a pull-plug detonator. Not only did McVeigh never say that but it wasn't even the government's theory. It was ATF's theory. What's more, it wasn't even in the chronology. Stringer had just thrown it in. It was a complete fabrication.

I've spent almost no time on ATF's theory because it's not germane to my story, but we knew the bureau's timeline and theory of the bomb itself was entirely different from the one the government would present at trial. The FBI had simply brushed it away. But here was Stringer advertising it as though it had come from McVeigh himself. You didn't have to be a rocket scientist to guess who had helped him with his story.

I had Stringer investigated thoroughly by a member of our staff. He reported that the daughter of an employee admitted (on tape) that Stringer acquired the material from her while she was having an affair with him. Allegedly, he'd had no intention of using it until after the trial, when he hoped to write a book about the case. But once *The Dallas Morning News* came out with its McVeigh confession, he apparently thought his own find would depreciate in value if he didn't act quickly. He called the William Morris Agency in New York, trying to get representation, and, failing that, tried to sell the story himself to *The New York Times* and other major publications. All of them turned him down, leaving him with *Playboy* and ABC. In fact, ABC denied having bought the chronology, for it is considered unethical for a news department to pay for information. Instead it bought Stringer, under the guise of paying him as a consultant. Other than his appearance on *Prime Time Live*, and one other on *Good Morning America*, I doubt he did much "consulting" for them.*

Within a week other stories started appearing: that McVeigh had failed a crucial question on a polygraph test; that McVeigh had participated in a bank robbery. These stories were inaccurate, but it was clear that suddenly, unmistakably, inexplicably, the media tide was turning. After almost two years of courting the media, of fighting to make sure Tim got a fair trial in that other court where they preside—the court of public opinion—I found my efforts undone in a matter of weeks. The story of Tim's confession circulated widely, continually, with little critical commentary, and whether it was true or false, the idea that he *had* somehow confessed worked its way into the consciousness of a public that gets its news from images, headlines, and sound bites while tuning out the fine print. Jury notices for our trial had gone out on February 14 to a thousand prospective jurors. Unless these citizens of Denver had taken a vacation to Mars, they couldn't have missed hearing something to the effect that McVeigh had "confessed."

The defense team, meanwhile, had divided into two camps. Personalities aside, I'd always been aware of the quasiphilosophical antipathy between the "case lawyers" among us and the "cause lawyers," but a few of us now panicked and wrote off the first, guilt-or-innocence phase of the trial. They assumed the worst. It was a foregone conclusion. They wanted to spend all our time on phase two in an effort to beat the death penalty. In the process, three people wanted to get rid of Stephen Jones. Judge Matsch wasn't about to let them do that, nor was I, because if three out of thirty-five wanted to get rid of me, that left thirty-two who remained steadfast. (With the full blessing of Judge Matsch, I could have fired the three, but I chose not to.) But what to do?

I've long been an admirer and student of the great French leader Charles de Gaulle. In May 1968, at the height of the student-

---

*Although the Court of Appeals rejected Tim's appeal, the Judges had scathing language for the lack of professionalism of X, Slover—himself a lawyer, though inactive—and Stringer. Said the Court in its published opinion: "The disclosure and publication of information obtained from documents purporting to contain confidential information between an individual and his attorney indicates a lack of self restraint and ethical compass upon the part of those individuals responsible for doing so."

inspired revolt that brought the French nation to the edge of the abyss, de Gaulle, the chief of state, suddenly disappeared. Everyone thought he was about to resign, where in fact he'd gone off with his family to the French military garrison at Baden-Baden, Germany, to make sure he had the support of the army. When he returned to Paris, the rebellion had already begun to run out of steam, and the Fifth Republic survived, as it does to this day.

The McVeigh case wasn't France, and I am hardly de Gaulle, but when I returned to Denver after dropping out for a couple of days, my mind was clear on what we had to do, and the minimutiny, such as it was, was over.

Two weeks before, under questioning by the media in the heat of *The Dallas Morning News* affair, I had pledged that we would not seek a continuance or a change of venue. But in view of what had happened since, we no longer had that choice. There was just no way we were going to be able to find and seat an untainted, open-minded jury.

On March 14, we filed with the court a "Motion to Dismiss, or in the Alternative, a Request for Abatement or Other Relief."

The exhibits were the key to our motion. We submitted fifty-two articles that had appeared in the Denver newspapers alone during the period from March 1 to March 13, each of which mentioned either the confession or the chronology. We also submitted transcripts from eighty local and national news reports that were broadcast in the Denver area from February 28 to March 13. With transcripts from CNN and the news programs of the other national networks, as well as clippings from national magazines that were widely distributed and read in Denver, we had an overwhelming factual case.

On the legal side, we were also on very sound ground. The underlying basis of our argument was the Sixth Amendment right of every accused to a public trial by an impartial jury. The U.S. Supreme Court has since limited that right, stating that jurors don't have to be totally ignorant of the facts or the issues involved in a case. Modern communications make that almost impossible in high-profile cases. But in its landmark 1961 opinion in *Irvin v.*

Dowd, the Supreme Court held that the right to a fair trial still required a panel of impartial, "indifferent" jurors. In a 1966 decision (*Sheppard v. Maxwell*), the Court elaborated on the issue, in a sense that fit our situation exactly: "Where there is a reasonable likelihood that prejudicial news prior to trial will prevent a fair trial, the judge should continue the case until the threat abates or transfer it to another county not so permeated with publicity."

In our case, there was probably no other county. But a continuance would have offered us obvious relief, and the Supreme Court had ordained it. Indeed there were those who found it so obvious that they thought *I* might have been the one who leaked the report to *The Dallas Morning News!*

But Judge Matsch was not one of them. In a court order dated March 17, that is, three days after our filing, he said that the trial would proceed as scheduled because "these articles have had neither the wide exposure or general acceptance that the Defendant's lawyers presume."

I don't know what the judge would have accepted as "wide exposure." I do know that we had asked him, under seal, for permission to employ a public polling firm in order to find out, before voir dire (juror examination) started, how many people in the greater Denver area had read and heard and remembered the stories. But the judge, even though he had authorized earlier polls, denied funding for this one.

A good jury member, he said in writing, "has to set aside any preconceived impressions or opinions. . . . There are always some who say this can't be done, that it is too much to expect people to disregard sensational stories about cases. I know better. I have been on this Court for twenty-three years, and I have worked with thousands of jurors in hundreds of trials. I know that most people are skeptical and distrustful about news reports, having seen many of them turn out later to be untrue."

As I hope I've made clear, I had—and have—enormous respect for Judge Matsch, for the way he ran his court, for his decency toward my client, for his no-nonsense, unceremonial style, for his constant effort, during the year and three months since he'd taken the case over, to prepare and assure a level playing field between prosecution and defense and a fair trial for the accused. This isn't to say I'd always agreed with him. Advocate that I am, I didn't think he came down anywhere near hard enough on the prosecution to produce discovery material. His point was that he couldn't order the government to produce what it had a constitutional duty to produce, meaning that, if prosecutors weren't going to do what the U.S. Constitution compelled them to do, they weren't going to do it if he ordered them to. He was right too, in a formal sense, even though, to me, he was putting form above substance. But in this instance—in denying our motion—I think he blew it.

From the very moment he took over the case, Judge Matsch had admonished lawyers on both sides about the media, reminding us that anything we said or did might prejudice a fair trial. I have mentioned this at several points in my story, and although, as I described, the judge tried to be lenient toward the defense when it came to "bartering" information, the nearer we came to the trial, the more restrictive he became. Finally, for the trial itself, he would impose a total gag order.

How, then, can one square this pattern of mounting caution with his eleventh-hour change of heart? Why bother imposing a gag rule if all the front-page stories of Tim McVeigh's "confessions" had no influence on the minds of "good" jurors? In its opinion upholding Tim's conviction the Court of Appeals did not address this apparent inconsistency. Possibly, because the inconsistency cannot be reconciled.

There was a terrible inconsistency in his ruling, and it has taken me time to understand, at least in part, what led to it. Judge Matsch, as he showed in so many ways, was an ardent defender of our system of jurisprudence, of our ideals of justice and the right to a fair trial. I think he also saw that system as under siege—not by the media alone but by lawyers and judges who dance to the media's tune and by a public that seems to look upon courtrooms as veritable fountainheads of scandal, drama, and high entertainment.

These last things are anathema to a man like Richard Matsch. Orderly, serious, stubborn, accustomed to being master in his domain, I think he would be damned before admitting that the media—the likes of *The Dallas Morning News, Playboy*, the American Broadcasting Company—could be so pervasive and so influential as to require a United States District Court—*his* court—to change venue for a second time or delay an important criminal proceeding like *United States v. McVeigh*.

Call it ego, if you will, but I think Judge Matsch looked on it as his obligation to try to uphold the traditional dignity of his courtroom against those forces that would turn it into a circus tent. By granting our motion, he would have been conceding that that dignity could no longer be maintained. By denying it, he undertook the task of proving that it could.

On March 19, 1997, 352 prospective jurors came to the Jefferson County Fairgrounds and completed a forty-page questionnaire concerning personal backgrounds, exposure to publicity concerning the case, and views on the death penalty. Their responses convinced me that, if Tim McVeigh was going to be convicted and sentenced to death, it would be because the minds of his prospective jurors had already been poisoned against him. But once Judge Matsch had the answers to the jurors' questionnaires, he said to me, "Mr. Jones, I know now we can seat a jury."

To which I replied, "Your Honor, I have no doubt that you will."

It may be too facile to say that on March 17, in denying our motion for a continuance, Judge Matsch also denied Tim McVeigh a fair trial, but, all things considered, I think it's true.

PART
IV

14

UNITED STATES V.
TIMOTHY JAMES MCVEIGH

We expected the trial to last a minimum of 180 days. It lasted thirty-six.

We expected the government to call as many as 327 witnesses. That was the number on the list they filed with the court. Instead, it called 141.

Prosecutors never called Tom Kessinger of Elliott's Body Shop, even though Kessinger had been responsible for the descriptions on which the sketches of John Does #1 and #2 had been based.

They never called Vicki Beemer, either.

They called Eldon Elliott and Eric McGown, but they never called his mother, Lea, manager of the Dreamland Motel. It was Lea who had recognized the sketch of John Doe #1. She had registered McVeigh. Now she too became a nonwitness.

They never called Jeff Davis, who delivered Chinese food for the Hunan Palace restaurant to a "Robert Kling" in room 25 of the Dreamland Motel. A nonwitness.

They never called David King, who lived in room 24 at the Dreamland Motel, or Connie Hood, who visited him there on April 17, 1995, or her husband, Donald Lee Hood, who drove her there that day.

They never called Hilda Sostre, a maid at the Dreamland Motel.

They never called Barbara Whittenberg of the Santa Fe Trail diner in Herington, Kansas, who'd seen a Ryder truck at the Geary State Fishing Lake on April 18.

They never called Sgt. Richard Wahl of Fort Riley, who'd taken his son fishing at Geary State Fishing Lake on April 18.

They never called Fred Skrdla, an attendant at the Cimarron Travel Plaza truck stop on Interstate 35 in northern Oklahoma.

They never called Richard Sinnett, assistant manager of a Sav-A-Trip in Kingman, Kansas.

They never called Kyle Hunt, a Tulsa banker, or David Snider, a warehouse worker in the Bricktown section of downtown Oklahoma City, or Mike Moroz or Brian Marshall of Johnny's Tire Store, or James Linehan, a lawyer from Midwest City, all of whom claimed to have seen the Ryder truck the morning of April 19 and/or John Does #1 and #2.

They never called Dr. Paul Heath. Dr. Heath was a psychologist with an office in the Murrah Building, and he was president of the Victims' Association. He claimed to have talked with Tim McVeigh in the Murrah Building barely two weeks before the explosion. He knew it was McVeigh because he'd made him spell his name for him. Yet while Dr. Heath was always fair in his public comments and is a credible person, on the day in question, Tim was in Arizona.

They never called Gary Lewis or Leonard Long.

They never called Margaret Hohmann and Ann Domin or Debra Burdick.

They never called Rodney Johnson.

They never called Daina Bradley.

They never called Roger Moore or Karen Anderson. Moore, the gun dealer from Arkansas and the alleged robbery victim, would be a mere whisper in the trial.

They never called David Williams, Roger Martz, or Thomas Thurman. These were the key forensic personnel from the FBI Lab, now discredited by the inspector general in their own Department of Justice. Instead they called Linda Jones, an explosives expert from Great Britain!

It was daring, it was high-risk. Who would ever have guessed that a case, already highly circumstantial, in which the federal government was asking the death penalty, would leave the jury *without a single witness* to Tim McVeigh's whereabouts between Junction City, Kansas, on Monday, April 17, and Perry, Oklahoma, at 10:30 A.M. on April 19? Nothing about the building of the bomb? No witnesses to Geary State Fishing Lake? Or to the truck ride from Kansas to Oklahoma City? Or how the alleged getaway car got to Oklahoma City? Or to the events at the Murrah Building? Or the morning of the bombing and the bombing itself?

Not a one.

Voir dire is the examination of individual candidates for a jury. It is conducted by opposing counsel in front of the judge. Judge Matsch had whisked us right through it. "Any good jury member," he said in writing, "has to set aside any preconceived impressions or opinions," and those panelists who wanted to be on the jury caught the signal and responded accordingly. Most of those who admitted thinking McVeigh was guilty, based on what they'd heard and read, were excused, but some gave clues to the fact that they'd heard the judge too well.

So, from Juror #522 (seat 5):

QUESTION: There have been some sensational headlines over the last ten months concerning the case. Can you tell me which ones you remember seeing?

ANSWER: Something about—something about an admission of something. That's about all I can remember, because again, I'm very concerned about the media and the sensationalism and the jumping on little tidbits of news and blowing them up.

And from Juror #32 (seat 6):

QUESTION: Do you recall any accounts of statements made by Mr. McVeigh to his counsel? Any news accounts of those?

ANSWER: Other than the news—you know, I didn't read the articles or anything, but hearing from work more than anything that, you know, statements were given—were given. But whether they're true or not, it could have been irresponsible media or it could have been the truth or a combination thereof. So again, like I was asked during the initial interview, stay away from that information. So I did.

QUESTION: But sometimes you couldn't help but either hear it or see—because it was there. Is that right?

ANSWER: Juror nods head affirmatively.

Or from Juror #267 (seat 7): "I did hear that Timothy McVeigh confessed but turned off the radio at that point, and then later heard on TV when I walked into the room where it was on that there was discussion of poor journalism and reporting. I know of recent there has been talk of moving the trial because of increased media coverage."

And, finally, from Juror #140 (seat 8):

ANSWER: Sir, I've seen very little of it. I just heard what—they had it on the Internet, and that's about it.

QUESTION: And do you use the Internet?

ANSWER: No, I don't. I just heard it on the—one of the news channels said that something came out on the Internet.

QUESTION: And what is it that you remember hearing that came out on the Internet?

ANSWER: That he'd confessed to the crime.

The above four, mind you, were seated. All of them eventually voted guilty. All of them voted for the death penalty.

Even the prosecution—scarcely the least biased of sources when it came to the question of the jury—conceded that of the ninety-nine potential jurors questioned during voir dire forty admitted to having knowledge of Tim McVeigh's alleged confession. One wonders about the rest. As the late Sen. Jim Rinehart, an old-style Oklahoma politician and lawyer, once said, if you locked up every prospective juror who lied on voir dire, the jails would be full twenty-four hours a day. But instead of allowing us to assemble a fairer jury, Judge Matsch limited us in questioning the jurors. Why? Well, he was determined to have his case and his courtroom on his timetable. But there was something more. If we probed too deeply, Judge Matsch's belief that he could, by weight of the authority and dignity of the court, overcome any preexisting prejudice in the jury box, would have been severely challenged. Also, the prospective jurors parroted Judge Matsch's remarks about their lack of interest in what the media reported. Their sensitive antennas had picked up the correct answer, which would withstand a challenge for cause. Too many responses that showed quite clearly that potential jurors had been influenced by media reports could have forced Matsch to admit, even to himself, that the trial could not be fairly held. Sometimes you want as much information as possible, and sometimes you don't. And thus our questioning was limited, and the trial proceeded.

A light snow was falling in Denver the morning of April 24— later on during the day it would turn into rain—and the whole downtown, or at least that part of it close to the federal courthouse, had been turned into an armed camp. There were police barricades at key intersections, police on horseback, even, someone said (although I don't recall seeing this myself), police with dogs, and there were checkpoints—at the entrance to the building, of course— where you had to show credentials. That morning, and every morning for the duration of the trial, I walked the gauntlet down 19th Street to the courthouse. Like the prosecution, I was under Judge Matsch's strict gag order. This didn't keep the media from waiting for me at the start of my promenade, with boom mikes overhead, half of their handlers walking backwards, and again at lunchtime, when I made a round-trip, and again at the end of the court day. The Byron Rogers United States Courthouse, named after the former congressman, was the new home of Judge Matsch. In fact, when the move of all the district judges took place, the only judge to stay behind in the old stately courthouse (renamed for retired Supreme Court Justice, Byron White) across the street was Richard Matsch, who, as Chief Judge, could pull rank and get away with it, but the demands and requirements of the McVeigh trial had forced even Judge Matsch to move. In the new building, he'd had a special courtroom outfitted for us—the courtroom of the future, someone called it. Each counsel table, and there were two to a side, had two computers that were wired to communicate not only to each other but, in our case, to the computer in our office in the Total South Tower. A kind of wall shielded the jury from the spectators' view, intended to preserve the anonymity of the jury members. Each side—typical of the judge's courtesy and thoughtfulness—had a large private room in the building, with toilet facilities, to which only counsel, not even courthouse security, had keys. We put work tables in ours, a refrigerator too. There were two sofas for the weary, and several comfortable chairs, and during every recess we and the prosecution would retreat to our respective rooms like boxers to their corners. There was, in addition, an auxiliary courtroom next door to the main one for the overflow, with audio feed but not video. The media people used it a lot, because they could come and go without causing any disruptions.

McVeigh had been moved from prison to the city proper, into a specially equipped, high security holding area in the basement of the building. There was a conference room available to us next to Tim's quarters, with soundproof doors, a telephone, a TV set, and a VCR monitor. Tim's cell resembled a Holiday Inn more than a prison, except for the television camera that kept its eye on him. He had an exercise room too, and a private bath—all rather unusual for a man being tried for mass murder. Yet once the trial began, he was stuck there for as long as it lasted. There were no windows, no way for the prisoner to tell the time of day except by the clock. In a study done for the U.S. Marshals Service, behavioral scientists have advised that an inmate deprived of sunlight and outside recreation, or even the ability to distinguish day from night, can encounter emotional problems, perhaps physical ones as well, leading to an eventual breakdown—which was the last thing anyone wanted for McVeigh. Such a breakdown could have resulted in a mistrial and an even more costly new trial. Everyone had planned for a long—not short trial. In addition, the facilities inside the courthouse didn't cost any more than it would have cost to transport Tim McVeigh every day from the federal prison to the courthouse and back again at night.

Each day, Tim was brought up from his quarters and escorted into the courtroom without shackles, and each day the routine was the same. I shook hands with him and we spoke for a few minutes, bantering easily. At night, one or more of us would be with him, either to work on the case or to relieve the tension. The marshals who guarded him—there were three at all times—were unobtrusive and cordial, never trying to interfere with our work, a credit to their service, and the accused—my client—was on his best behavior from day one. After two years of waiting for his day in court, he was polite, quiet, and, once in the courtroom, totally wrapped up in the proceedings.

The morning of April 24, Joe Hartzler opened for the prosecution. He gave a strong, forceful, and utterly predictable statement, highlighting the catastrophe itself, introducing the evidence, introducing their twin stars, Lori and Michael Fortier, coming down hard on the motive issue.

"McVeigh liked to consider himself a patriot," he said, "someone who could start a second American revolution. The literature that was in his car when he was arrested included statements from the founding fathers . . . people like Patrick Henry and Samuel Adams." He continued: "Well, ladies and gentlemen, the statements of our forefathers can never be twisted to justify warfare against innocent children. Our forefathers didn't fight women and children, they fought other soldiers. They fought them face to face, hand to hand. They didn't plant bombs and run away wearing earplugs."

Balanced against the cowardly demon were the victims. In Hartzler's vision, the trial wasn't just about Tim McVeigh, it was about the victims too, and inevitably, as though unable to resist it, he told the story of Tevin and Helena Garrett, the one-and-a-half year old, who didn't survive, and his mother, who did.

And then it was our turn.

"Like Mr. Hartzler," I said, after introducing myself to the jury, "I begin where he began."

As he said, it was a spring day in Oklahoma City, and inside the office of the Social Security Administration located in the Alfred P. Murrah Building, a young black woman named Daina Bradley was feeling the atmosphere a little stuffy and warm. So she left her mother, her two children, and her sister in line and she wandered out into the lobby of the building. And as she was looking out the plate glass windows, a Ryder truck slowly pulled into a parking place and stopped. She didn't give it any particular attention until the door opened on the passenger side and she saw a man get out.

Approximately three weeks later, she described the man to the Federal Bureau of Investigation's agents, as indeed she did to us and to others, as short, stocky, olive-complected, wearing a puffy jacket, with black hair, a description that does not match my client. She did not see anyone else.

She turned around and went back into the social security office, and then, in just a matter of seconds, the explosion occurred. It took the life of her mother and her two children and horribly burned her sister.

And so the trial was joined. I spoke the rest of that morning about McVeigh's background and much of the afternoon about the Fortiers, the telephone debit card calls, the key witnesses from Junction City. I went over each piece of government evidence methodically, and each witness to come. Still assuming he would be called, for instance, I talked about the discrepancies between Tom Kessinger's various statements and how they'd changed as he'd met with investigators and prosecutors. And then I took on the FBI Lab, highlighting their shoddy work and comparing the work they did on the Murrah bombing to "forensic prostitution."

"If Tim McVeigh built the bomb and put it in the truck," I concluded, "our proof will be that his fingernails, his nostrils, his hair, his clothing, his car, his shoes, his socks, would have it all over them. They don't. Out of 7,000 pounds of debris, there are fewer than half a dozen pieces of evidence of a forensic nature; and we will go over each one of them with you. And our evidence will be that they do not prove Mr. McVeigh guilty or a participant in this bombing."

Normally, I believe that opening statements should be relatively short, but in this instance, given the length of the prosecution's witness list, I feared the government's case could take months, and I wanted badly to impress on the jurors' minds and memories the fact, as I put it, that "every pancake has two sides." I also wanted to make clear that the victims and their plight were as important to the defense as they were to the prosecution. I told of the doctors, led by Andrew Sullivan, chief of orthopedic surgery at the University of Oklahoma Medical School, crawling through the rubble to amputate Daina Bradley's leg while millions of people all over the world watched on TV, and then I recited the names of each and every one of the 168 deceased. It took longer than eight minutes. I called it the "Pearl Harbor" of my generation. But the question remained, and I put it to the jury squarely:

"The question is, did they get the right man?"

I t was day two before I realized that the government had something totally else in mind.

They'd let it be known—at least there were rumors to that effect—that prosecutors were going to open with one of the Fortiers. I seriously doubted that. For one thing, either Fortier would have been too vulnerable to cross-examination. And sure enough, they began instead in a more traditional, predictable way, a few witnesses first, then, with photographs and diagrams and mockups of Oklahoma City and the Murrah Building, a careful, high-tech presentation of what had happened the morning of April 19.

At some point that morning I briefly left the courtroom on some task, assuming the government would be putting on more of its foundation witnesses. I'm not sure how long I was gone, but when I came back, I ducked into the auxiliary courtroom first, where there was just the audio feed. I had more business to attend to outside the courtroom—I'd only stopped to see what was going on—but suddenly I realized that a couple of people in the group listening there—they were members of the press—had tears running down their cheeks. They were literally weeping.

Someone was testifying. It turned out to be Helena Garrett. She was talking about her little boy, Tevin, age one and a half. Ms. Garrett worked in the Journal-Record Building, just across the parking lot from the Murrah Building. She had two children, Sharonda, a five-year-old, and Tevin. She dropped Sharonda off at school on her way to work, and she delivered Tevin to the day care center in the Murrah Building a few minutes before eight. That particular morning, she remembered, he cried when she started to leave, so she'd stayed a few minutes, consoling him.

That was the last time she saw him alive.

It was an unbearably moving story, and it lended emotion and drama to the prosecution's inevitably dry presentation of the bombing. But it took me a day or two, after the prosecution had introduced another victim, then another victim, to realize the design behind it.

Of course we objected. The parade of victims to the witness stand, moving as their stories were, and sincere and truthful their testimony, was simply not relevant as a matter of law to the issue of Tim McVeigh's guilt. Justice, after all, is blind—blind to sympathy,

blind to compassion, blind to agony. Justice is blind to these consid-
erations so that they do not influence or prejudice the search for the
right verdict under law. But despite Judge Matsch's admonitions,
the prosecution either couldn't or wouldn't control its witnesses.
Meanwhile, Judge Matsch himself had been bitterly criticized by
some of the victims on national television, even on the editorial
pages of the Denver papers—this, mind you, was a man whose own
young daughter had died a tragic and horrible death in Hawaii—
and there was a limit to what he could do. He gave us a standing
objection, meaning that at least we didn't have to stand up and say
the awful word, "Objection!" over and over again, and he admonished the prosecution repeatedly, and they would promise not to do
it again. For a day or more, the trial would resume its normal
course: presentation of evidence, examination of witnesses, cross-
examination of witnesses. But then, somehow or other, on some
pretext or other, usually at the end of the day or just before the
weekend break, there in the witness chair would be yet another victim, telling his or her tale of anguish. It was the forgotten man of
the prosecution, Pat Ryan, who emerged from the shadows to lead
these witnesses through the telling of their stories, and their effect
on the jury was immediate, dramatic, and indelible.

These, after all, weren't lawyers or cops or experts telling what
had happened. These were ordinary people, talking to the members
of the jury, who were also ordinary people, about the horror and the
pain that had literally torn up their lives. Their testimony was like a
tide. And the tide became a flood, and the flood threatened to engulf
all of us. Even me.

One day, the sister of the only victim I had personally known
took the stand. Her parents were longtime friends, and they had lost
one of their two daughters. I had had to object—successfully, I
might add—to the reading of a short eulogy by the deceased
woman's father, my friend of thirty-five years, who had carried his
daughter's ashes in a small urn and wanted to tell how he had carried
her home from the hospital, in these same hands, the day she was
born. But as I listened to the surviving sister testifying about the
special qualities of her lost sibling, I almost lost my composure, for
I, too, had carried my daughter home from the hospital in my
hands. I was sitting facing the jurors. I could look into their eyes as

they could look into mine. And then I felt a hand on my knee. With-out shifting my gaze, I knew that in that moment Tim had reached over in an effort to comfort me.

What, I wonder, would the jury have thought—would the world have thought—if they had seen that small gesture?

Early on the morning of Monday, May 12—it was during the examination of Michael Fortier—a juror approached the clerk of the court and handed him a note, asking if they could speak privately. Jim Manspeaker complied. Thereupon the juror related an exchange between two jurors that had taken place during a recess the Friday before.

ONE JUROR: I hope I'm not the only holdout.
SECOND JUROR: Oh, I think we all know what the verdict should be.

Confiding in Manspeaker, the juror said she'd had nightmares all weekend, thinking about it.

At the end of that day's afternoon session, Judge Matsch gave an extrastrong admonition to the jury, leaning hard on the point that they shouldn't discuss the case with anyone, including their fellow members. Then he reported the incident to counsel for both sides.

The juror in question, Judge Matsch speculated, was just trying to be funny. I thought otherwise. Obviously, the juror was deeply disturbed.

Funny or not, I immediately moved that the juror in question be dismissed and that the first alternate replace him.

The judge disagreed. The prosecution, of course, sided with the judge. The extrastrong admonition he'd just given the jury, they opined, ought to suffice.

Judge Matsch listened, and then he ruled.

"I'll stand on what I've done," he said, referring to the admonition. "We'll see what happens."

In view of what did happen, I've often been asked why Judge Matsch failed to act. Didn't he know full well that by not removing the one juror he was jeopardizing the ultimate verdict?

I'm sure he did know. Although the juror in question later denied having made the remark, I'm sure he made it. I'm sure he meant it too, and not in humor but in dead seriousness. But what the juror said gave the judge a problem. He hadn't said, "*I* know what the verdict should be." He'd said, "*We* know what the verdict should be." Just removing the one juror who'd talked out of turn would have left open the question Who was *we*? Short of a hearing in which each juror and each alternate could be requestioned, there was no way of knowing how many of them were included in the "we," that is, how many had already made up their minds.

In other words, we were back at the old challenge to Judge Matsch's belief that the jury—*his* jury—could be impartial and untainted.

The truth was that by this point—with the prosecution's case unfinished and the defense yet to be heard from—many of the jury members *had* already reached a verdict.

For better or worse, I'm not flogging a dead horse, either. After the trial and verdict, Rob Nigh wrote a long and masterful appeal to the Tenth Circuit. It ran more than two hundred pages, only a few of which were devoted to this incident. Oral argument was heard during spring 1998, when the panel of judges had a chance to pepper counsel with questions concerning the issues raised in the written document. Guess which issue drew the most animated questioning from the judges in oral argument?

It was the story of what this one juror said, and what Judge Matsch did about it.

T he factual part of the government's case was pared down to a minimum, and it went fast, like a film that's been edited to a jump-cut pace—presumably so that no one would notice the gaps and the inconsistencies. Into the courtroom on the third day came the 250-pound rear axle of the Ryder truck that had been found a block away from the blast. Out went the axle and in came Glenn Tipton, the salesman for VP Racing Fuels, who claimed that a man had approached him at a racetrack outside Topeka, Kansas, in October 1994 and asked him about buying a quantity of anhydrous hydrazine, which is a mixture of rocket fuel and nitromethane. Tipton claimed to have reported the incident to ATF at the time. (The prosecution offered no such corroborating evidence.) He was "90 percent" sure the man who approached him was Tim McVeigh. (Better than 50 percent, I suppose, but less good than 100 percent.) No matter that the government's own experts never claimed anhydrous hydrazine was used in the bomb; the witness was already gone.

Motive, as we'd expected, played a big part, relying heavily on the testimony of Jennifer McVeigh, even more so on the Fortiers, who, whatever Joe Hartzler had said in the past, now became the star prosecution witnesses and the core of the case. Jennifer McVeigh clearly cared about her brother, and it pained her to have to bear witness against him, but that probably lended credence to her recital of his violent expressions of anger and hatred toward the government. The Fortiers were another matter. They were both capable of great expressions of remorse now—Lori because she admitted she could have stopped the bombing with a phone call, Michael for having once lied to his father(!) about Tim. Or so he now said. But if it was believed, their direct testimony was obviously devastating to us.

Carefully prepared by Rob Nigh, I tore into them on cross-examination, Michael in particular. I made no secret of the fact that I didn't like him. A worm of a man. I demonstrated that virtually everything they'd claimed to know about the bombing had been on television and in the papers—easily accessible to them—long before they'd "corrected" their statements. They had discussed, and the FBI's hidden microphones had recorded, how they were going to make millions on their stories and that would be their ticket out of hell. (Hell was Kingman, Arizona.) I played the tapes of the wiretaps for the jury, letting them hear Michael's boasts that he was the key man, interspersed with spurts of profanity that were as dumb as they were arrogant, and I leaned hard on the benefits of plea bargains for both of them—for Lori obviously, because she walked away scot-free, but also for Michael, even though it will be the next century before he follows her.

By the time I was done, an impartial jury would have been suspicious of everything the Fortiers had described—the trip to Oklahoma City and Kansas with Tim, the Roger Moore robbery, the makeup of the bomb, and so on. And theirs, it must be remembered, was the *only* testimony presented in the government's entire case that spoke to Tim's alleged plans and his execution of those plans, the only testimony, in an otherwise sparse exposition, that linked the angry brother on Jennifer McVeigh's e-mail and the alleged mastermind who had exploded the Murrah Building.

We also tore into the government's forensic evidence. We wanted—no doubt about it—to put the FBI Lab on trial, believing that the inspector general's report as a whole depicted a long-term pattern of arrogance and shoddy, scientifically unacceptable performance that put the mistakes made in the Oklahoma City bombing into sharper and incontrovertible perspective. But Judge Matsch, in a very narrow and legalistic ruling, confined us to only a small part of the chapter in the report concerning the Oklahoma City bombing itself, and he would do the same thing later, when we called Fred Whitehurst as a defense witness. The jury remained ignorant of the larger scandal that had called all the FBI's forensic work into question and of Whitehurst's role in exploding that scandal.

Still, even within the confines of the judge's ruling, Chris Tritico struck home. The government's handling—or mishandling—of key elements of evidence left it wide open to attack on the contamination issue. To cite but one example, Tim McVeigh's clothes—the T-shirt and jeans he was wearing at the time of his arrest—made the trip from the courthouse in Perry, Oklahoma, to FBI headquarters in Oklahoma City to the FBI Laboratory in Washington in a brown paper bag, folded over in a cardboard box. God knows who touched them, or handled them, or sneezed on them, or did what with them, en route. Then, once inside the lab, these items, and McVeigh's knife and earplugs, were left to the devices of Roger Martz, who made his "visual" examination of the evidence because he didn't need a microscope. Even worse were the wild discrepancies between the tests Roger Martz had run on the evidence and the results of Steve Burmeister's testing when he came back to the lab from the Oklahoma City bomb site. Martz found a residue of pentaerythritol tetranitrate (PETN) on McVeigh's knife, whereas Burmeister didn't. Burmeister found PETN on the T-shirt and the jeans. Martz didn't. Burmeister found nitroglycerin on the knife. Even putting aside the issue of contamination—that these tests had come out differently strongly raised the possibility of contamination—why nitroglycerin? Nitroglycerin didn't even fit with the government's theory of the bomb's makeup. And why, for that matter, PETN? Because PETN is a component of detonating cord. The government was convinced Tim McVeigh had cut detonating cord with the knife found on him at the time of his arrest. And why was that? Not because it'd found traces of PETN at the bomb site, or on recovered pieces of the Ryder truck, but because detonating cord had allegedly been stolen in the famous Marion, Kansas, quarry burglary!

The PETN fiasco was a classic example of how the FBI Lab had worked "backward," and the villain of the piece (whom the prosecutors also didn't dare put on the stand) was David Williams, the erstwhile hero of the World Trade Center investigation who had subsequently been castigated and totally discredited in the IG's report. Williams, it will be remembered, had been in charge of the forensic investigation into the Oklahoma City bombing, and he was Burmeister's boss. It was Williams who'd "decided" that the Ryder truck bomb was an ANFO bomb—not because of any forensic evidence but because of the 4,000 pounds of ammonium nitrate the FBI could prove had been purchased from the Mid-Kansas Co-op and the single McVeigh fingerprint on the receipt found in Terry Nichols's house. Otherwise, the main charge inside the Ryder truck could have been any number of other explosive combinations and cocktails. To this day, neither the FBI nor anyone else—other than David Williams—has been able to tell us with any certainty the bomb's makeup.

But there was worse—in a sense, far worse.

Williams, who was Burmeister's boss in the investigation, had changed Burmeister's reports. This had come out in the IG's report, and it came out again at the trial. With regard to Tim McVeigh's knife, Burmeister had written, "The result of an instrumental examination of residues removed from the blade portion of the specimen was consistent for the presence of [PETN], but the presence of PETN could not be confirmed."

Anyone familiar with legal or accounting or scientific jargon knows that the phrase "consistent with," as used above, is a loaded deck. It is indefinite. It is a policeman's term, not a scientist's. It suggests something might be, but then again it might not. It suggests that something can't be ruled out, but neither can it be confirmed.

That was the meaning of what Burmeister had written—that the presence of PETN couldn't be ruled out but that it couldn't be confirmed either.

But it wasn't good enough for Williams, who, in what I believe may have been a criminal act, changed it to read: "Traces of PETN were located on specimen Q18 [the identification number for the knife], however could not be confirmed."

"Consistent with" now becomes "located." The PETN is now there on the knife, it is definite. What the "could not be confirmed" is still doing there, or what it now meant, would remain a mystery had not the inspector general himself asked the same question. The IG, in fact, had zeroed in on it. What did "could not be confirmed" mean in this new configuration?

David Williams himself had to admit the answer. In an earlier draft, it hadn't been there at all, he said. But Burmeister, to whom he showed it, had objected to the falsification of his report. He'd insisted that "could not be confirmed" be included. So David Williams, presumably in an effort to be accommodating, had simply stuck it back in!

Poor Burmeister! His colleagues discredited, the whole FBI Lab tainted (whether or not Judge Matsch wanted the subject aired), it fell to Burmeister to be the government's sole witness from the lab, now put in the position of having to defend the lab from charges of bungling and falsification. It should be remembered too that Burmeister, even though he had the formal technical training every FBI Lab investigator ought to have (but didn't), was still an underling and now in the position of having to defend his bosses and, as "acting" chief of his unit, Burmeister had to know his career with the FBI was on the line, but so was his reputation for integrity in the broader scientific community outside the FBI. Although he didn't fall on his sword for them, he managed to soften his own criticism of what they had done. And while Chris Tritico could, and did, go after him on cross-examination—Chris was able to point out, for example, that anyone who shoots guns regularly (as Tim McVeigh did) is likely to have PETN residue on him, just as he or she is likely to wear earplugs—Burmeister stuck doggedly to his story of the "hits" they'd made when examining McVeigh's clothing. It would be up to us, on direct examination of our own experts, to bring out the fact that no one, including the

FBI, had forensic proof of the makeup of the bomb itself and that therefore Burmeister's so-called hits really meant nothing at all.

By the time our experts from London and elsewhere were done shredding the practices and reputation of the FBI Lab, there wasn't much positive left in the government's forensic case. In another trial climate, and even despite the restrictive muzzle the court had put on us, I'm sure a more open-minded jury would have seen it for what it was—too tattered and tarnished to be convincing of anything, much less of Tim McVeigh's guilt beyond a reasonable doubt. But it is well-nigh impossible, with a jury that already "knows what the verdict should be," to convince its members of anything that runs against the grain of what they've decided.

One fellow Oklahoma lawyer who served as a self-appointed legal commentator for television criticized our defense by saying he had "called more witnesses in a drunk driving case" than I did in defending Tim McVeigh against a capital indictment. What he neglected to mention was that he wouldn't have called any of those witnesses in his drunk driving case if the judge had told him he couldn't.

But my fellow lawyer was right too. Our defense only took three and a half days.

It often happens, I should point out, that the defense in criminal cases puts on no case at all. Gerry Spence secured the acquittal of Randy Weaver and his codefendant in the Ruby Ridge case without calling a single defense witness. The government, in that instance, failed to prove its charges, and Spence's skillful cross-examinations only underlined it. In fact, a prosecution case is almost always longer than the defense reply.

But it is very hard to counterpunch when the other side throws so few punches. Many of the witnesses—the Tom Kessingers, the David Williamses—whom we'd been prepared to attack and impeach so wholeheartedly that not even this jury could ignore it, had simply never been called. The government knew we were ready for them. It was a silent acknowledgment of our thorough preparation. In theory we could have called them ourselves. We could, say, have subpoenaed Lea McGown, the manager of the Dreamland Motel, and even though she would have been hostile to us, we could have probably forced her to admit that, yes, she'd told the FBI back in 1995 that she'd seen a Ryder truck in the motel parking lot *the day before* Robert Kling had rented his at Elliott's Body Shop. But at the same time, either during direct examination or during the prosecution's cross-examination, McGown would have identified McVeigh as the man who'd rented room 25 and who'd signed the register and so on. In other words, if the prosecution had called McGown, we could have poked holes in her testimony and created a reasonable doubt in a reasonable jury's mind. But as a witness for the defense, she would have appeared, upon cross-examination, to have been substantiating the government's case more than challenging it. Almost as a rule, cross-examination threatens the case of the party that originally calls the witness. It was a subtle but important distinction.

So the government called no eyewitnesses to the Ryder truck at or near the Murrah Building. Not a single person put Tim McVeigh at the crime site. Prosecutors knew that we would be able to focus the jury's attention on discrepancies and contradictions between witnesses. Worst of all, they didn't bother with the many witnesses who claimed to have seen a second man because this would have reopened the whole question of John Doe #2 and others unknown and the inadequacies and failures of the FBI investigation. To the prosecution in the McVeigh trial, John Doe #2 and others unknown simply didn't exist.

Although we did call Daina Bradley, who'd seen the olive-complected man—John Doe #2—get out of the Ryder truck on the passenger's side moments before the blast and who testified that the driver was not Tim McVeigh, Pat Ryan, in the counterpuncher's role, got her to admit that she'd had a history of mental problems, that she'd lived in a mental hospital for almost ten years, that she'd been on heavy medication in those years. The medication, in a side effect, had given her bouts of memory loss. And, she admitted, the harrowing experience of the bombing—the loss of her mother, two children, and sister—as well as the emergency amputation of her own leg—had made her need counseling again. Presumably this was enough for the jury to disregard her testimony. Ironically, though, her memory was consistent with much of the evidence: Two men renting the Ryder truck, the descriptions given by others of John Doe II, the unidentified leg which might have belonged to the bomber, and so on.

onsidering everything that had happened on evidentiary issues till then, I can't say I was optimistic that we would ever be able to get our Philippines material in. But I was determined to try. Just as the trial was about to begin, I sent Jim Hankins over to the Philippines. Jim wasn't going to be needed in the courtroom, and I had a delicate mission for him: To ascertain, first hand, if Edwin Angeles would repeat in court the statements he had made on tape the previous fall and if Jim himself found him a credible witness.

Jim came back pessimistic. Angeles's story had since been "embellished." The underlying facts were just as in the statements he'd made on video the previous November to his Filipino interrogators. He had met the Farmer, who was clearly Terry Nichols. Angeles remembered the place of the meeting and some of the specifics. He could hardly disavow all these things, since they had been taped. But like a repentant sinner, or a defendant turning cooperating witness, he knew how to sink his own testimony with additional and often implausible statements. Clearly, he had no desire to leave his prison. Who would protect him if he did? Not the Philippine government, certainly. And the American government had made it clear to his captors that it wanted them to give zero cooperation to the McVeigh defense. It was one thing for him to talk to an investigator in the comparative safety of his own cell, another to answer a subpoena in a far-off courtroom in front of the international media. The first might get him into trouble. The second was tantamount to signing his own death warrant.

I didn't hold out much hope, in any case, that Matsch would willingly issue a subpoena (in this I was right), but I wanted the record to reflect that he had refused. Again, there was a part of this incident that was a telling point in why the defense costs, borne by the taxpayers, became so great. I requested my local congressman by letter for a copy of a treaty between the United States and the Philippines which set forth the rules to obtain a deposition of a Philippino citizen for use in an American Court. His office refused to help because I was Tim McVeigh's lawyer. I guess—notwithstanding very generous financial support from me in his past political campaigns—that I was reapportioned out of his district when a Federal Judge appointed by Ronald Reagan, on the advice of conservative Senator

Don Nickles, named me to represent Mr. McVeigh. So I had to assign an attorney to track down the document and obtain it, at a cost of about $1,200.00 to the taxpayers. At least the congressman wasn't a hypocrite. He didn't stand up on the floor of the House of Representatives and criticize our defense expenses when he could have helped, in a small way, to hold them down. The hypocrisy of the position of Senator Nickles didn't bother the senator though. He said the public would be "outraged" at defense expenses, moved to limit them, and then steadfastly refused even to acknowledge or answer several letters we wrote him, and his co-sponsor, Senator Inhofe—in an attempt to hold down costs—requested their assistance in obtaining documents and other matters from the government.

Much more central to the defense, though, was Carol Howe.

At no time did the FBI consider Andreas Strassmeir or Dennis Mahon a subject of the Oklahoma City bombing investigation.

The question must be asked again and again: If that was so, then why not? One effect of the Carol Howe revelations had been to send us back, again, through hundreds of thousands of individual documents, which we were now able to scan and review quickly. And we'd found some nuggets among them. All during the time the American people were being reassured that there was no foreign involvement in the bombing—just Tim McVeigh and Terry Nichols and possibly John Doe #2—our State Department had been burning up the cable lines to the U.S. embassy in Bonn, Germany, seeking information about Andreas Carl Strassmeir, a/k/a Andy the German LNU. And we discovered, furthermore, that the diplomatic security service of the State Department had even distributed in its counterterrorism section photos of Strassmeir as a suspect in the Oklahoma City bomb—with the Oklahoma City bombing investigation code number on the leaflet!

At no time did the FBI consider Andreas Strassmeir or Dennis Mahon a subject of the Oklahoma City bombing investigation.

Were they narrowly defining the term "subject"? Or was it that Strassmeir or Mahon or Millar, or two of the three, or all three, were informants and that therefore the FBI stayed away?

Whatever it was, we were about to explode it. When Carol Howe took the stand, the doors would open at least a crack, and when they did, the American people would discover that government law enforcement agencies had had prior warning of the bombing and had failed to act. The fat would be in the fire.

On the Sunday before we were scheduled to begin our presentation, Clark Brewster, Howe's lawyer, flew up from Tulsa to meet with us. In March, the government had finally indicted her in the Viefhaus case. The charges were willfully making a bomb threat (in a taped telephone message), possession of a "nonregistered destructive device" (the materials for a bomb), and conspiring with Viefhaus. That the charges were spurious wouldn't come to light until the summer, in a trial that lasted less than a week, when the Tulsa jury acquitted Howe on all counts, but the government, presumably, had decided that by not indicting her it was giving credence to the idea that she had been an important informer. But if it thought she would go away quietly or be intimidated enough to plea bargain, it had miscalculated.

That Sunday, Howe was somewhere in Denver. Brewster hadn't permitted us to meet or question her, and indeed there was a potential hitch concerning her testimony. The rules of federal criminal procedure prohibit lawyers—defenders or prosecutors—from subpoenaing witnesses they know will invoke the Fifth Amendment in front of the jury. But Brewster and we had a working lunch that Sunday and spent the afternoon going over the questions we would ask, the answers Howe would give, and any trouble spots Brewster wanted us to stay away from. Brewster also brought us more papers from Judge Burrage's court in Tulsa (where the Howe case was tried). One was evidence that ATF had not known that the FBI had its own investigation of Elohim City going on until late February 1995. To top that, there was the document in Angela Finley's handwriting stating that Dennis Mahon, according to Carol Howe, had blown up a truck in Michigan using a 500-pound ammonium nitrate bomb that he placed either under or inside the vehicle. There was also an ATF memorandum to the file confirming that Mahon, Strassmeir, and others at Elohim City had connections abroad with neo-Nazis in Germany and other European countries.

Why hadn't we been shown this by the prosecution during discovery?

In any case, by the end of that working Sunday, we had made a deal with Clark Brewster.

Carol Howe wouldn't plead the Fifth Amendment. She would testify.

Rob Nigh and I were psyched. We'd been through weeks of the government's parade of witnesses punctuating the emotional out-pouring of the victims of the bombing. But now it was our turn, and all those people who'd accused us of blowing smoke, all those, including those on our own team and those in the jury box who took the verdict as a foregone conclusion, would now have to sit back and listen. We had a key witness. At long last, the McVeigh defense was about to take center stage.

Until Judge Matsch decided otherwise.

He had already told us that if we wanted to call Howe he wanted to be informed ahead of time and hear what we had in mind.

So at 8:00 A.M. Monday morning we met with him by appoint-ment in chambers. Beth Wilkinson was there too.

I presented, in detail, what I thought Howe would say on the stand. Under Judge Matsch's questioning, Beth Wilkinson rebutted. Of course, she professed to know nothing about the truck bomb in Michigan. The judge seemed puzzled by that. Was there friction—rivalry—between the ATF and FBI? Would one have kept informa-tion from the other? No, Wilkinson said. She'd interviewed Agent Finley herself, she said. She thought it might have been her fault. If the handwritten note was in Agent Finley's file, she (Wilkinson) must somehow have overlooked it herself.

Judge Matsch wanted to know where I was going with Carol Howe's testimony. I said I wouldn't be able to put the Elohim City people in front of the Murrah Building on April 19, 1995. For that matter, the government hadn't been able to put Tim McVeigh in front of it either.

He understood that. But did I have any other real evidence that brought them closer to the actual planning of the bombing?

The truth was that I could bring them as close as the government had brought Tim McVeigh. I had found a group of conspirators who had actually planned to bomb the Murrah Building, and one of the leaders of that plan had been executed in a federal penitentiary on April 19, 1995, the same day as the building blew up. The same "evi-dence" that was brought to bear on Tim McVeigh, minus the "cor-rected" statements of the Fortiers, could be brought to bear against Elohim City, even to their proximity to Oklahoma City. They too had read *The Turner Diaries* and given it away. They too hated the federal government. They too (in the person of Dennis Mahon) had experimented with ammonium nitrate bombs, and where Tim and Terry had failed, they had succeeded. And so on, right down the line.

But was there nothing else, the judge asked?

No, I said. He already knew we hadn't been able to close the circle, any more than the government had been able to close it against Tim. If we'd had all this information a year and a half ago, when we should have had it as discovery material, then it was possible we would have closed it by now. Furthermore, although I was well aware Judge Matsch didn't want to delay the trial, I was sure the government was still withholding pertinent information.

So there we stood, with the trial due to resume at 9:00 A.M.

Suddenly, I realized what was coming. It was devastating. Two years of effort, of expense, of struggle to get information, evidence, were about to be brushed away as by the flick of a hand.

"Well," Judge Matsch said, "we've had a number of disclosures concerning Mahon, Strassmeir, Elohim City, and now some additional information from Carol Howe. But my ruling is that it's excluded, not sufficiently relevant to be admissible."

Not sufficiently relevant to be admissible.

But how could that be? Judge Matsch had always said the criminal trial was a test of the government's evidence, but did that preclude the defendant from presenting evidence that another party was guilty?

In a sense, there had been three trials of Timothy McVeigh, and one could argue that his fate was decided in the absence of his trial jury. The first of these took place in the grand jury deliberations at Tinker Air Force Base in summer 1995. The second, and much the most important, took place in the mind of Judge Richard Matsch. Had Carol Howe testified, and we'd been permitted to extrapolate and elaborate from it in all its implications, it would have made a difference. (It clearly *would* make a difference in the trial of Terry Nichols.)

So why did Judge Matsch do it?

To put it differently: A man was on trial for his life in the judge's courtroom. That being the case, how could he take it upon himself to declare Howe's testimony irrelevant and inadmissible, when, on the face of it, it was highly exculpatory? How, in other words, could he play both judge and jury?

It is a question I can't answer definitively. Only Richard Matsch can, and I doubt he ever will. The fact was this: The Carol Howe testimony wasn't *irrelevant*; it was *anomalous*, that is (with reference to the dictionary), it would have deviated from the normal. There hadn't been anything like it before in the trial. There hadn't been a whiff, all during the government's presentation, of Elohim City or of the prior knowledge issue. And I think, at the end of the day, that the judge simply didn't want anomaly in his courtroom. The same reflex that had made him so obstinate about holding the trial when and where he had scheduled it came into play now with regard to what evidence and testimony he would allow. By the judge's lights, the jury selection had been orderly, the trial had been orderly, the jury's deliberations would be orderly, the verdict would be orderly.

In that sense, allowing Howe to testify would have opened the doors to chaos. It would have constituted a direct threat to his authority.

As I've indicated before, I hold Richard Matsch in very high regard. Of all the judges I've pleaded before—they must number in the hundreds by now—he is surely in the top tier. As the western historian, Walter Prescott Webb, would say, "he was a breed so rare." I am well aware, having experienced it myself, of the corrosive effect of the media, of the terrific pressure he was under, of the clamor outside the gates. But in the *United States v. McVeigh*, I wondered whether it was Judge Matsch himself who tried the case before it ever went to the jury—*his* jury—whether it was *his* verdict, as expressed in his decisions and his rulings, that condemned Tim McVeigh.

There was little enough left for us afterward. We called our experts—Fred Whitehurst, T. K. Marshall, and company—and Daina Bradley, as mentioned, and we presented the theory that the extra leg belonged to the bomber himself, and poked enough holes in the government's theory of the bombing to drive, say, a small Ryder truck through it. In my summation, I reviewed it all, one last time:

- The Daryl Bridges debit card. There was no way of telling who had made any of the calls charged to it.

- ◆ The Mercury Marquis, or as Tom Manning, who sold it to McVeigh, had called it, "the roachmobile." A fine getaway car for a criminal mastermind. But who had taken the plates off? Not Tim McVeigh.

- ◆ The Eldon Elliott identification of Robert Kling and the absurdity of McVeigh registering at the Dreamland as McVeigh, using the Nichols address in Decker, Michigan, but renting the truck as Kling. *If* it was McVeigh.

- ◆ The FBI Lab and all the missing experts the government hadn't called.

- ◆ Daina Bradley and the absence of other eyewitnesses.

- ◆ The extra leg, and the likelihood that it had belonged to the bomber.

"Someone blew up the Murrah Building," I said. "But more likely than not, several people were involved. They had skill and training, and they didn't get it out of some book that talks about mixing it in an oven."

It was clear to me, as I spoke, that the government had failed to prove its case beyond a reasonable doubt. But were the jurors listening? After all, they already knew what the verdict should be.

They were out three days. I'm not sure what took them so long, but I think most people were happy about their finding.

Guilty.

Guilty as charged, on all counts.

A t least with regard to phase two of our trial—the sentencing— Judge Matsch was consistent. Tim McVeigh had been convicted of all the charges the government had brought against him, and now it was up to the same jury to determine his punishment.

In planning the defense of our client, we were aware of the strategic tension between arguing before the jury that our client was innocent, and then, if the jury found otherwise, arguing that notwithstanding their finding of his guilt, we, as his lawyers, would be asking them to spare his life. Our research showed that with the exception of one case in North Carolina, the details of which were provided to me by James Coleman, Ted Bundy's former lawyer, no defendant in recent times has ever been given any sentence other than death in a jury trial—where the death penalty was an option—when the jury found that six or more first-degree murders had been committed by the defendant.

My view on the dilemma was—contrary to what some others urged—that our best chance for Tim was to defend vigorously the first stage of the trial, that is that the government's proof was not sufficient to prove him guilty beyond a reasonable doubt. The fact that the jury spent four days deliberating on the question of his guilt or innocence, and only overnight on the sentence, would seem to confirm the wisdom of that strategy.

Some public defenders give up a defense on the first stage of a capital case in order to spare their client's life because they recognize that a defendant and his lawyer may lose credibility after vigorously maintaining his innocence, and then, in effect conceding his guilt in the second stage while trying to save his life. There probably are cases where that strategy may be appropriate, but I am uncomfortable with it. In any event, it wasn't appropriate in Mr. McVeigh's case. With 168 people dead, including eight law enforcement agents and nineteen children under the age of six, the chances for him getting anything other than the death penalty if found guilty were extremely remote, if not simply impossible.

As time wore on in our preparation, and we discovered the weaknesses in the government's evidence in the first stage, which I have outlined here, we reconfirmed our earlier decision. But, if we lost that stage—and we ultimately did—we had to prepare for the second stage. Clearly a conventional mitigation defense would not work. For a while, I seriously considered presenting a general philosophical argument against the death penalty in any circumstances. The most eloquent and moving argument for this line of thinking was one I heard on Sunday morning in the beautiful Scottish Episcopal Church, St John's, across the street from my hotel in Edinburgh, Scotland. On that morning. the priest, with a famous English political name, Neville Chamberlin, delivered a sermon with this theme: Mercy is a greater virtue than justice. I spent a lot of time talking to him about this theme which appealed to me as a

Christian, and I read some of the literature and considered the recent examples of the commission on truth and reconciliation in South Africa.

Ultimately, however, I decided that this defense would probably not be effective and that a political defense would be best. The actions taken at Mt. Carmel outside Waco by our government, as I have outlined, were so horrible and wholly against our constitutional and legal traditions, that I felt that if the jury bought the government's case with its theory that Mr. McVeigh committed the bombing because of his anger over the events at Mt. Carmel, the jury was entitled to know precisely what those events were which drove that anger. But, Judge Matsch and the Court of Appeals disagreed.

We tried, again, to introduce the Carol Howe testimony. Although it might not have convinced the jury of Tim's innocence, certainly, as we argued, when it came to deciding on his sentence, the idea that he might have been a tool in the hands of others unknown and had been caught, whereas others had escaped, ought to have been a mitigating factor in the jury's deliberations. Similarly, the idea that the government, or a branch or branches of the government, might or ought to have had prior knowledge of the bombing and had failed to take the necessary precautions would have had an obviously mitigating effect.

But Judge Matsch, having already decided it was irrelevant, wanted no part of it. Carol Howe's testimony remained inadmissible in the second stage.

The defense also wanted to introduce Waco. Since the government, in developing a motive for McVeigh, had made much of his anger over Waco and his alleged desire to avenge the Branch Davidians, we wanted to show that in the eyes of many Americans, including witnesses, Waco had in fact been a crime committed against Americans by the ATF and FBI. In other words, Tim had not been alone in his feelings, and when it came to condemning a man to death, the possible moral legitimacy of his outrage, if not of his act, should be taken into consideration.

I tried explaining it this way: A man stands trial and is convicted of murdering an individual he believes participated, or caused or aided, in the destruction of his neighbor's house and the killing of his neighbor's children. Surely it is relevant to punishment if, in fact, the accused is right, that is to say, the person he killed did burn his neighbor's house, did kill his children.

Waco, in this sense, I maintained, was mitigation. It was highly relevant.

But Judge Matsch, oversimplifying, proclaimed, "I don't intend to try Waco here at this trial," and he allowed us only a very limited, insufficient exposure of that tragic event.

The Supreme Court of the United States, in its 1991 decision in *Payne v. Tennessee*, determined that the Eighth Amendment to the U.S. Constitution does not prohibit victim-impact evidence in the penalty phase of a capital trial. But it was extremely careful, and very clear, in that decision about limiting and restricting such evidence. The high degree of emotion and emotionalism inherently associated with such evidence could not, the Court cautioned, be permitted to overwhelm the jury's responsibility to make a reliable judgment. It was the lower court's responsibility to strike and maintain a balance, and it was what Judge Matsch was trying to do when, after the return of the verdict in the first stage, he advised the prosecution, the media, the witnesses, and indeed the world at large, that there would be no "lynching" of Tim McVeigh in his courtroom.

But as Rob Nigh and Dick Burr wrote in their later appeal to the Tenth District:

Nearly every victim-impact witness strayed beyond the limit expressed by the District Court [Judge Matsch]. Not only was "the empty chair" [of the deceased victim] acknowledged, but the effects of that empty chair, in riveting, emotional poignant, heart-wrenching detail, were allowed to flood the courtroom. The "grieving process, the mourning process," which the Court expressly prohibited—and the compelling emotional need for witnesses to pay homage to their loved ones and so find some way of sharing their intense pain—rolled over everyone, much like it had in the guilt phase, but with no restraint, with the sense instead that it had been sanctioned by the Court.

Again, why Judge Matsch allowed it, in clear violation of the Supreme Court's ruling, I cannot say. He made no effort to stop it. It lasted a week. Jury members cried and wiped their eyes. The effect was again of a flood, and it left us, and especially Dick Burr, in a deep hole.

Dick is a fine writer and a moving speaker, and he had worked weeks, months, in upstate New York and elsewhere, interviewing prospective witnesses, choosing from among them, coaxing them to come to our courtroom in Denver, preparing for this moment. He'd assembled teachers from Tim's school days, childhood friends, army buddies, and he had home movies, and Tim's divorced parents, Bill McVeigh and Mickey Frazer, who wept on the stand and said, "I am pleading for my son's life. He is a human being, just as we all are."

This was Dick Burr's theme, that Tim was "one of us," a phrase later mocked by Joe Hartzler and, still later, taken by Rick Serrano as the title of his book about the case. Dick talked—eloquently—of love and compassion. He gave full voice to the age-old question of those who have fought the death penalty: "When hate leads to killing, do we abandon our commitment to love and compassion by killing the killer?"

As I listened to Dick, I couldn't help but recall the words I had once heard from Father Chamberlain on a Sunday morning in Scotland in St. John's Episcopal Church: "Mercy is a greater virtue than justice."

All for naught. He could have been Demosthenes and Isaiah and Jesus all rolled into one. I joined Dick in summation, pleading that life imprisonment was a worse punishment than death. But the spirit of the day was elsewhere—in the ghosts of the victims perhaps, and also in the cry of vengeance that was like a voice out of the terror during the French Revolution:

"Tell him he is no patriot. He is a traitor, and he deserves to die."

The speaker was Beth Wilkinson, in summation, and pointing her finger at Tim McVeigh.

The jury agreed with her.

On June 19, 1997, the twelve men and women returned their penalty verdict.

Tim McVeigh would be put to death.

On September 8, 1998, the United States Court of Appeals of the Tenth Circuit upheld the verdict and sentence.

15
GOING HOME

In a way, Tim McVeigh set me free.

I went on the road with Sherrel in the immediate aftermath of the trial, but I was aware of Tim's discontent, aware too that two people associated with the defense were encouraging him to get rid of me so that they could take my place. In fact, in July I had already told Tim that I did not wish to be his appellate counsel unless he specifically wanted me to. I had told him that I was going to write a book to express my strong convictions about the case and that I wished to withdraw, unless he truly wanted me to represent him on appeal.

Unfortunately, Tim then gave an ill-advised interview to a Buffalo newspaper. He said, among other things, that I was betraying him now by writing a book, and he asked what I had accomplished for him, after all, other than to get him the death penalty. He criticized my strategy and competence. In doing so, he revealed previously confidential information. But I have restricted my discussion in this account to nonconfidential information, almost all of which is already in the public record. Matters personal to myself or my family do not, of course, relate to my representation of him. Tim suggested, in addition, that Judge Matsch and I had met secretly and that we had lied to him.

Although I had little objection to Tim's blowing off steam at my expense, he had insulted Judge Matsch gratuitously. In addition, he had in my judgment come perilously close to breaking all of the attorney-client privilege on his own, which could have opened everything in the case to public scrutiny.

In any case, it was time. I had represented Roger Dale Stafford for eight years before his execution, and Tim McVeigh full time for two and a half years. When the curtain comes down, so to speak, it is time to get off the stage. Furthermore, I believed Rob Nigh eminently capable of representing Tim through the appeals processes and securing the appointment of whatever assistance he needed. God knows the judge had given him ample material to work with in his conduct of the trial. If there ever were an Oklahoma state trial or—it is not beyond the realm of possibility—a retrying of the federal case, well, then the ruling court would have to appoint a new defender.

I, myself, after the verdict on June 19, set off on a circuitous trip around these United States in an effort to recover emotionally. Part of the time I drove by myself; sometimes Sherrel joined me. For more than two years I had lived as though in a giant fishbowl, the media passing on news of my every sneeze, and I'd learned to hold my emotions in tight check. During that time, I'd been totally, all-consumingly focused on the pursuit of one goal—a fair trial for my client.

Now it was over, and although I felt that I had done just about everything that could be done, it was hard not to feel as though I had failed.

Terry Lynn Nichols was tried in that same courtroom before a new jury. I kept abreast of the proceedings from long range, and I was aware that Judge Matsch changed a number of key rulings from our trial and that Nichols benefited enormously from them:

1. He relaxed considerably the restraints and constraints on voir dire—the individual examination of prospective jurors—which gave Mike Tigar five weeks instead of three and much more leeway.

2. He instructed the jury on lesser included offenses. This gave them the possibility of finding Nichols guilty of manslaughter, which they eventually did. In the McVeigh case, the jury received no such instruction.

3. He permitted Carol Howe to testify while still refusing to allow her to explain that she had been an undercover informant for ATF. What his rationale was, I can't say. Nonetheless, she testified that she had seen McVeigh at Elohim City—which was news to me.

4. He permitted testimony concerning "others unknown." We had tried so hard to introduce such evidence—John Doe #2, the Philippines connection, Elohim City, Dennis Mahon, Andrew Strassmeir—but Judge Matsch had turned us down, not only in the first stage of McVeigh's trial but even after the jury had decided upon conviction, when it was crystal clear that such evidence had direct bearing on the issue of the death sentence. The judge made a crucial error in my judgment. He rectified it for Nichols.

5. Although Judge Matsch had turned down almost all of our requests to restrict what the government could say about Tim McVeigh's political background and beliefs, he restricted such testimony in the Nichols trial. What was admitted was carefully circumscribed and without unnecessary elaboration.

6. Most important of all, Judge Matsch put absolute brakes on the use of emotional testimony in the first stage of Nichols's trial. There was no more about the emotional impact of the bombing upon the families in the first stage, and testimony that clearly elicited emotional responses, testimony concerning the children and pregnant women who died, was reduced almost to the vanishing point.

The timing of these reconsidered decisions was very beneficial to Terry Nichols' defense. The Court of Appeals upheld all of Judge Matsch's contrary rulings in the McVeigh trial. But the Nichols' case was tried before the appeal decision was public. Had the timing been reversed, i.e. Tim's conviction upheld before Terry Nichols stood trial, it may well be that Judge Matsch would not have changed any of these rulings which benefitted Terry. In which case, Terry Nichols' verdict may have been the same as Tim's. Guilty on all counts and the imposition of the death sentence.

I don't know what caused the judge to change his mind. I like to think our motion and a 250-page brief for a new trial played a role. Perhaps it persuaded him to reread the opinions in *Payne v. Tennessee* and other cases we cited as precedents that clearly cast doubt on his rulings concerning the emotional-impact question. But I think something else came into play too, and I will come back to it.

Terry Nichols was helped in other ways as well. One very major factor was that his trial came second. The public clamor for blood, for eye-for-an-eye justice, as represented by the victims' testimony in the McVeigh trial, had been answered by the McVeigh death penalty, and the anger, the outrage that had focused on McVeigh from the very beginning had been assuaged. In addition, Nichols's lawyers sat in during every day of our trial and so were able to "go to school" on the weaker portions of the prosecution's case. When these subjects came up in Nichols's trial, Mike Tigar and Ron Woods attacked brilliantly.

But in the end the verdict was only a cosmetic victory for the defense. The government had offered Nichols, three times, a life sentence with Bob Macy, the state prosecutor's approval, but Nichols had foolishly rejected it. He still got a life sentence, but now Macy was not bound by the verdict and said he would seek the death penalty against Nichols.

Nichols was also helped by overconfidence on the part of the prosecution and changes in personnel. After McVeigh's guilty verdict, Joe Hartzler quit and went home to Springfield, Illinois. Undoubtedly he thought he'd be appointed to the federal bench— certainly, I would have thought so—but his day in the sun rose and fell with the thanks of the president and the attorney general, the loving thanks of the victims, and his trial victory. Illinois's two Democratic U.S. senators, Carol Mosley-Braun and Richard Durbin, quietly passed him over in favor of their own candidates for federal judgeships, and President Clinton apparently didn't see fit to intervene. New lawyers, who had not been present during the first trial, were brought in to prosecute Nichols, and they were at once overconfident and less effective, which in turn made Judge Matsch less patient.

There were, in addition, two developments during the Nichols trial that embarrassed the government and diminished its credibility. One was the testimony of Karen Anderson, Roger Moore's girl-friend and/or business associate, who was introduced to support an exhibit that supposedly listed all of the weapons that had belonged to Moore before the robbery, which, the government maintained, Terry Nichols had carried out. As Mike Tigar was quick to point out, one of the weapons on the list had in fact been purchased by Nichols at a gun show several years before. There were only two possible explanations: Either the weapon in question, which Nichols had bought once, had somehow ended up in Roger Moore's house in time for Terry Nichols to get his hands on it again, this time by robbery, or Karen Anderson's "list" was an after-the-fact job and that the famous Roger Moore robbery wasn't a robbery at all. In any event, this was a stunning blow to the prosecution. As to what happened to the FBI agent who was supposed to double-check the "robbery" data, I can only assume he is now presiding as resident of the FBI station nearest the North Pole.

The government also let itself be bamboozled by Tigar with regard to another witness. This man claimed under oath to have seen a Ryder truck at Geary State Fishing Lake on the afternoon of April 18, 1995. In a photograph handed to him by the defense, he identified one of the individuals as a man he'd seen around the Ryder truck. The government, of course, had had the right to inspect all the exhibits, including this one, before their use in the trial, but they had missed the fact that the person the witness identi-fied in the photo, who was of some prominence in Kansas extreme right-wing circles, happened to have been in jail on April 18. The government had time to investigate and learn the identity of the person in the photograph before it was called upon to present any rebuttal evidence, but, for whatever reason, it either didn't, or if it did, was so overconfident it let it go.

I continue to be convinced, as I've said, that the government's case against Nichols was, or should have been, stronger than the one against McVeigh. Specifically, it had that initial nine-hour state-ment to tear into. Considerable portions of it could be proven false, which led one, inexorably, to the conclusion that the lies had to have been a perverse form of admitting responsibility. In addition, Nichols lived close to Junction City, which was the hub of pre-bombing activity according to the government's theory, and as one of his jurors said afterward, the average person just doesn't keep such quantities of explosives, detonator cord, and similar objects lying around his residence. Very late in the day, in fact, just before Nichols's sentence was pronounced, a forensic psychologist hired by the prosecution, Dr. Reid Meloy, advised Judge Matsch that "in the case of the Oklahoma City bombing, Mr. Nichols was the strategist and Mr. McVeigh was the tactician." Although Dr. Meloy, to my knowledge, had never examined Nichols or Tim McVeigh face-to-face, he wrote that "throughout the records [provided by federal authorities] there are numerous descriptions of Mr. Nichols' ability to carefully plan, consider his options carefully, focus on details. . . . Mr. Nichols, thirteen years older, provided the stable anchor for the conspiracy to unfold."

This was the Terry Nichols I too had seen. But the government, it appeared, failed to convince the Nichols jury of this characterization.

The *Rocky Mountain News* once called me a "competent country lawyer," Mike Tiger "brilliant but arrogant." Both definitions are correct. Mike's arrogance was amply expressed, before the trials, by the disparaging remarks that he made in public about me, but his brilliance was on the courtroom floor, and it expressed itself in different ways. I even read, and was persuaded that it was true, that one of the jurors who held out against the death penalty for Terry Nichols felt that Tigar had somehow singled her out. She felt flattered by his questions during voir dire and by his special glances during the trial.

For all these reasons, the Nichols jury came up with a skewed and divided verdict that owed little to logic. In declaring Terry guilty of conspiracy but not of the crime of mass destruction itself, the jurors were obviously trying to sidestep the death-penalty question, and when it came to phase two, they were unable to agree on Nichols's sentence and passed responsibility for it back to Judge Matsch—a process that, as I shall relate, led in 1998 to one of the most curious and revealing exchanges of the two trials.

Meanwhile, I went home, back across eastern Colorado and western Kansas, as I had numerous times before, through Limon, Burlington, Caruso, Colby, Hays, Pratt, Medicine Lodge.

Even though I'd been physically absent from Enid, the psychological gap seemed much wider, and I felt a little like a veteran of some second civil war, straggling home to my former life from far-off battlefields. Just south of Anthony, Kansas, just before crossing the state line, there is a small rise in the road. This time I stopped, pulled off to the side, and got out of the car. From this position, I could look down on northern Grant and Alfalfa Counties in Oklahoma. The wheat fields were being readied for planting. I could make out barns, houses, and, here and there, a tractor, an occasional pickup—all symbols of normal life. That was what I wanted. Just as we could now get rid of most of the security arrangements, including the shotgun I'd kept under our mattress the two and a half years past, so I wanted our normal lives back. It took some doing.

I wasn't sure how many people would want Tim McVeigh's lawyer representing them and the Democratic Party tried to make an issue of my contribution to Governor Keating's campaign—some people even tried to persuade him not to come to my home, but these were minor irritants. Old friends such as Bob and Pat Anderson and Nancy and Frank Davies invited Sherrel and me to their homes for dinner. I slept late more often, rejoined the Enid Rotary Club, and once again served as lay reader in the St. Matthew's Episcopal Church.

One of the ironies of having been in the spotlight in our society is the assumption people make that you've filled your coffers in the process. As for me, personally, I was paid $125 per hour. My normal rate had been $175. The same went for all the lawyers in my office, each of whom billed the government for less than their hourly rate. In 1994, the year before I undertook McVeigh's defense, my gross income had been in the low seven figures. After all business expenses, I had a very comfortable six-figure income. Now, by the time I came home, my law practice was shattered. We had all of three open case files. Ours was a litigation firm, and I had been the so-called rainmaker, that is, the lawyer who brought in the bulk of the business. With me gone, the practice had essentially dissolved. Now, at age 57, I had to start over. Some clients didn't want to come back. They didn't think it wise to have as their lawyer the man who represented the worst mass murderer in American history. I found myself in the courthouse defending people accused—yes—of drunk driving, working on divorce suits, personal injury claims, title work, and probate. A few insurance companies started coming back, and once again I was representing Phillips University, the *Enid News and Eagle*, Jumbo Foods, and Luckinbill Contractors, but my income was but a fraction of what it had been, and we had two children still in school. So what did I do? I did what Americans do in emergencies; I refinanced my home, which had been almost paid off.

I'm not complaining, mind you. But *United States v. McVeigh* did not do much for the Jones family bank balance.

Nor did it provide a stepping-stone.

In August, at the American Bar Association convention, I had breakfast with Merrick Garland, now a judge in the prestigious U.S. Court of Appeals for the District of Columbia Circuit, who asked me what city I was moving to. When I told him I was going back to Enid, he was absolutely incredulous. He, like some members of the media, just couldn't believe that I didn't intend to use my new notoriety to jump-start a big job with some large law firm in Denver or San Francisco or New York or Washington, D.C. Even if I'd wanted to, I'm not sure I could have. For one thing, we'd "lost" the case. For another, I didn't come with a batch of litigious clients in my briefcase. But I didn't want to, which was the point. I was an Oklahoman. I live and practice law in Oklahoma because I want to, I live and practice law in Enid because I want to, and if that makes me some kind of an anomaly in contemporary society, well, then that's what I am.

I love Oklahoma. There's no place I'd rather be.

The high cost of the McVeigh defense—it exceeded $15 million— will appall some and enrage others. There were, as I see it, two main causes. One was the complexity of the case and its far-reaching strands. (We weren't the only ones, as I've indicated, to send investigators into the Philippines.) A proper defense required experts in a number of specialized domains, and some of our experts demanded— and deserved—fees that greatly exceeded what we lawyers made. But the second, I would venture, more costly factor was the enormous expense of discovery, to which the intransigence and the obfuscations of the government greatly contributed. The main reason it took us two years to get to trial was that the prosecution kept us in the dark as long as it dared, even after. As I hope I have demonstrated, the prosecutors' stalling tactics and lies forced us into cascades of paperwork, motions upon motions upon motions, endless court appearances.

Each of these motions and appearances took time, and time, in legal proceedings, brings quickly to mind the ticking meter. For both these reasons, we had seventeen lawyers, sometimes with the help of experts, sifting through hundreds of hours of electronic recordings, 30,000 witness statements, 156 million entries in telephone records, 1 million hotel registrations, hundreds of pages of medical records for hundreds of victims, 100,000 photographs, more than 500 hours of videotape, more than 400 hours of audiotapes, and tens of thousands of pages of FBI Lab reports. We defended more than a hundred ancillary actions, filed either in the case or separately, by victims, by organizations claiming to speak for victims, by strangers, interlopers, even media organizations. We went to the Tenth Circuit a dozen times. We examined literally thousands of would-be exhibits.

But this high cost is a direct product of our legal system. In 1790, one of the first laws passed by the 1st Congress was the Crimes and Offenses Act, which provided that anyone facing a capital sentence in federal court was entitled to a lawyer "learned in the law" in order that he might make his "full defense." The concept was expanded and elaborated until the 1960s, when the Supreme Court decided that the due process clause of the Fourteenth Amendment required court-appointed counsel in criminal prosecutions. As a result, there are now some thirteen thousand lawyers on the criminal justice list in the various federal courts of the nation who will accept court appointments, as well as federal public defenders and lawyers available to represent state death row prisoners in their federal habeas corpus proceedings. The states, in addition, have their own systems.

For my Birthday in 1997, my wife asked our friend and local artist, Vicky Jackson to paint the following words placed onto the mantle of the fireplace in our library: "The justice of a society is measured not by how it treats its best citizens but how it treats its worst." Sherrel said that that sentence distilled my philosophy as a trial lawyer, and so it does. In today's world, the cost in dollars of giving a defendant like Tim McVeigh a full defense is going to be high. So, by the way, will be the cost of prosecuting him. Yet we have tried lynching, and most of us have found it wanting.

But there are still greater costs built into our current system of justice that have nothing to do with dollars and cents. In *United*

States v. McVeigh, there were two, and, I am tempted to say, in hindsight, they were inevitable:

1. The government's investigation remained incomplete.

2. Tim McVeigh did not get a fair trial.

I have said in the course of this book, as I said in the heat of battle in Judge Matsch's courtroom, that I was convinced the prosecutors were holding out on us. I still believe this to be so. I believe there was exculpatory material it either had or knew of that was denied us, particularly having to do with the prior knowledge issue. But it is also likely that there was evidence they themselves couldn't get hold of. At least five government agencies investigated aspects of the bombing: the FBI, ATF, INS, the State Department, and the CIA. The prosecution only controlled one of them, the FBI, for both worked for the Department of Justice. Their access to the others and to their information was problematic. Furthermore—and this was key—*they had no motivation to do so.*

For example, we ran into the CIA's footprints at several key junctures during our own investigation. We knew it'd been interested in Strassmeir. We knew it'd been notified, at least twice, of the phone call Vincent Cannistraro had received from his Saudi Arabian contact. And you didn't have to be a spook to surmise that CIA files were alive with information on Islamic terrorism in the Philippines. But we couldn't get near any of it. Whenever we tried to get the prosecution, or tried to get Judge Matsch to get the prosecution, to obtain information from the CIA, we were told there was none. What had they done, Judge Matsch wanted to know? They'd written letters, came the answer. And the answers? The answers, also by letter, were that the CIA had nothing relevant in its files.

Well, I'm sorry. You know and I know that if the prosecutors had really wanted to find out what the CIA had in its files, they'd have gone straight up the chain of command to Janet Reno, then across town to the White House, and the White House would have done its own arm wrestling with the CIA. This is precisely what *should* have happened. Wasn't one of the points of the exercise—the months of investigating, the weeks in the courtroom, the thousands of man hours, the millions of dollars—to make sure that the Oklahoma City bombing had no sequel? Or was the Justice Department, in the wake of excruciating embarrassments like Ruby Ridge and Waco, only and purely interested in obtaining their conviction so that from the attorney general on down all could walk away from the table, congratulating one another on a job well done?

Laurie Mylroie, who, it will be remembered, was a consultant to the McVeigh defense, expressed this theme brilliantly in an article in *The National Interest* about the World Trade Center bombing, which is just as applicable to the Oklahoma case.

"A high wall," she wrote, "stands between the Justice Department, including the Federal Bureau of Investigation, on the one hand, and the national security agencies on the other. Once arrests are made, the trials of individual perpetrators take bureaucratic precedence over everything else. The Justice Department inherits primary jurisdiction, and the business of the Justice Department is above all the prosecution of criminals."

Mylroie made the point that national security agencies are denied critical information because the Justice Department and the FBI refuse to share with them. I'm sure this is true. But the reverse is equally true, and to the McVeigh defense, that "high wall" constituted a two-way, bureaucratic Do Not Enter sign, as impenetrable as the Berlin Wall during the height of the Cold War.

Laurie Mylroie also wrote, "By responding to state-sponsored terrorism solely by arresting and trying individual perpetrators, the U.S. government, in effect, invites such states to commit acts of terror in such a way as to leave behind a few relatively minor figures to be arrested, tried, and convicted."

This scenario may well have described, with disturbing accuracy, the Oklahoma City bombing case.

We know that "others unknown" were no figment of the federal grand jury's imagination. As much as the government may have tried to sidestep and duck the issue that others beside McVeigh and Nichols had participated in the bombing, it was built into their own presentation of the facts all during spring and summer in 1995. We, during our later defense investigation, came very close to proving it ourselves. The government, in denying it in order to "win," and quite probably to hide its own failure to act upon prior warnings, simply left the door wide open. In time, I am afraid, Timothy James

McVeigh and the Oklahoma City bombing will join President Kennedy's or Dr. Martin Luther King's assassinations as a feast for conspiracy theorists of all kinds and stripes, and the condemned man in a celebrated trial will become, yet again, a poster boy for the darker side of our society.

T he Terry Nichols jury, as I mentioned, was unable to agree on a sentence in the second stage of their trial. Therefore the burden of sentencing the convicted man reverted to the court. In spring 1998, Judge Matsch made a kind of judicial "proffer" to Terry Nichols. The only way Nichols could avoid life without parole, he said, was for him to name names. If Nichols would identify "others unknown" to the court and provide some answers, then Matsch would consider a lighter sentence.

Nichols failed to respond. Accordingly, on June 4, 1998, Judge Matsch pronounced the sentence of life without parole.

I may have known Richard Matsch only since the fall of 1995. However, I believe I know him well enough to affirm that he never would have made such a proffer speculatively or frivolously or to gain attention for himself. And even if he was simply responding to some boast of Nichols or some feeler put out by his lawyers, he never would have done so publicly.

Unless, that is, he too believes, in his heart of hearts, that others unknown are out there.

Could it be that Richard Matsch, persuaded by evidence he refused to let our jury hear, has himself become a conspiracy theorist?

IN CONCLUSION

I come back to my client.

To raise the question of whether Tim McVeigh did or didn't get a fair trial will seem irrelevant to some, and in the heat of frustration, in the course of struggling to defend him as best I could, I sometimes felt I was the last person in America who cared about fair trials. This was presumptuous, even egotistical on my part. It was also rather bullheaded.

A lot of us care. We wouldn't be Americans if we didn't care, and if we ever stop caring, then all the laws and institutions we and our forebears have created to protect the ideals of liberty, equality, and justice will crumble, and we will be back to lynchings and hangings and mob rule.

Of course, Tim McVeigh didn't get a fair trial. But that said, I think there are times—instances—in our society when our nobler instincts give way to a more visceral, quasireligious need. The Oklahoma City bombing was such an instance. It was a shock to our national psyche. It was the worst single act of terrorism in our history. It struck at our heartland. Our first human response was one of revulsion and revenge, as epitomized in the pledge of that most political of human beings—our president—to get the death penalty for the perpetrators. We demanded catharsis.

In that climate the first man accused was almost bound to be "it." In hindsight, I would go so far as to say that the minute Tim McVeigh was led out of the Noble County Courthouse in manacles and the orange jumpsuit he was a condemned man. He was the first caught, he was the demon. Terry Nichols always played second fiddle.

For the next two years, McVeigh's defenders and Judge Matsch were alone in trying to protect McVeigh's constitutional right to a fair trial. Our Justice Department could have cared less; the media checked which way the wind was blowing. And then, late in the day, for whatever reasons, Judge Matsch himself abandoned the cause.

X also helped deny Tim a fair trial, and so did Pete Slover and Stringer, and so, as I've described, did I. But I'm not sure, in hindsight, that anything we did do, or didn't, would have changed the result. I have little doubt but that most members of the McVeigh jury had already made up their minds before the prosecution and defense delivered the opening statements. But if there were hold-outs among them or some who heeded the judge's admonitions to refrain from judgment until everything had been heard, their resolve was washed away in the flood of tears that swept the courtroom as victims told their stories. In their rage, their anguish, their sorrow, the victims made the jurors their surrogates. From that point on, the verdict was an inevitability.

I come back to the beginning. I am hearing that Cassandralike remark Susan Otto made when she and John Coyle handed over the McVeigh defense to me in May 1995.

"When you know everything I know," she said that day, "and you will soon enough, you will never think of the United States of America again in the same way."

I've never asked her what she meant, but her words have echoed in my mind at various junctures. When I visited Waco, for instance, and tried to imagine why it had been necessary for the Branch Davidians to die. When, later, I discovered that the federal prosecutors had been lying to us. Or when, that night after X left my apartment in Denver, I pondered the corrupt power of the media. Or when, finally, I stood on the courthouse steps right after the sentencing and spoke briefly to the media, with the wind in my face and the pain inside.

In her wonderful novel, *To Kill a Mockingbird*, Harper Lee's fictional lawyer, Atticus Finch, tells his daughter, Scout: "...Simply by the nature of the work, every lawyer gets at least one case in his lifetime that affects him personally. This is mine." Well, Tim McVeigh's case is one of mine.

Our polls at that point showed that the death penalty had never been more popular. Other polls, at the same time, showed that the majority believed the government had botched the investigation and that there were other conspirators on the loose.

Bread and circuses.

I'm thinking about Rome. I'm thinking about what it might have been like to have been a county-seat lawyer (whatever he was called then) in the days of the Roman empire, when the great ideals of the republic had given way to power, venality, and display, when, for better or worse, there was no turning back. The McVeigh case did that for me, and I grieve, in my quiet way, not for Tim—whose fate is now in the hands of the United States Supreme Court and, possibly, other courts of appeals in the future and, also possibly, the Oklahoma grand jury—but for what the case told me about the ideals of American jurisprudence: due process, the right to a fair trial, the rule of law.

On June 22, 1998, that is, the first anniversary of the death penalty verdict, a reunion took place in Oklahoma City, some of it on the site where the Murrah Building once stood. There, before the television cameras, members of the McVeigh jury mingled and embraced with survivors and members of the victims' families, many of whom had testified at the trial. Those of us who saw it on television—and the reunion received widespread media coverage—could only be moved by it, by the outpouring of emotion on both sides. But it also served to remind us of a troubling truth—that once the victims began to testify in the Denver courtroom the previous year, Timothy McVeigh never had a chance.

I have no quarrel with a jury's right to pronounce its verdict, only with the way the McVeigh jurors appeared to have arrived at theirs. In my judgment, they did not convict the right man. My real quarrel is with the federal government. In that respect, I suppose, I have become somewhat like my former client, and this troubles me too because I am sworn to uphold the U.S. Constitution, and I believe fervently in our law, in the rule of law, in our systems of justice and jurisprudence. But I saw little concern for justice in the functioning of the Justice Department, less respect for the law, still less passion for the truth, no interest whatsoever in fairness. What I saw instead was an arrogant clan of bureaucrats hell-bent on "winning," skilled at spin, brazen in their efforts to conceal their own mistakes.

This, to my mind, smacks very much of Rome, the Rome of the Empire, and it makes me fear for the health of our great republic.

In *United States v. McVeigh*, an enormous wrong was committed. As a result, the whole truth about the worst case of domestic terrorism in our history will likely never be known. The government certainly, but much of the public too, seem satisfied with that outcome, at least for the moment, but I believe they are wrong. Whatever happens to Timothy McVeigh or Terry Nichols, the American people need to know what happened to themselves, that terrible morning in April 1995.

We need to know and we don't know.

The Murrah Building is gone, the dead have been buried, two men have been convicted. But the mystery remains.

Here ends a story not unwarranted in this incongruous world of ours—innocence and infirmity, spiritual depravity and faire respite.

Herman Melville, from an early draft
of *Billy Budd Foretopman*

ACKNOWLEDGMENTS

In representing Tim McVeigh, I had the support of so many people that I hope I do not inadvertently omit someone from this list of acknowledgments. If I do so, please do not attribute it to me as an act of ill-grace or that I have forgotten you, simply tax it to poor memory.

My mother and father instilled in me certain values and beliefs that furnished the core of my attitudes and philosophy, and they made it possible by their love and affection for me to live in a wholesome environment and attend good schools and to develop an interest in law and politics. My debate coach, Mollie Martin, Jeanne Wootters, my high school counselor, and Jim McBride, my history teacher, all significantly influenced my interest in speech, debate, politics, and the law, and each gave of their time and interest in encouraging me in my high school years and beyond. Their influence is with me almost a half-century later. But man is not influenced just by people he meets, but also by what he reads. In my case, John F. Kennedy's *Profiles in Courage*, William Kunstler's *The Case for Courage*, Earl Conrad's beautiful biography of William H. Seward, *Mr. Seward for the Defense*, William Harbaugh's *Lawyer's Lawyer: The Life of John W. Davis*, Daniel Kornstein's *Thinking Under Fire*, and especially Edward Bennett William's classic *One Man's Freedom* all shaped and molded me and my character. These stories of lawyers who defended unpopular causes against great odds and overwhelming condemnation left their mark on me. I may have thirsted or longed for such a challenge, and if I did, I certainly got it the night Judge Russell called me.

The late E. T. Dunlap, chancellor of the State Regents for Higher Education, and Gov. Henry Bellmon's executive assistant, Drew Mason, made it possible for me to attend the University of

Oklahoma Law School. W. J. Otjen Sr., who came to Oklahoma when it was still a territory and was a leader in Oklahoma's politics, having served both as a Republican member of the state's house and senate and almost elected governor in 1942, and Frank Carter, the last lawyer in Enid to be admitted to the bar by "reading the law," gave me my start in Enid, as did Ken Martin, Grant Harris, and Milton Garber.

My wife of twenty-five years, Sherrel, has become known in Enid among our friends as the "defender's defender." Through hopeless political campaigns, controversial criminal cases, unpopular civil liberties cases, Sherrel has defended me. Her style, quiet manner, gracious hospitality, and loving consideration not just of me but of my parents, and her unselfish support of everything that I have done professionally and politically, made it possible for me to take on the most controversial and unpopular of cases. No man could have defended Tim McVeigh unless he had an empathic and supportive wife, and I certainly have that. No less important were our children. For John and Stephen Mark, grown and away from home, having a father involved in such a controversial case was not particularly onerous. For Rachael, away at Westminster College, my work plus her internship in Washington with an old friend, Letitia Chambers, convinced her she should pursue law school. However, my youngest child, Edward, still in high school, had to bear witness and accept the taunts, challenges, criticism, and sarcasm of some of his classmates. That his teachers understood may have made it somewhat easier for him. Edward never complained, and he bore silent witness to my work.

I was also gifted with a highly competent, loyal, and professional office staff. My personal secretary, Renae Elmenhorst, who had been with me for more than a decade, worked as though the clock did not exist. Karen Olds, our receptionist, who had to field thousands of calls, many of them from the media, and Karen Warner, Bob Wyatt's secretary, all earned the respect of outsiders for their patience and good work. Trish Pierpoint, who suffered a stroke shortly after we moved to Denver, Shelly Hager, Kathryn Irons, Desi Milacek, and Mahemala Spragg all helped carry the burden. Becky Blasier, our accountant, supervised the preparation of our monthly vouchers and billings as well as those for the experts and witnesses. Less than one-half of 1 percent of our billings were questioned by the court review staff, and even those were usually resolved easily. Becky was responsible for seeing that not only were we paid on time but so were all of the third party vendors and experts who were helping us.

Then we assembled the lawyers. Rob Nigh, whom I had known for many years, and Bob Wyatt, were the first two I contacted to get help. The other members of Jones, Wyatt & Roberts: Mike Roberts, Andy Murphy, Jeremy Lowrey, Julia Allen Sims, Jim Hankins, Amber McLaughlin Gill, Robert Warren, all recognized the case was the greatest challenge of their professional careers. Two very experienced trial lawyers, Chris Tritico, of Houston, and Cheryl Ramsey, of Stillwater, Oklahoma, joined our team about two months before the trial started. These individuals gave unstinting loyalty to me, as did my researcher and "minister without portfolio," Ann Bradley, who served as my "eyes and ears" where I could not be and helped me manage, to the extent we could, our sometimes turbulent relations with the media. Jeralyn Merritt, a Denver, Colorado, lawyer, proved of invaluable assistance in locating experts and tackling difficult issues such as eyewitness identification and the government's use of handwriting experts. Maurie Levin, an Austin, Texas, lawyer, also helped with the punishment phase of the trial. Kevin McNally, one of two lawyers authorized by the Federal Defender Service to provide assistance to court-appointed lawyers in death penalty cases, was enormously resourceful and helpful to us. Richard Burr and Mandy Welch, of Houston, Texas, and Randy Coyne, a law professor at the University of Oklahoma and an academic specialist in the death penalty, were also members of the team.

Ann Seim, a longtime personal friend and a highly competent office manager for many private physicians, was brought on to be project manager to supervise the filing, recording, and office operations of the McVeigh defense team. She did an outstanding job, as did Steven England, a recent member of the Colorado bar, who got us ready every morning with our papers and files and brought everything back at the close of day. Scott Anderson, a recent graduate of Phillips University, was with us from the beginning and helped with computers and filings.

Sam Guiberson, the resourceful expert for attorneys on court ordered electronic interception and recordation in Houston, Texas, provided our litigation support. The real guru of the computer and the person whom we relied upon endlessly was Chuck Miller. Chuck was absolutely the most talented computer expert I have ever seen. He was on call twenty-four hours a day, seven days a week, and he moved to Denver with us while his wife was finishing up her residency in ophthalmology. Chuck not only was a whiz with computers but also a personable sort though quiet and dignified of manner. Sam Guiberson also brought in a number of very talented lawyers to assist with litigation support and electronic interception analysis. These were Margaret Vandenbrook, Lorraine Derbes, Maria Ryan, Francesca Castaldi, Michelle Mears, and Kristan Tucker. Nic Merritt, Daphne Burlingham, Kelly Cherry, Rebecca Winters, Leah Kling, Chad Wold, Sarah Lee, John Jones, Heidi McLemore, Hoss Parvizian, Michael Grote, Trent Luckinbill, and Alicia Carpenter also assisted the defense either in staff positions or as law clerks.

Then there were our expert witnesses. Dr. Keith Borer, Dr. Brian Caddy, Dr. John Lloyd, Dr. Jehuda Yinon, Sid Woodcock (bomb trace analysis experts), Michael K. Crawford, M.D. (expert who conducted physical examination of defendant), Dr. Roy Godson (terrorism expert), David V. Foster, M.D., John Smith, M.D., and Seymour L. Halleck, M.D. (determined defendant's competency for trial) and assisted by the clinical psychologist Anthony Semone, Ed Simonson, Danny Lee Fong, and Brian McDaniel (consulting experts on the telephone records), Dr. Stephen Sloan (expert on terrorists and terrorism), and his assistant, Seth Meisel, Dr. Kent L. Tedin (assisted with change of venue motion), Linda S. Thomas (expert in vetting other side's experts), Peter V. Tytell (questioned documents), Gary L. Wells, and Elizabeth F. Loftus (eyewitness identification issues), Professor M. Yasar Iscan (consulting and expert testimony regarding unidentified leg issue), Aaron Zelman (gun control), Frank Davies and Dan Harris (architects), Peter DeForest (tool mark examiner), Mark Denbeaux (document examiner), Hammet Photography, Emricks Moving and Storage of Enid, Ikon LDS (coding and scanning), Tammy Krause (victim impact), George Krisvosta (tool mark examiner), Litidex (scanning and coding), Herbert MacDonnell (fingerprints), Peter McDonald (tire imprints), Patricia Matthews (filming), Mike McNulty (assault on the Branch Davidians), William McQuay (fingerprints), Richard

Murray (venue), James Pate (Waco), Skip Palenik (micro trace analyst), Donald Streufert (victim impact), Rimkus Consulting Group (chemist), Anthony Rockwood (weather), Jasa and Dahl Towland (venue), Richard Sanders (audio and video), Alan Scheflin, Howard Zehr (victim impact), Laird Wilcox (penalty phase), Wiss, Janney, Elstner Assoc. (engineers), Kathy Roberts (photography), Joe Taylor, president of Broadcast News of Mid-America, Inc., Michael Stout (voir dire), Donald L. Hansen (government's evidence concerning the bomb), J. Neil Hartley, Lee Norton, and Lisa Moody (investigation of mitigation factors), Tom Owen, president of Owl Investigation, Inc. (reviewing videotapes, magnification and enhancement), Skip Palenik (micro-trace analyst), Stuart Wright, Dean Peet, and Dick Reavis (expert on issues concerning Branch Davidians), Ann Cole and Sandy Marks (jury selection experts), Art Reed and James D. Weiskopf (reviewed military records), Dr. T. K. Marshall (autopsies), John H. Wootters Jr. (consulting expert on firearms and weapons), Jack Zimmerman (Waco events), and with special gratitude for Father Neville Chamberlain of Edinburgh, Scotland.

Marty Reed and Wilma Sparks assisted us with investigative leads in Oklahoma and Kansas. David Fechheimer and Josiah "Tink" Thompson of San Francisco were two of the best private investigators I have ever been associated with, as are Blair Abbott and Christine Hoover, a husband-and-wife team from Arizona. By the time it was over, Blair and Christine knew Michael and Lori Fortier better than they knew each other and who helped us put together the cross-examination, which in my opinion was one of the best of my career.

Kingsley Napley in London and its partners who assisted us, John Clitheroe and Christopher Murray, provided invaluable assistance, as did John Bates, a retired inspector for Scotland Yard Special Branch, and Ray Tilburey. Richard Post, a former CIA employer, and Laurie Mylroie, author of a best-selling book on Saddam Hussein, together with Dr. Roy Godson, all provided invaluable assistance and resources on terrorism. Finally, there are some individuals here and abroad whose identities are of necessity held by me "in petto". Retired intelligence officers, active journalists, foreign government officers, and diplomats, retired and others still at their post, and representatives of diverse religious and political organizations, here and elsewhere, have requested anonymity. For their counsel, time, and advice, I am grateful.

To the judges of the United States District Court for the Western Judicial District of Oklahoma, especially its chief judge, the Honorable David L. Russell, classmate, friend, fellow member at the bar and before his appointment, fellow Republican activist, I am indebted for their confidence in appointing me to represent Mr. McVeigh. To the clerk of the court, Robert Dennis, for the federal court in Oklahoma City and especially James Manspeaker, clerk of the United States District Court for the District of Colorado, and his staff, Madelyn Henetz, Debra Hansen, and Esther Bell, there are no words to describe adequately my appreciation for their help, guidance, patience, and professionalism. I would be remiss if I did not acknowledge U.S. Marshal Tina Rowe and her first deputy, Larry Homenick. Larry had already gained considerable fame for his work in the Christopher Boyce case (the "Falcon" from the Falcon and the Snowman investigation). Then there were all of the deputy marshals who guarded our client and provided security, and there were those in the Denver and Oklahoma City Police Departments who provided security for me, as did the men and women of Professional Security led by David Pritchett of Enid who were hired by the court to provide security for my home, family, and office.

I must acknowledge the greatest personal and professional debt to Chief Judge Richard Matsch of the District of Colorado. After the trial, I was frequently asked whether I missed all the drama and excitement. "Truthfully, I don't" I replied, "but I miss Judge Matsch." In my life I have been privileged to know some very exceptional men: my father, the historian Walter Prescott Webb, Congressman Paul Findley, Oklahoma City attorney D. C. Thomas, *Raymond v. Humphreys* and Richard Matsch. Judge Matsch's reputation is deserved. He is tough but fair. He does not suffer fools gladly. But I seldom saw a flash of temper that wasn't justified. He tried to give Mr. McVeigh a fair trial. I believe he failed, but it was not for lack of trying, and I recognize that history may come to a different conclusion, as has the court of appeals, but in my opinion Pete Slover's article ruined any chances for a fair trial. Perhaps it never really existed given the widespread public condemnation of my client before the trial commenced. But Judge Matsch did everything he could to see that this most important case was tried fairly in accordance with the rules in our constitutional system. He worked long, hard hours. He moved from his beautiful offices and chambers to a more austere location. He adequately funded the defense. He built a whole new courtroom with state-of-the-art technology, and he insisted that my client be treated with respect, and by his generosity he protected the lives of the members of the defense team and my family, and he supported our work in his published opinions and in his oral statements from the bench. He is the model of propriety and rectitude, learning and fairness, for every judge. The chief judge of the Fourth Judicial District of Oklahoma, Ray Dean Linder, and his predecessor, Joe Young, are very much judges in the tradition of Richard Matsch. All of the judges and lawyers before whom or with whom I practiced, of the Fourth Judicial District of Oklahoma, comprising nine counties in north-central Oklahoma, and others such as Judges Lee West, Carmon Harris, Elvin Brown, and Charles Wilson, prepared me, each in his own way, during thirty years for my work as Tim McVeigh's lawyer. No less important were my law school professors, such as Frank Elkouri, Leo Whinery, Eugene Kuntz, and Maurice Merrill, and those lawyers who were role models, Harold Singer, Earl Mills, Bill Berry, Lynn Bullis, E. B. Mitchell Jr., and D. C. Thomas.

The Enid newspaper, whose publisher at the time of my appointment was Ed Hauck, and its editor, Jerry Pitman, by the fairness and balance of its coverage of my appointment and the subsequent trial, performed a valuable service in educating the community in which I live of the professional honor that requires a lawyer to accept an appointment in a controversial criminal case when tendered by a judge.

And finally to my client, Timothy James McVeigh, whom I spent more time with for two and a half years than probably any other human being, including my wife. At the end Tim and I parted on somewhat acrimonious terms, but no one should judge him harshly for that, least of all me. I understood, as they say, where he was coming from. And no amount of acrimony or unpleasantness could change the fact that Tim McVeigh was my client, and I owe him the highest duty of care and consideration. I found him completely different from the public caricature. Others from time to time attempted to interfere with that relationship and to advance their own personal agenda rather than Tim's interest, although conveniently they persuaded themselves that their agenda and Tim's interests were the same. We worked together. It was a great privilege and honor to represent him, as I said, I know his story.

For the reasons set forth in this book, I do not believe Tim McVeigh should have been found guilty. There is honest and, in many cases, compelling doubt as to his guilt, and under our system he is entitled to the benefit of that doubt. Nothing I write herein should in any way be considered as evidence of any opinion of mine that he is anything other than not guilty.

The attorney-client privilege and the rules of confidentiality have been scrupulously preserved in this book. I obtained legal opinions from outside counsel and guidance from the Oklahoma Bar Association about what could and could not be included. The material discussed is in the public record of the transcripts, filings, testimony, exhibits, arguments, or media coverage, except for a very few things that are generally known even if not specifically mentioned in the public records. Where Tim McVeigh's thinking or words are used it is because, in those few instances, there is no attorney-client privilege because Tim made the comments to third persons.

Many times I was asked, "Did he do it?" or did I think Terry Nichols was involved. Not only can I not answer the first question because of professional constraints, there is an even more compelling reason: I was not there. I do not know. Certainly it seems clear to me that both men were entitled to the benefit of the doubt. Had they been tried in England with its restraints on pre-trial publicity and been judged strictly on the evidence I believe both may well have been found not guilty. In Scotland the verdict would have been slightly different, "not proven." I am content to leave it there. My purpose is not to argue Nichols's guilt, but to assert that Tim McVeigh did not receive a fair trial and that the government withheld exculpatory evidence from the defense and crucial facts bearing on its own responsibility from the public.

The decision to write this book was made only after the completion of Mr. McVeigh's trial in June 1997, after informing Tim, Rob Nigh, Dick Burr, and Judge Matsch, among others, of my desire to have other counsel appointed for the appeal. Having devoted more than two years full-time to Tim's defense, and confident in Rob's ability to serve as appellate counsel, I felt it was time for me to return home to my family and law practice. Prior to the July decision, I had spoken to no publisher, nor had I signed a book contract or an agency agreement, about any book on the case. Nor had I negotiated for one, nor did I have any personal plans for one. I did not represent Mr. McVeigh so I could write a book. The success of the government in hiding or containing some of the facts herein in our criminal case, in civil litigation, with the media, and persuading Sen. Arlen Spector not to hold congressional hearings on the subject, all convinced me that the only way the truth would come out would be in a book that I might write. After Terry Nichols rejected Judge Matsch's invitation to tell what he knew in return for a reduced sentence, I was even more convinced the means of justice were being used to defeat the end of justice. However, I have acted as I have here, not to the prejudice of my client, but because the full truth is his best hope.

During most of the preparation of this manuscript, Renae Elmenhorst was my secretary, as she has been for many years. Toward the end of the project, she moved with her husband to another city in Oklahoma, and she was succeeded by Susan Brooks, who completed the project and typed the manuscript, and to them I am indebted for their spelling checks, long hours, and hard work in putting the manuscript together in a form suitable for the publisher.

I am especially indebted to Peter Matson, my literary agent, who carried this project forward for me after I decided to go ahead. Peter, a well-known literary agent associated with the Sterling Lord Literistic Agency, took me in hand and introduced me to the ways of the New York publishing world and provided encouragment and support when it really counted. I was introduced to Peter through a mutual friend, Ann Bradley, who was involved in the early stages of assisting me with the manuscript before she returned to Georgetown University Law School. I am also grateful to Arlene Friedman for her early and enthusiastic support of the book.

Peter Matson steered me to a man whom I knew only by reputation: Peter Osnos, the publisher of a new house, PublicAffairs. Osnos I knew from his work as correspondent and later foreign editor of *The Washington Post*. I had read his coverage from Moscow and Indochina. His work at Random House with such authors as Markus Wolf, Peggy Noonan, Anatoly Dobrynin, and Robert S. McNamara all commended him to me. He made trips with me to Oklahoma and Kansas to visit the sights associated with the bombing case firsthand. In addition, Peter and his wife, Susan, had me to their family home in Greenwich, Connecticut, one cold Sunday afternoon for dinner. But what finally sold the deal in my mind was not just his professionalism and a sense that here was a man who could guide me through the preparation of a book that would cover a number of sensitive subjects he had tackled through his career. It was also the influence that men such as Ben Bradlee and I. F. Stone had on his career. Also, PublicAffairs, as a new company, could not afford to pay big advances. I had already received one from another publisher, but we parted company amicably. So I agreed to pay it back, I was released from my obligations to them, and I went with Peter Osnos. A brash New York reporter–book publisher and a small-town lawyer from the Midwest may be a combustible mix, but I have not been disappointed and a hundred times over found my decision—made with the encouragement of Peter Matson—to have been the right one. Finally, but not of least importance, in signing with Peter Osnos, I met my coauthor, Peter Israel, himself a writer and former publisher (of Putnam) and my editor, Geoff Shandler. The opinions herein are mine and mine alone, but Peter Israel and Geoff took my undisciplined and inexperienced writing and patiently guided me to a finished product that I am satisfied tells the story of the bombing conspiracy in a way that I hope convinces the American public that we did everything we could for Tim as his lawyers yet disturbs them enough that they will demand answers from their government.

Stephen Jones
Elmstead
Enid, Oklahoma

ABOUT THE AUTHORS

Stephen Jones is a fifty-eight-year-old Enid, Oklahoma, attorney whose practice is limited to trials and appeals. He attended the University of Texas, graduated from the University of Oklahoma Law School in 1966, and was admitted to the Bar that same year.

In 1964, he served as research assistant for Richard M. Nixon, and in 1967 was legal counsel to the Governor of Oklahoma. From 1966 to 1969, he worked as administrative assistant to Congressman Paul Findley and special assistant to Senator Charles Percy. In 1968, he was a member of the United States delegation to the North Atlantic Assembly.

From 1970 to 1974, he was general counsel for the American Civil Liberties Union in Oklahoma. He was the Republican nominee for Attorney General of Oklahoma in 1974 and for the United States Senate in 1990. He also served briefly as Republican State Chairman.

Stephen was a member of the Oklahoma Supreme Court Committee on Civil Jury Instructions, associate editor of the *Oklahoma Bar Association Journal*, and a member of the Oklahoma Court of Criminal Appeals Rule Committee. In 1979, he was appointed Special United States Attorney to investigate allegations of criminal wrongdoing by the Administrative Director of the United States Court System. He served as a judge in a temporary division of the Oklahoma Court of Civil Appeals.

Stephen practices law in Enid where his clients are typical of those of a county-seat lawyer in the Midwest, but he also serves as general counsel for Phillips University. A substantial portion of his practice is devoted to commercial litigation. He is the author of a book on Oklahoma's political history, and scholarly monographs on France and China, and Southern Republicans.

On May 8, 1995, he was appointed by the United States District Court to serve as the principal defense counsel for Timothy James McVeigh, charged in the Oklahoma City bombing case.

He is completing a biography of Chapman Revercomb, a Republican United States Senator from West Virginia in the 1940s and 1950s, and planning a biography of Charles R. O'Conor, the forgotten nominee of the Democratic Party for president in 1872. A two volume work, *Oklahoma Criminal Law, Practice and Procedure* will be published by West Law Book Publishing Company in 1999. He is married, the father of four children and lives today in Enid, Oklahoma.

Peter Israel is the author of nine novels. He was president and chairman of the Putnam Publishing Group during the 1980s, and he has served on the boards of the Association of American Publishers and the Mystery Writers of America. Most recently, Mr. Israel assisted the late Arthur Liman with his memoir, *Lawyer,* which was also published by PublicAffairs.

INDEX

PublicAffairs is a new nonfiction publishing house and a tribute to the standards, values, and flair of three persons who have served as mentors to countless reporters, writers, editors, and book people of all kinds, including me.

I. F. Stone, proprietor of *I. F. Stone's Weekly*, combined a commitment to the First Amendment with entrepreneurial zeal and reporting skill and became one of the great independent journalists in American history. At the age of eighty, Izzy published *The Trial of Socrates*, which was a national bestseller. He wrote the book after he taught himself ancient Greek.

Benjamin C. Bradlee was for nearly thirty years the charismatic editorial leader of *The Washington Post*. It was Ben who gave the *Post* the range and courage to pursue such historic issues as Watergate. He supported his reporters with a tenacity that made them fearless, and it is no accident that so many became authors of influential, best-selling books.

Robert L. Bernstein, the chief executive of Random House for more than a quarter century, guided one of the nation's premier publishing houses. Bob was personally responsible for many books of political dissent and argument that challenged tyranny around the globe. He is also the founder and was the longtime chair of Human Rights Watch, one of the most respected human rights organizations in the world.

.   .   .

For fifty years, the banner of Public Affairs Press was carried by its owner, Morris B. Schnapper, who published Gandhi, Nasser, Toynbee, Truman, and about 1,500 other authors. In 1983 Schnapper was described by *The Washington Post* as "a redoubtable gadfly." His legacy will endure in the books to come.

Peter Osnos, *Publisher*